AJ

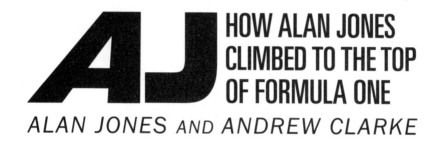

HOW ALAN JONES CLIMBED TO THE TOP OF FORMULA ONE

ALAN JONES AND ANDREW CLARKE

EBURY
PRESS

An Ebury Press book
Published by Penguin Random House Australia Pty Ltd
Level 3, 100 Pacific Highway, North Sydney NSW 2060
www.penguin.com.au

 Penguin
Random House
Australia

First published by Ebury Press in 2017

Addresses for the Penguin Random House group of companies can be found at
global.penguinrandomhouse.com/offices.

National Library of Australia
Cataloguing-in-Publication entry

Clarke, Andrew, author
A J / Andrew Clarke with Alan Jones
ISBN 978 0 14378 383 1 (paperback)

Jones, Alan, 1946 November 2–
Automobile racing drivers – Australia – Biography
Automobiles, Racing – Australia
Formula One automobiles

Other Creators/Contributors:
Jones, Alan, 1946 November 2 – author

Cover design: Luke Causby/Blue Cork
Cover photographs: photo of Alan Jones by Bob Thomas/Getty Images; photo of Williams
FW07B by National Motor Museum/Heritage Images/Getty Images
Typeset by Post Pre-Press Group, Brisbane
Printed in Australia by Griffin Press, an accredited ISO AS/NZS 14001:2004
Environmental Management System printer

Penguin Random House Australia uses papers that are natural, renewable and
recyclable products and made from wood grown in sustainable forests. The logging and
manufacturing processes are expected to conform to the environmental regulations of the
country of origin.

While this book is a very personal story, it is also one that couldn't have been written without the thousands of people that helped during my career, many of whom you will read about in these pages. I owe them all a great debt, but it is one I trust I repaid on the track.

Contents

Foreword by Bernie Ecclestone

I got on very well with Alan. It was usual for the drivers to be competitive and this also included the teams. We all loved him. I will tell you how Alan came across as an Australian; a lovely guy but do not try to push him around. He was aggressive on the track and when he was in the car, look out. When he was not racing, he would fight for what was right and wrong for him to be competitive. Otherwise, Alan was not aggressive at all.

Alan's World Championship win is so different to what the sport is today. The people are different, team owners and drivers are in a new environment and times have changed since Alan was racing. Alan could not exist today. He was friendly with everyone in the sport. Both the teams and drivers in those days would help each other out.

When he was at Williams and I owned Brabham, if either of us was in trouble, the teams would help each other. Frank would say, 'I need some help from you,' and we would assist. The same can be said for when we approached Frank at Williams. Today the teams and drivers do not talk to each other. It is not an Alan Jones time environment today. We did whatever was necessary to get the most competitive piece of machinery and then the drivers would do whatever they could do to win races. But, in doing so, in a different environment than today.

Today, if somebody wants to do something there are 2000 lawyers involved. Alan was not a guy who wanted a profile and to get in front of the press and have his photograph taken. He was not that sort of a driver. He was very friendly with people but did not seek publicity and things like that.

Alan represented Australia in a great way when he was racing in Formula One. Look at the percentage of people in Australia as compared to Europe. I think the percentage of those that Australia has had and been good at their job is probably higher than most places. Things have changed.

Alan as a driver steward is great. He is happy and sensible. He makes the right decisions, I am sure. We miss Alan. I miss him. I really do miss him being around all the time.

Foreword by Sir Frank Williams

I have been privileged to have employed some of Formula One's greatest drivers since I started in the sport in the 1960s. Alan Jones played a very important role in my professional life and will forever have a place as a central figure in Williams' history.

Alan joined a Williams team in 1978 that was very much an unproven force in Grand Prix racing. Alan came on board at a time when my co-founder Patrick Head and I had just relaunched Williams with a fierce determination to make the team a front-running contender.

Alan was deemed a solid and reliable driver at the time, but he had never really had the opportunity to get behind the wheel of a truly competitive car and show his potential. He didn't have what you would call the classic Grand Prix racing frame; at first glance he looked uncomfortably big to be a Formula One driver – certainly by today's standards. But Alan did possess raw pace and a knack for pulling out his best when he needed it most. Both qualities are very hard to come by and cannot be taught, in my opinion.

In 1978 we gave him a car that was extremely reliable and well engineered, but perhaps a year out of date compared to our competitors because it didn't have the 'ground effect' design that proved such a performance enhancer. Regardless of this limitation, Alan did enough to make heads turn both within the team and across the paddock. In 1979 we gave him a car that was capable of winning races, the FW07, and he used it to good effect and really helped put himself, and Williams, on the map. Despite some early reliability problems, we won four races that season and finished third in the Championship.

It was in 1980 in the FW07 that Alan really showed his qualities and ultimately won the Formula One World Championship. His battles with Nelson Piquet in the Brabham that year stand out in my memory. Yes, Alan was fast, but this was combined with exceptional mental fortitude; he was awed by nobody and would go toe-to-toe with his fellow drivers and never back down. With Alan Jones behind the wheel of your car, you knew you were getting 100 per cent commitment at all times. He had natural car control and his driving style matched his character; rugged and no nonsense.

On a personal level, he was a real man's man and very personable. His boisterous personality fitted in well with Williams and he developed a very good relationship with Patrick Head and myself. I know Patrick found his style particularly beneficial. He was never the sort of driver that buried himself in the detail, but what he did have was a knack for giving Patrick direct and useful feedback that could be easily actioned. He would come back after a session and have a clear idea of what he liked and disliked, what was working and not working, and this is always very helpful to a Technical Director.

As our first ever World Champion, Alan will always have a key place in the history of the Williams team. His skills, combined with Patrick's engineering genius, proved a formidable double act and set us on the way for further success in the years to come. His decision to retire from the sport in 1981 came as a surprise to myself and Patrick, but his native Australia was where his heart was and it was clear that he wanted to return. Having said that, he was a racer through and through, so it was no surprise to me that Alan soon found his way back into a racing car on an ad hoc basis in the years that followed.

Modern Formula One drivers are a very different beast to Alan and his contemporaries; with 24-hour media and greater corporate commitments, it is inevitable that we do not often see personalities and characters come to the fore in the way that we used to. Alan Jones, though, will always go down as one of the sport's good guys and a very talented racing driver in an era that witnessed some of the sport's finest going head-to-head.

1

From the Beginning to England

I DIDN'T GO racing for anyone other than myself and, to a lesser degree, my team. I didn't crave fame – in fact, I worked hard to avoid it, although I did enjoy some of its trappings. In my early years, I made it clear to anyone who employed me that I was there to race and to race hard enough to win. If you couldn't help in that quest, I was going elsewhere.

I believe I acted throughout my career with honour and stuck to the values I have held since my early years. I have never wanted anything more or anything less than has been agreed. If we do a deal, I expect you to honour your part of the agreement, just as I will mine. My old man also taught me manners come cheap. They cost nothing. Everyone deserves respect: a waiter, a bellboy, a cleaner – say thank you and don't take those people for granted. I've tried to stick by that all my life: not to be arrogant and to treat all people the same way. In many ways, despite my dad's flaws, I did learn from him . . . in some ways I am more like him than I ever wanted to admit.

We are all affected by our parents, consciously or subconsciously. I was born in November 1946 and I was only 12 when my parents split up and my father, Stan, went broke a decade later. Those events were big lessons for me, and helped shape who I became, even if I didn't know it at the time, even if I don't fully understand it today, 60-odd years later.

My parents' marriage was volatile. I remember the police coming to the house a few times. The old man was a fantastic bloke. He had a heart as big as Phar Lap: you'd be going along with him and he'd see a homeless person and he'd stop and give him five quid. But he'd rather a fight than a fuck half the time, and was a bit inclined to give Mum a biff, which upset me. She'd call the police and they would come around and then there'd be a full-on blue in the house with him and the police . . . he wasn't scared of having a go at them either. In fact, I don't think anything frightened him, but he was extremely kind to me.

While it upset me, there was nothing I could do, so you just carry on like it wasn't happening. I don't think I was ever the sort of kid that would say, 'Mum, could we sit down and have a talk? I'm a bit worried about the old man hitting you.' I wasn't even that person as an adult. It was never discussed.

But I am not my father, just as my son Jack is not me. Jack is totally different to me; he doesn't care about motorsport for instance. He loves his soccer and he has a beautiful temperament – unlike me. He might turn out to be a real prick, I don't know, but at the moment, he's a lovely boy. I worry for him though, because boys like him get into trouble they are not looking for.

Whereas Zara, his twin sister, she contributes to most of the aggro in the house. I brought some sushi home one night and it was the wrong sort. She got stuck into me, so I threw it in the rubbish. To which she sarcastically said, 'Oh, welcome back.' She's not scared of giving it to me. Zara is me and Jack is Amanda, their mother, which makes life interesting.

So I didn't suck my thumb and curl up in the foetal position upstairs at night, thinking about it; no, I just rolled on. That's the way it was, that was the kind of man my father was and I couldn't change it, so I had to wear it. Mum too. I remember him for all his good characteristics, not his bad habits. You might consider that to be denial – I don't know about that, nor do I care. The one thing I did take away was that I would never hit a woman, and nor would I allow a woman to be hit if I could do anything about it.

Dad was raised by his grandfather in Warrandyte. He was a bastard in the true sense of the word and he was self-made because of that. I'm sure his childhood was tough; everything he had or did, he created himself.

My mum, Alma, was typically Irish, stubborn as a mule and never taking a backward step ... something to do with the red hair I suspect. She'd rev Dad up something shocking, call him something and that would be enough for him to give her a whack. It wouldn't stop her though – if you gave her a backhander she'd just come back for more, mouth off even louder. He was volatile and had a very short temper ... it didn't make for a good mixture.

Mum was one of three girls – Auntie Maude, Auntie Nell, and Mum. There was a brother too, Jack, who got killed driving his truck up at Ballarat. When that crash happened, the old man had a brand-new Jaguar XK120, and he ripped off the governor – the device that limited its speed – and screamed up there. I used to go in the truck with Jack quite a bit, its name was Leaking Lina. He was a lovely guy.

They were a reasonably close family, which was obviously different to Dad's. When Mum and Dad used to go out for dinner, they'd drop me around to Nanna and Pops. I'd go to the local pictures when I was there, because in those days you could walk down to the picture theatre at night by yourself, even as an eight-year-old. I'd be too scared at my age to do it now.

It's funny, I look back on my childhood now and can see how abnormal it was, but at the time I had no idea. I thought Dad and his girlfriends was a normal thing. When they got divorced I ended up living with Dad, which was unusual at the time. Still is. Mum was keen for it to work, and if I'd had a choice that is what I would have asked for too, so everyone was happy. The old man pretty much got what he wanted most of the time, and this was just another example. We were living in East Ivanhoe, in Melbourne's north-east, and he had the Holden dealership in Essendon, over in the north-west, about 20 kilometres away.

Mum went off and married a man called Wally, and then my parents became the best of friends. The old man and I would go around to their place for roast dinners and the like. Most people would say, 'Christ, what a weird set-up that was.' I didn't really see any problem: it worked.

Mum was a very good mother and wife. Without fail, every day when she was with Dad, she'd stop housework at a certain time, have a shower, get fresh clothes on, put the perfume on, and get dinner ready. She always made sure she was well presented and looked good when Dad came home. Unfortunately, half the time he never came home, which was a bit of an issue. She knew he mightn't, but she got dolled up anyway, come what may.

Mum was fiercely loyal: she would always stick up for me and would do anything for me. She was in charge of choosing the places for my schooling. I started at All Hallows, a Catholic primary school in Balwyn, and then I went to Burke Hall, the junior school for Xavier College . . . again Catholic. My mum was the Catholic in the family; her father's name was Paddy O'Brien, which speaks for itself.

I was certainly no scholar. I thought I was far too good and clever to worry about sitting down and learning anything. How the hell, I thought, was Latin going to help me buy and sell cars, or race them? Which of course Latin – and everything else – does, in a roundabout way. But when you're Mr Smart Arse aged 13, you don't think about education or getting help from anyone. My objectives as a child were strictly those of the day I was living in; tomorrow didn't exist.

Dad was the sort of person who really couldn't give a shit about religion. If Mum had said she wanted me to go to a Jewish school, he would've said, 'Yeah, right-o, whatever. As long as he's out of my way and being educated and he's happy.' She was the one that wanted me to go to Xavier. Burke Hall was in Studley Park Road, which wasn't too far from where we lived, and then from there I'd go to the big school for the rest of my education . . . well that was the plan.

I won't say I was expelled, but I think the school suggested to Dad that it'd be better if I finished my education elsewhere. Then he sent me to Taylors Business College, which was basically a place for kids that had been asked to leave private schools, so that their parents could hold their heads up in their social networks and say, 'Oh no, he's going to a business college.' Which was just bullshit. It was on the sixth floor of a building in the CBD of Melbourne.

I finished off my last year or so of schooling there, but for me it just didn't matter. I was a shocking student, I wasn't academic at all. It was a complete waste of time – not that I want my kids to have the same attitude. But I knew what I wanted to do.

I had something other kids didn't have. Racing was my chosen goal; my father was a racing driver and because Stan Jones was known to be good, I could also be good. I grew up with his mates and his mates' sons, and every last one of them was going to go racing, too: which they invariably didn't. But for me, there was this great big billboard in my mind that said, I've got to do it. School, in my eyes, was of no value. I wanted to be a racing driver and that was it. All this was just filling in time.

My Catholicism didn't last. Burke Hall turned me off. They used to strap me for blowing my nose the wrong way. You didn't have to do much and those pricks would pull out these long straps they kept in shoulder holsters. They were leather with steel in them, and they used to soak them in vinegar just to make the leather a bit crisper. You'd have to hold your hand out and you'd either get two, four or six of the best, depending on how much you flinched.

The trick was to try and pull your hand away, so you took a lot of the sting away. You had to time it perfectly, because if the prick thought you did it too much, he'd go again.

One day during catechism, where we'd be taught religious knowledge, Father Brown belted the shit out of me for not knowing why Jesus was kind and gentle. I thought, 'Hang on, this prick is his representative on earth, and he's belting me up for not knowing why Jesus was kind and gentle.'

That's when I became an agnostic.

There was a lay teacher, Mr Tilley. He hit me with a ruler and cut my eye open once. The old man was so angry he flew up there and dragged him out of the classroom. Mr Tilley was screaming like a sheila. Dad whacked him, which not too many parents at Burke Hall or Xavier would do. But what others would do didn't ever stop him.

The school didn't do anything about it because Dad was going to press charges for assault on me if they did. After that Mr Tilley used to shit himself every time he saw me; he wouldn't come anywhere near me. Good.

*

I like to take things as they come. I always believe that tomorrow is another day. It doesn't matter how bad things get today, you go to bed and tomorrow is another day, another opportunity.

It's like in my racing career – I was always able to sleep well the night before a race because I wasn't overthinking things. You'd get to the circuit and some drivers would say, 'I didn't sleep last night.' I used to think, 'Jesus, why tell me that? You've just shown me a chink in your armour.'

I used to say, 'Oh really? I slept like a log. In fact, I slept in,' which I didn't. Those mind games are part of the game. I was competitive. I looked for every advantage. I looked for weaknesses in my opponents.

That was something I got from the old man, as was the whole motor racing thing. It was in my blood, if you believe in that concept, which I am not sure I do. You'll find out why soon. The old man was good enough to be offered drives for Ferrari and BRM, but he had a young son and a business that was going quite well, so he turned them down.

One of the guys he was racing and beating was Jack Brabham, who did take those opportunities, went to Europe and won three world championships. The truth is though, the old man could drive Brabham into the weeds. And he did so. When Brabham was New South Wales champion and Dad was Victorian champion, they had a grudge race at Holden's home, Fishermans Bend, in Melbourne, just the two of them. When Brabham crossed the finish line, my old man was already out of his car sitting there drinking a Coke. I admire everything Brabham did, but I reckon my old man was as good or better as a driver.

Dad took his regret for not taking those opportunities to his grave, especially after his business went broke and he was left with nothing. I didn't want to die with regret. I didn't want to live under a question mark of 'what if?' My old man died wondering whether he should have gone to Europe or not; there was going to be no question mark over me. I decided I'd go over, give it a good go and if I turned out a failure, I could still look at myself in the shaving mirror and say I'd given it a go, had some fun and had some stories to live on. But the old man died with the question hanging there.

*

As I said, I lived with Dad when my parents split, but I really just spent a lot of time with housekeepers and nannies, because Dad used to go off to work and never got home until late. More often than not he was in at Mario's in Exhibition Street having dinner with his girlfriend or something, and he used to leave me to my own devices. The housekeeper was supposed to make me do my homework, which I didn't. I used to lock myself in the bedroom – she thought I was doing homework, but I used to climb out the window and go down the street. But I conned them into thinking I'd spent the last two hours in my room studying. They'd swallow it and tell my old man what a good boy I'd been, and he'd be pleased and say, 'Good boy, Alan.' I learnt the world was a con; it never bothered me to abuse their confidence.

I was learning some important life lessons. Firstly I was becoming independent, which made moving to Europe, and doing what I needed to do at the age of 19, a lot easier. The second was about the con and the sale. I was good at that.

I started driving cars when I was 15. No, that was not legal. I used to drive myself into Melbourne for Taylors College, park up in Collins Street, and then walk down to school. Eight times out of 10, I never made it to school; I used to drive somewhere else.

Racing was there very early in my life. I started out in billy-cart racing when I was seven or eight. To race a billy-cart the first thing you need is a great big hill. You sit in your billy-cart at the top and race others to the bottom. Yongala Street in Balwyn, where we lived then, was perfect, as was Balwyn Road. They even used to have a soap-box derby there, which was great. You couldn't do it these days with the amount of traffic, but back then it was different. Cottee's, loved by kids throughout the land for their cordial, had a special billy-cart with all the jazzy wheels and bodywork, and the old man bought it for me. I raced it and took home my fair share of wins.

I was born into an environment where my father was racing cars and I would go to as many races as I could with him. We went to the 1954 New Zealand Grand Prix at Ardmore, flying TEAL Airways in a Douglas DC-6B with four propellers on it. I always remember Ardmore because the train went through the middle of the town. It's funny how things stick in your mind. There was a big pool there where I went swimming. I had a Saint Christopher medal around my neck – the patron saint of travellers – and a Maori girl came up and ripped it off me. I also went to an outhouse there and there was this huge spider, the biggest I had ever seen in my life.

Ardmore certainly left an impression on me, especially when Dad won the race. That was a big deal, the biggest win of his career at the time. He beat some big names in some pretty special cars – Brabham in a Cooper, Ken Wharton in a BRM, along with a pile of Alfas, Ferraris and Maseratis. Dad was in the Maybach Special, an interesting Australian car, certainly not in the same league as those others. It had its fair share of dramas on the weekend, but came through in the race.

We always had racing people calling around to our house. People like Bib Stillwell and Bill Patterson came around for pleasant Sunday mornings and they'd all have a few drinks. I think the modern thing now would be brunch, but I don't think there was too much food involved.

I grew up in an environment with car-racing people, and that's all I ever wanted to be – a driver. A winner. A champion. I didn't go racing to hang around the pool or play golf. I was there to win.

When I did go to Europe, I made a conscious decision to forego a lot of things. I couldn't go around to Mum's and have a roast dinner on a Sunday for instance. No-one was going to get in my way. I was going to do what I wanted to do, and that was it.

So I think what I got was an attitude. People say, 'It's in the blood.' And OK, it may be, but I don't think you inherit it.

Christian, my first son, is adopted, and he's a bloody good driver. It's not in the genes. You look at most Formula One drivers – they don't have racing fathers. So you don't need it and you don't inherit it.

Dad more or less did his own thing when I was growing up. On several occasions, he made the fatal mistake of leaving the car keys lying about. One such car was the ex-Dan Gurney two-door Galaxie that was raced in England. I used to pinch it and scream around the neighbourhood.

I came home from school one day and one of the neighbours said, 'Alan, can I see you for a minute? Tell your father to stop testing that Ford race car because the coppers are onto him and they're going to lie in wait.' I said, 'Oh, thank you very much, that's great. Thank you.' That was a lucky escape.

Dad didn't want me to start racing too early. I think I was 13 when he bought me an Azusa kart from America. We had quite a bit of success with that one. Because he had no idea what he was doing, he also bought me another go-kart, which had twin 125cc engines. Little did he know that the maximum capacity allowed was 200cc – and this had 250. It went like a bloody rocket ship, and although it couldn't race it was fun. It also meant that when I got into the 100cc one, it felt like I could get out and walk faster.

Most of the tracks were converted drive-in theatres, full of undulations. There was one out in Broadmeadows, at Melbourne's northern tip, and a really good one at the Puckapunyal army camp up the Hume Highway that hosted the Victorian titles.

Dad would send me off with one of the mechanics from his dealership to look after me. One of his secretaries, Elsie Pretty, had a go-kart she used to race. One day when I broke mine she lent me hers and I won the Victorian title in it. It was a Rainey kart, built by a guy called Maurie Rainey, who was a dwarf. His daughter used to race as well. Good little go-karts, actually.

Dad never really used to help me as such. Although he did buy me the go-karts. He also let me drive his Cooper Climax and bought me my first competitive car, a little Mini 850 I raced at the Geelong Sprints in my first ever competitive outing in a car. But that was it.

No sage words of advice, just the brutal truth on what I did wrong. He used to abuse me if I didn't win, or if I did something wrong. He never really praised me if I did anything good. I don't know whether he helped me or not.

It wasn't a nurturing, 'Listen to me, son, I can teach you something' type of relationship; he just wasn't that sort of a person. He'd rather get his mechanic to come and help me. It's a bit like when we used to go to the Melbourne Show; well I say we, but it wasn't really. He got his secretary to take me and he'd give them a handful of money and tell them to buy me some bags and make sure I was happy. He would no more think about taking me himself than flying to the moon.

That's just the way he was and to a certain degree, I'm a bit like that. You learn things at an early age that just aren't that easy to unlearn.

I'm not big into the parent-teacher interviews or going to the father's days at the school and all those sort of things. I'm just not into it. Sometimes I think I should be, but it's not me. Thank God I've got a wife that does do all that – it means I don't have to.

I developed into who I was at an early age, and that is pretty much it. I was a shit of a kid, I used to fight all the other kids. Exactly the sort of kid I don't want any of mine to be.

Dad's business was going quite well and he was going all over Australia to race, with me in tow. But running a car dealership in Australia in the 1960s is not like what it is now. You couldn't hold more than one franchise at a time: if you were a Holden dealer, that was it; you couldn't do Alfa or Fiat as well. You also couldn't own more than one Holden dealership. When he was racing on the Gold Coast once, he bought another Holden dealership off a guy called Jack Moran, and then he bought Tweed Motors a little later. General Motors got in touch with him and said, 'Hey, you can only have one. Pick which one you want to keep.'

Unfortunately he kept the Essendon one.

It's a funny old world, I'll tell you. Dad raced the Maybach on the Gold Coast, at a race track in Ashmore – and years later, I bought an industrial complex at 73 Ashmore Road, not knowing it was exactly where the pits were for the race track. He had a big shunt there too. He was going over a bridge in the Maybach 2, which had its fuel tank behind the rear axle. As the fuel load dropped, the back got light and he went over the bridge and off she went into the trees. The Maybach was cut in half. All Dad got was a cut chin – and maybe concussion, because he was still sitting there with the steering wheel in his hands, saying, 'How am I going?'

Then he went back to Moran Motors and they all got into the grog and tore crabs apart and that is when he bought that dealership.

These days I live on the Gold Coast, which is where I used to go just about every school holidays. I'd bring the dog up, we'd go down the beach. It wasn't very developed then: there was the old ski gardens with the go-kart track out in the middle of the cane fields, which I went to as often as I could. The weather was good, and that was what I remembered most, which is why I moved here.

*

I was quick in karts and starting to win other races as well as that Victorian title. Karts were great for someone like me, who wasn't very technical: if I take something to pieces, you can absolutely guarantee there'll be something left over when I put it back together. If I change a light bulb, I think I've done a major job.

You couldn't change gear ratios or anything serious on karts. You could change sprockets, make it go a little bit harder down the straight or a bit more out of the corner, and you could play around with tyre pressures, but that was it. What you were doing was honing your race craft. You're lining up people, you're going deep, going in under brakes and all that sort of stuff. Whether you know that or not, you're learning that for the next level of racing. It was all stuff that I took with me.

Feel, perception and judgement are the biggest assets that a driver can have – and a nice big set of balls helps too. You need to be willing to take a bit of a risk – and you do have to take a risk every now and again. If you don't, you're not going to get anywhere.

I was very happy to take risks in the kart. I used to ride over people and I wasn't scared of banging wheels. I would do whatever was necessary to win. If it meant having somebody off, I'd do it. That sounds bad, but so be it.

Back then in karts, as it was for a long time here, it was 'Stan's son' that was going OK. For the last 30 years or so it's been the other way around: he's 'Alan's dad'.

Even with the Jones name and even with the wins, it wasn't easy and I don't think it ever is in car racing, especially if you want to drive Formula One. There were hundreds of thousands of young drivers around the world chasing one of 20 drives, and I was just one of them. A bag full of cash – which I didn't have – makes it easier, but you still have to be good.

Fortunately, I was one of those people that was often in the right place at the right time, and used the equipment I was given to show my ability. With that I was able to keep getting into the right cars.

Some of the guys Dad got to help me were pretty handy too. I'll never forget the day the old man sent Otto Stone to help me in a race up here on the Gold Coast, when Dad was racing a Maserati. Otto was the chief mechanic on the Maserati, but there he was looking after young Alan. I took my karting as seriously as he did the Maserati.

That day I jumped into the lead early and was half a lap in front of the field. Otto was leaning over the fence going, 'Slow down, don't win by too much. Slow down.'

I go around the bloody track and who should be hanging over the fence but the old man saying, 'Speed up, you little . . .' There was a lady next to him saying, 'Look at that little smart arse, he's slowing down.' To the old man, that was a red rag to a bull; to him, that was embarrassing.

So he's there saying speed up, Otto's saying slow down.

In the end, I slowed down, and then I copped another lesson in life: the kid behind me screamed past and won. Then I got abused by the old man, and I said, 'Otto was here, you told me to take notice of him.' I would have won by a lap had they left me alone. But I learnt my lesson: the only bloke who knows what's happening is the driver, and that's me. Even to this day, when people say this, that and the other thing about what is going on in a race car, the only bloke that really knows is the driver.

I learnt that your attitude must be to win at all costs. Nice guys don't win, I'm afraid. By the time I was leaving the house for a race, I was starting to turn into a nasty and aggressive person. It didn't matter whether I was on the plane or in a hire car, I was going somewhere to win, not make friends.

I'm a bad loser, simple as that. I'm very, very competitive – and not just at car racing. When I was driving for Williams I'd go up to Frank Williams' place and play tennis – and I used to smash my racquet and carry on. I'd get very upset. Same with golf; I used to throw my clubs and have little dummy spits . . . my wife refuses to play with me. It wasn't because I was being beaten, it was because I couldn't manage the shot that I wanted. I didn't know why I wasn't able to hit that ball like Greg Norman. If he can do it, why can't I?

I was hard on myself, which is one reason I retired early. If I didn't qualify in the top four, you couldn't talk to me. I used to go back to the motel in a shocking mood.

I was also superstitious, although I wasn't developing too many little quirks in karts. If I had parked in a certain spot in the car park and I got on pole, I'd try to get that spot the next day or the next time I was at that track. I happened to have a red pair of underpants on one day and I thought, 'These are quick,' so from that time on, I always used to race with red underpants. I always used to hop in and out of the car from the left-hand side. Just stupid little things.

Don't ask me why, but I always liked it when I saw an ambulance. I would say 'ambulance' under my helmet. Fortunately I didn't need the ambulance much in my career or life.

The closest a car ever came to killing me had nothing to do with racing. I was playing tag with my cousins on the median strip in Hoddle Street – Melbourne's main north-south road, would you believe. I was rolling around on the ground, and I rolled off the median strip onto the road. A car's tyre went past my head so close I felt it brush my hair. I could have been squashed or killed easily.

I'm not a religious person, probably not game enough to be an atheist, so I'm an agnostic, and I'm sitting on the bench until He comes and tells me otherwise. I am a believer in destiny, and I think that just wasn't my day to be squashed under a wheel.

*

I loved every part of my racing back then. I spent quite a bit of time with people who worked for Dad, like Otto. It is funny looking back about the ones I remember and why . . . it wasn't always about what I learned from them, it was often just something that was different. Like Otto's wife always used to give us toasted sardine sandwiches – and I've never forgotten Otto's K3 MG, which was a beautiful maroony coloured car, stunning. Then there was John Sawyer, who had a moustache and always wore the flat hat like the English wore back then.

Dad was a hero to me at the time and he was fuelling my desire to get to Europe. I do remember him saying to me, 'Get over there and give it a go. Australia will always be here, it's not going anywhere. You can always come back.'

I didn't get much fatherly advice from him, but that was the best advice he ever gave me.

I watched Dad racing a lot and thought he was the best. When he won the Australian Grand Prix at Longford, in 1959 in the Maserati, I did the lap of honour with him sitting on the back above the fuel tank.

This was all amazing, and it just kept the dream growing, which made Mum a bit nervous. She used to get nervous when Dad raced, but she didn't make it to many of my races. There was one race with Dad where they all took off and they were rubbing wheels and smoke was coming off the tyres and she just screamed. Motor racing was really dangerous back then, many drivers died, but she never tried to stop me, even though she probably didn't want me to do it. She knew trying to get me to study was a lost cause, so she just let me be.

As I got older I started taking on some paid work. One summer I worked with a racing driver and car builder named Ernie Seeliger at his workshop in Richmond – and very quickly discovered I didn't like working on dirty engines, or anything that was dirty. Which is why I never really liked rallying, because it was too much mud and dirt everywhere. When my son Christian was doing his go-karting, all the bloody grease and chains and sprockets, I hated it. When he went into Formula Ford, I thought, 'How good is this?'

Then I started working for the old man selling cars. That was more me, I thought it was better to bullshit than to clean. It was less strenuous and I sweat too easily. It suited me. For example, cars used to come in many shades of grey. If we were out of the one grey and the customer wanted it, I'd say something like 'That's good because it is popular with the undertakers' – and they'd happily take the other one which amazingly we had in stock. It was good to be earning my own money and having some financial independence.

This was all before I could even get a licence in Victoria. I went to Adelaide to get my licence at 16. I used 18 Kitchener Avenue, Dulwich as my address, where a mate of the old man's who was also a car dealer lived. He let me use the address – but as I said, I was driving before I even had that licence. The old man gave me a Morris Minor convertible, painted it iridescent green and put in a gold interior and gold wheels. You'd swear he was bloody Greek or something. I was horrified, but what could you do? He gave me a car, and I wasn't arguing.

When I turned 17, I got a licence in New South Wales. A guy called Laurie O'Neill organised that out at Five Dock. Then when I was 18, I finally got my Victorian licence – and then I got pulled up for the first time. Go and figure that one out.

I had a 300 Healey, a Triumph TR6 then a little Austin-Healey Sprite. On Saturday afternoon we used to get a big bag of chips and a Coke and then we'd all get in a courtyard somewhere, jack the cars up, take the wheels and tyres off, clean under the guards, nugget the tyres and the soft tops and get them just absolutely immaculate. Then we'd go out that night and get pissed and start doing figure eights on the local oval and get covered in shit. On Sunday morning, the cars were dirtier than before we started cleaning them on Saturday.

There was quite a gang of us. John Lyall was one, Brian McGuire was another. Brian's father was Dad's spare-parts manager, and we ended up going to Europe together the first time; the second time I went back with John.

I remember parts of that second trip vividly. Olivia Newton-John was there with fellow singer Pat Carroll and a model named Frankie Lightfoot and that was fun. Olivia was going out with Ian Turpie, who was a TV celebrity, but I knew him because he also used to race a little Mini with me. So there was a bit of a crowd of us on the ship, and when we got over there, I hooked up with Brian again and we got an apartment. That starts a whole new story, which we'll get to soon.

I had finished with karting now and was moving into cars.

We bought this repossessed Mini that had the engine and gearbox sitting in the boot. Dad gave it to Brian Sampson at Motor Improvements and said, 'Do this up, because we'll race it.' I think he thought, Morris 850, it's not going to cost much. I know he shit himself when he got the bill, but Brian did a great job. We resprayed it silver-grey and put black wheels on it. It was a lot better to look at than the green Morris, that's for sure.

I entered that car in the Geelong Sprints, which was my first ever competitive outing in a car. It wasn't a complex race, a standing half mile race with a big curve – you don't have to be too clever to go fast like that. I won my first outing.

Then I started racing it whenever I could. Calder Park was easy because it was close, but Winton and Hume Weir took some effort. The old man had done all of that when he was younger, car on a trailer and travelling the countryside. He did warn me about the drive to Hume Weir: 'Watch those bridges on the way home, because if it's wet, those wooden bridges get very slippery.' And he was right, I lost the car on one of them and was spinning down the road with the trailer and the Mini on the back. Never touched a thing and ended up pointing the right way. I thought then, maybe there was a God, as I escaped another near miss.

I was doing OK on the track though and was winning races. But I was hungry for more.

The old man had the Cooper Climax in the garage and I managed to persuade him to let me use it for a picnic meeting at Calder Park. It was a nice friendly scene, those meets. The oil companies like BP, Shell and Castrol had their tents up and every driver had a contract, even if it's only worth ten quid and some oil; but that made us contracted drivers and that's a step up from the bottom. All you had to do was put a badge on your overalls and on the car, then after the race pick up a steak sandwich and a beer from them.

In the mornings there would be sprints, and road races in the afternoon. I entered the Cooper in everything and the little Mini in a lot too. I blew everybody into the weeds in the Cooper: there weren't that many kids at the meeting with a Cooper Climax.

The racing was serious; at least I took it seriously, going up the night before and staying in a real motel! I felt I was on the way up; also I was living up to what was expected of me – I was Stan Jones' boy and I was expected to win. But when I look back on those days, I'm amazed. I didn't have any proper driving goggles, so I wore sunglasses. If you'd got a stone through those glasses, you'd be history, but you just don't think like that when you're young.

I loved that Cooper Climax. It was powerful and an open-wheeler. I thought, 'This is me, this is what I've got to do.'

The karts put me in fairly good stead when it came to this sort of car. Being an open-wheeler, I could see the wheels and tyres and that didn't affect me all that much. The gear stick was on the right-hand side, which was unusual for me, but it was quick. I'd probably think it's a piece of shit now, but in those days I thought it was the ant's pants.

I did about two or three race meetings in it. For me it was just check the tyre pressures and race; it was somebody else's job to make sure it was tracked up with everything pointing in the right direction. People can't believe that I'm not mechanically minded, but I am seriously lacking in that area, which is why I love my Lexus – you get in and it goes. As to how to make it work – no idea.

Then the old man's dealership went broke.

He had literally hundreds of cars on the lot; his money came from turnover. Which is fine when things are going well. Then came the great credit squeeze of the early 60s: the cars were on the lot, but he couldn't pay for them. Selling cars back in those days was like stocking shirts in a haberdashers: you had to have what the customer wanted on your lot. When the Major with his RAAF whiskers drives up and says he wants pink upholstery with green stripes, he wants that car right away, in time for a drink at sundown. If you don't have it, he moves along and buys it from someone else.

Dad went under, like thousands of others. I found his fate instructive: the smart man doesn't put all his eggs in one basket.

In hindsight, the warning signs were there. Elsie Pretty, the secretary, once said to me, 'Alan, have you thought about doing something else for work, because your father might not always be here.' After I understood everything that was going on, I thought, shit, she was trying to give me a message. Of course, I was too young and stupid to pick it up.

Until that point I'd been terribly spoiled; now I learned life wasn't all a bed of roses. If Dad hadn't gone broke, I would certainly be a bigger bastard and probably wouldn't have been much of a racing driver. I was an obnoxious little bastard as a kid, a big-headed little shit. When Dad was in the money, I was going to a private school, driving a sportscar at 16, living in a nice house, going to Surfers Paradise for my holidays and the son of a famous man. A prescription for disaster. Next minute, no MG, no Surfers Paradise and three-quarters of the old man's friends have vanished, owing him money. Now I've seen both sides of the coin.

His going broke dragged me down to earth. It taught me things can go wrong as well as right; and to be kind to people on the way up because you may meet them on the way down. Mainly, it taught me not to worry about what other people are doing or thinking: my job is to look after me and mine.

Dad lived every day as if he wasn't going broke. I don't think he could help himself. He drank a bottle of scotch a day. Then it was three-hour lunches and back at work for an hour and knock off for dinner.

If there was racing at Southport, he took his mechanics up there, he took their wives and girlfriends and pretty much anyone else he could find, paying for everyone and everything. They still call him the Last of the Big Spenders – he handled money as though it were going out of fashion. He was a player, a player as wide as he was tall. He was colourful and strange; he was a character. Dad didn't cope very well and he went from bad to worse. He started a Chrysler dealership, but that didn't work. Then he ran a consignment business where he didn't have to buy the stuff, he just sold other people's cars. Between you and me, I think there might've been the odd time where he forgot to pay them for the car.

So Dad was broke, which was bloody inconvenient for me. That's when I went overseas. I think he thought to get me out of the joint to save us all the embarrassment. He was going to send me some money for me to continue on my merry way. After the first couple of slightly delayed payments the money was always coming, like a cheque in the mail.

I stopped at Madrid on the way to England and the money wasn't there. I had $50 to my name and I had to book into a hotel where they supplied bed and breakfast, because that's the only way I was going to eat. When I booked in and stayed the night, I got up the next morning and had my continental breakfast and that was it for the day. There was no lunch, no dinner, nothing. I couldn't check out because I didn't have enough money to pay the bill, so I had to keep staying there.

I used to walk down to American Express to check if the money had come through. I was there four or five days and to this day I know Madrid like the back of my hand. I didn't eat.

I stopped having the breakfast because I'd try and sleep in as much as possible so it would make the day shorter. Hard to believe, but true. Eventually, I got the money.

But Dad never really recovered. He had lived on a diet of daily excitement that eventually did him in early, with strokes, heart attacks and dreadful blood pressure. He was about to turn 50.

2

England Take Two . . .
to Formula Three

I WENT TO England for the first time in 1966, a 19-year-old with my mate, Brian, off to build motor racing careers in the motherland. We went by boat and it stopped in Djibouti on the north-east coast of Africa, opposite Yemen. They speak French and Arabic there, which was news to me. It was a bloody eye-opener and let me know the world outside Australia was a little bit different to what I knew. Or expected. For two well-to-do boys from Melbourne, that place was just something else – and the sort of place I hoped I would never see again. Fortunately we didn't stay too long before the boat headed off for the Suez Canal and onto Athens before finally dropping us on London.

That was more us . . . for a start, everyone spoke English. I got a job at Selfridges department store selling fireworks. Brian and I shared an apartment for a while, as young Aussies did. We both wanted to go racing, but we had no idea how to do it. Neither of us had any serious plan, which was pretty much the story of my life. I never really had a plan for anything. Still don't.

I just figured things would all play out all right; after all they always had. I had a mate with me, and that helped, even if we were naive. It wasn't like I was on my own and getting lost in the middle of Kangaroo Valley, or Earl's Court as the locals preferred to call it, with my suitcase on the side of the road.

So we did the London thing for a little while and then we toured the Continent . . . desert boots, jeans and a Bedford Dormobile – well, a Kombi actually. We slept across the seats in the back, we hadn't bought the camper version, had we? So sleeping bags and a pillow across each of the back seats. We had a few cooking utensils and we'd go to camps to have a shower. The usual Aussie 60s trip – except our trip was designed around racing tracks and car races trying to get in as many races as we could. We went to some sportscar races at the Nürburgring and also made it to a couple of grands prix and got down to Monza in northern Italy, where I had my first brush with fame and *the* lifestyle.

We even managed to get hired as extras in the film *Grand Prix* by John Frankenheimer – but don't ask me how. Frankenheimer was a big name then – he'd directed *The Manchurian Candidate* and *The Birdman of Alcatraz*. James Garner starred in *Grand Prix*, as did that bloody French actor Yves Montand. He used to stack on the turns . . . he was so full of himself and a complete wanker. And there were motor racing people everywhere for this movie, with racers acting as consultants and driving cars for scenes.

Bob Bondurant was one of those consultants, an American racer in Europe to race sportscars. He was trying to crack onto some of the girls who were travelling with us, so we got to know him quite well. We were staying in the camping area at Monza and that meant we got to meet and become friendly with other parts of the crew too, including Garner's hairdresser. I'll never forget him, even if I can't remember his name.

We were sitting around one day and he said, 'Do you want to try this?' I said, 'What is it?' He said, 'It's some hash.' I'd never had anything like that, and I took it because I'll try pretty much anything at least once – well, I wouldn't try heroin or any other hard drugs, but this seemed OK. I remember getting some apricot juice and thinking, 'This is the best apricot juice I've ever had in my life.'

Extras eat well too. We'd get up in the morning, have our salami bun and coffee and go across to the track and be in the movie.

Naturally I bumped into someone I knew, Buzz Buzaglo, from Balwyn just like me, but a couple of years older. I raced him in the billycarts down Balwyn Road and he had been in Europe for a little while trying to work his way to the top. I probably could have learnt a bit from him if we weren't having such a good time.

After we were finished with the movie, we stuck with Bondurant for a bit, which got us some access around European racing tracks. We were looking around and trying to work it all out for when we went back to England.

We'd met some important people and made some reconnections, like with Bruce McLaren, who Dad used to race against. Bruce was a Kiwi who finished second in the World Championship to Jack Brabham in 1960 and then third a couple of years later.

I went out to his factory at Colnbrook just near Heathrow Airport, where he was building his very first sandwich construction chassis, which is two thin pieces of aluminium with some stuff in between them . . . I told you I wasn't technical-minded. He cut a bit off and gave it to me. After that it was dinner at his apartment, and we ate T-bone steaks, an absolute rarity in England back then. They were so rare you had to pre-order them from the butcher because he wouldn't carry any in stock.

Bruce drove me back to the station and I took the train home. A fantastic bloke who fired me up even more to get into racing. He was dead only a few years later, killed during testing at the age of 32 – but the team he started still bears his name.

One other person I met in London at the time was a young 'counties girl' named Kay, and we'll talk about her a bit later. Let's just say for the moment that she got pregnant and I was the father. I was already on my way out of England and I was happy to leave her with my flatmate Joe, who was her new boyfriend. I think it actually worked out better for all of us: she was with Joe for 20-odd years and moved to Tasmania with him and had another couple of kids. At that time I would have been a shit father.

Back in Australia for my resetting, which I needed, I worked for Bob Jane rather than the old man. I was selling Jags and Saabs and I had a Saab to drive as part of the job. It was one of those shocking front-wheel-drive two-stroke things. Brpbrpbrpbrpbrp. Jesus it was bad . . . but I still sold them.

I worked there for a year before Dad's business started to struggle and by now I desperately wanted to get back to England. I *had* to get back to England, it was the Mecca of motorsport, and still is. So I packed the bags and jumped on the boat and eventually made it over for my second take at it . . . a little bit wiser and way more motivated.

During my short stay back in Australia I had met Beverley, my mother's hairdresser. Mum organised for me to go to a party that Bev was throwing and I went around to her flat and knocked on the door. She looked at me and said, 'Yes?'

I said, 'I'm Alan Jones.' To which she replied, 'Yeah, so what?' I thought, 'Jesus, nice bitch this is, Mum.' Anyway, I went into the party and one thing led to another and we started dating. We argued quite a lot and we were in and out of the relationship. She left for England with some friends while we were in an on phase, and I went down to see her ship off at Port Melbourne. When it was time to get off, I didn't. I stowed away to Sydney. I went into the cinema and sat in a seat there for a while and then just walked around the boat. When we got to Sydney I waited until a family was walking off and I joined them. I had to get back to Melbourne, but that was all a bit of fun.

Bev was waiting for me and when I eventually arrived in London, we carried on like we hadn't missed a day. Then I hooked up with Brian again and we got a place together at Greenhill Apartments with some other Aussies. It was a bit upmarket for us, given we had no real money and no job – it had a doorman for heaven's sake – but it was in a great location, so we set up a story. Remember the con?

I was a grazier's son, our mate Peter Caines-Buchanan was an accountant and Brian was a doctor. We fed them enough bullshit to get the apartment. I'll never forget the day we moved in. We pulled up in these mini vans with kangaroos on the side – the look on the doorman's face said it all, 'Fucking hell, what's going on here?'

The doorman was right. We used to party all night, sleep until midday, then go down to the pub and continue partying all night. London in the late 60s was everything everyone has ever said about it. I did feel for the poor bugger that used to have to climb the steel staircase out the back of the apartment to collect the rubbish – there were so many empty beer bottles he would have had to make a few trips to get them all.

I had really put on some weight during my year back in Australia, and all this boozing wasn't helping. I was 16 stone – 100 kilos – and I had to shake that off pretty quick smart. I've always been prone to a bit of weight gain. Murray Walker used to call me 'the big burly Australian' in his TV commentary – and that was when I weighed in at 76 kilos. James Hunt used to call me 'Big Al' when I was in my prime. Christ knows what they'd call me now.

Brian already had a small business selling mini-vans, so I joined him in doing that before we expanded to vans converted for camping that we sold to poor unsuspecting Australian and New Zealand tourists. It was the equivalent of backpacking today, and the young tourists would come over and want a campervan to drive around Europe. We started with the Dormobile with the windows in their sides and the hard wooden seats. We'd put a little Primus stove inside and a couple of rolled-up sleeping bags, then paste the back windows with stickers as though the vans had already been everywhere there was to go. From there we sold the holiday, the beautiful castles of Germany, the history of France, and the romance of Italy – and they wouldn't look too closely at the vans.

We had these vans parked near a tube station in Earl's Court and put up a 'For Sale' sign with a phone number. Earl's Court was all that Aussies coming into London knew at that time; to them the rest of London may as well have been Djibouti. By the time we got back to Greenhill from making a sale, the phone would be running hot and we'd have to jump in the car and go back to Earl's Court.

As they headed off on the big adventure, we'd always ask when they were coming back and then spin a line around my sister coming over around that time and we'd buy the van back for her.

This was all well-constructed too. 'We know it is a good van and if you look after it we can virtually give you your money back.' They'd come back OK – usually the day before they were flying out, keeping the van as long as they could because of our 'deal' to buy it back. Then we'd spin a line – my sister couldn't make it over – to make it seem we didn't need the van anymore. 'We don't want it.'

You could see their mouths hit the ground. I know this is shocking car salesman stuff, but we'd do them a favour and buy the car we didn't need – for about 500 or 600 quid less than what they paid for it. As soon as they were out of sight, hose it over and get it down to Earl's Court with the For Sale sign back on it, with the 500 or 600 back on it and off we go again. Selling a car once is good – twice is great. Brian and I were generally clearing 500 quid a week each, and some weeks even more than a thousand, which in 1969 was a lot of money.

It was so easy, we thought the business would last forever. Which it might have, if we'd taken it the least little bit seriously.

Both Brian and I were into motor racing. Well into it. All we lacked was a car, and I knew I just had to have a racing car and the opportunity to go out and do my thing. There's a way to go about getting into racing; it doesn't depend strictly on yourself. You have to know the trade people, because they supply you and can perhaps sponsor you; you have to know the circuits, because that's where you're going to drive; and, above all, you have to drive, because that's why you exist.

We had to have a car, so we bought a brand new Merlyn Formula Ford and rented a house in Ealing. We also bought a Volkswagen tray back that was designed to carry the car. We headed off to Brands Hatch for some testing and started to get into it all.

As much as we were making, we were spending . . . and more. I was using one credit card to pay for the other credit card, and if we needed a new set of tyres we bought it and worried about the money next week. Welcome to racing.

We were doing a bit of testing and racing, one week me and the next Brian. To me the Merlyn was very similar to the Cooper of Dad's I had raced, it seemed to have as much power and it was on skinny little tyres. It was a great little car and I felt very comfortable in it. But Brian wrote it off in a crash, which was a bit of a setback. We didn't waste it though: we took all the pieces, the engine, the chassis, the wheels, the gearbox and put it all together again just like Humpty-Dumpty – and offloaded it. Not that I had much to do with it given my mechanical skills, but the flat looked like a garage for a while.

Next I bought a two-year-old Lotus 41 that was ready for Formula Libre. I stripped the whole car down and had the chassis sand-blasted and the paintwork enamelled. I made it into a bloody beauty. But beauty doesn't win races; a car in working order does that. I neglected to check that they'd taken all the sand out after they'd done the face-lift. I had a gorgeous little car, all gassed up and doing nicely, and then I threw six engine bearings in a row.

Finally, we worked out why the bearings were going – bloody sand – and I devised a new scheme. I would make my Lotus fit Australian specifications, take it back home, flog it and come back to go Formula Three racing off the money I'd made. That was the plan, anyway.

One day I was out at Brands Hatch testing. Everything was going sweetly and I was putting in respectable times. Good enough, anyway, since I was new to my car, new to the sport and a relative newcomer to the circuit. It was a Wednesday and Brands Hatch was a muddle. Open practice and the circuit was filled with every kind of car under the sun: Formula Fords and what not all over the track.

The pits were on the left-hand side of the circuit going up into the paddock for this sort of test day, rather than the right. Ahead of me there was this bloke who was a bit slower than me: no problems, pass him nice and easy on the right. Except that he suddenly decided that he would turn into the pits, which for a test day weren't the same as a race day. I was inexperienced. At the time, I thought the main thing was to miss him: so I went round him – right round him, winding up off the track, in the grass and into a tyre bank. The Lotus was a complete write-off. End of big sale in Australia. End of Formula Three plan. End of AJ's career?

I was back on with Beverley then and being a good, loyal girl, she'd decided to come out to Brands to see her man taking his car out. She arrived just in time to hear this big bang and see me lying in the grass, swearing my head off about how I was going to kill the bastard that cut across me. It wasn't just the anger. There was also the sadness. There was my Lotus, all lovely, all resprayed, a mess in the grass, just like me.

That Lotus had a spaceframe chassis and you had to put your feet underneath a bar to use the pedals. When I hit the fence, my feet came back and I had broken the instep on my left foot quite badly.

Finally they got an ambulance to me and took me off to hospital. It was my first shunt and the hospital must have been built in the Boer War. They took me into casualty, and there was this lady doctor standing over me, screaming. 'You should stop doing this criminal thing,' she said. I could sympathise; she'd had another driver in the week before and she didn't want a bloody mess in her clean cubicle after last week. So she went on yelling at me about didn't I know what would happen to me if I persisted in my fatal course? Finally, I said to her as politely as I could, 'I'll tell you what, Madam, you get on with your job and I'll get on with mine.' Or words to that effect.

Reluctantly, she took out a pair of scissors and was about to go to work on my brand new Nomex overalls. It was my turn to yell at her: she wasn't going to snip at my valuable equipment. She desisted, helped me up on to the operating table and said she wouldn't be long. I lay there with my leg hurting like hell for at least 10 minutes listening to the rattle of tea cups in the next room. Finally, she came back and they put plaster on my leg. The week after, I went to have it checked in Chiswick and they said, as doctors love to say, that they'd done it all wrong the first time.

So they did it again. They cut off the plaster with me grimacing through it all and the doctor told me not to be such a sook . . . I offered to trade places to see who the bigger sook was. I wasn't in the best of moods.

He replastered it and put a rubber thing on the heel, and said, 'You'll be able to put some pressure on that in a week or so.' Two or three weeks later I couldn't put any weight on it at all, the minute it looked like touching the ground, pain shot up my leg. He had got it wrong too.

Today I still walk with a limp from that and it is progressively getting worse too. I should have gone to St Thomas', which is a special bone hospital, but I didn't know that at the time. Apparently, I should have had a V cut into it and a bone graft, which I didn't. So now they want to seize it up to reduce the pain, but I'd rather deal with the pain than limp worse for the rest of my life.

Not daunted by a little broken leg and yet another setback, Brian and I bought a pair of Brabham BT28s – BT28-25 was mine, BT28-16 was Brian's – and did a deal with Ron Tauranac, who was the 'T' in 'BT', for kits to turn them into BT35s (and then BT38Cs), which had their fuel tanks on the side, inboard brakes and a few other updates. We got our engines from Vegantune, and the guy that ran that, George Robinson, turned out to be instrumental in my pathway to Formula One. I got on with him really well, and often just rang for a chat at night.

We bought an old furniture truck, painted it orange with black lettering. We called ourselves AIRO – Australian International Racing Organisation – which was rather grandiose and, as it turned out, a bit of a mistake. People thought we were *the* Australian international racing organisation while we were just a couple of Dormobile salesmen bullshitting our way through it all, but we did OK.

We had some hair-raising experiences in that truck – it would run out of brakes going down a big hill and we'd have to get ready to jump out.

Three big things changed for me just before that season began. Firstly, Dad moved over to stay with me so I could help look after him. He'd had heart attacks and strokes, and he wasn't the physically commanding man I remembered. His speech was all slurred and he needed a walking stick, which would come in handy given his temper hadn't changed.

Everyone thought he was pissed all the time, but he wasn't. He used to go off to the auctions and buy cars for us to re-sell. He used to take it as a personal thing if anyone else was bidding for the car. He'd win the auction and then he'd start on the other bidder . . . 'Yeah, fuck you.' Some things just don't change.

A couple of times he brought them home and the right-hand side had dents in it because he was on the left-hand side and he never saw them. I'd be the one that'd have to get them all fixed up, advertise them and then sell them for him. I'd be negotiating a deal and go back inside and say, 'He's offered such and such.'

'Tell them fuck off,' he would say, offended someone would offer so little for something he had no attachment to. I'd said, 'Dad, it's a profit, take it.' 'No, fuck off.'

It was easier when it got to the point where he couldn't do any of that.

The second was the opportunity to race in Brazil, which came about through a mate of mine, Brian Kreisky, who operated a management company in Europe called Promoto and was a nephew of former Austrian chancellor Bruno Kreisky. Brian was a bit of a wheeler and dealer of the time, and made millions out of motorsport video and TV broadcasts. He was close to Bernie Ecclestone, before dying in 2000 in a plane he was flying from Blackbushe.

Brian had been approached by somebody in Brazil to supply drivers and Formula Three cars for a series they were running over the British winter. He was given the job of choosing the drivers. I was in.

It was a three-race series. They gave it a fancy name, given the previous year they had run the South American Tournament at Interlagos, and it was being run to prove to the rest of the world that the Brazilians could conduct an international championship event. They were setting their sights on a Formula One race, and this was the showcase.

It was held mostly at Interlagos starting on 10 January 1971 with a non-championship race in Porto Alegre and the final event at Tarumã at the start of February. It was a quick series, I didn't win it or anything but I did enough to raise a few eyebrows.

I was about 24 when I hit Brazil and I'd never been anywhere much except England and a bit of continental Europe. I'd tried to forget Djibouti. It seemed somehow miraculous to find myself in a place that was so profoundly different. I'd never even heard of Sao Paulo before. I went there expecting to see mud huts and when we flew in I was staggered. I couldn't believe the size of it. It's bigger than New York. All I wanted to do when we landed was hit the town. I'd brought my dad with me and Jim Hardman, my mechanic, and while Dad slept off the trip in our hotel, Jim and I went out for a walk. I think we knew what we were looking for. Fortunately, or unfortunately, our hotel was just up the road from a nightclub, and of course we had to venture in.

No sooner had we sat down at a table and ordered a few beers then there were half-a-dozen birds sitting down all round us, groping us under the table. As long as you drink, the girls are there to keep you happy. The women of Brazil are beautiful. I'd never struck anything like this in my life and I turned to Jim and said, 'How long's this been going on? And why have I been missing out?'

It was my very first taste of international glamour and I fell for it. Because I was out enjoying myself too much, I got a really bad dose of sunburn, and that made it hard to get the belts done up properly when I was in the car. It is one of the reasons I avoided pools for the rest of my career.

Before we left for Brazil, I thought to myself that I'd better take the races seriously. I suppose I was evolving, slowly. These were, after all, my first major professional races, and I had travelled halfway across the world for them. I hadn't quite got the Vegantune deal across the line in time for this, so I bought myself a year-old super engine from a guy called Brendan McInerney. This was going to be my *pièce de résistance*, but it barely got through the first weekend. I wanted desperately to do the right thing. I wasn't brilliant in the first two races at Interlagos in Sao Paulo when the screamer let me down. Thankfully I'd taken the old engine down as a spare and it turned out to be better than the screamer anyway.

When we got to Porto Alegre, Jim and I nodded knowingly at each other and said, 'OK, let's put the wings on for this one.' Porto Alegre was not about top speed as much as Interlagos; now we needed grip, so on went the wings.

I was about fifth quickest in practice, and afterwards Dave Walker, a fellow Australian who was about to race in Formula

One with Lotus, came up to me in the pits asking me how things were going. I said very nicely thank you; I was quite pleased with myself and, I might add, with the friendly attention of a real big-time racing driver like Dave. 'Well,' he said, laconically, 'I think you could do a whole lot better if you put your wing on the right way, because you've got it on back to front!'

With that little bit of exact science under my belt, I managed to get onto the front row with Walker and everybody was tickled to death and running about as if they didn't know what had happened. I knew, and I think Dave was wise to it as well.

We were all celebrating our triumph when Peter Warr from Lotus came round to our garage and started to examine my wings, because I was as fast as his driver. Peter figured that had to be because my car was bent. He sniffed around, took out his tape measure, announced that I was a centimetre too wide and he was going to protest the grid position. My old man didn't take kindly to any of this and even though his speech wasn't all that clear by then, his walking stick made his point perfectly clear.

The old man chased Peter right out of our garage and only narrowly missed cracking his skull. Which wasn't from lack of effort. I was appalled at the time, but I laugh now. We sawed a centimetre off the wing and I was running sixth in the race when my gearbox gave out.

So we had this great adventure in Brazil. Interlagos was a highlight, a brilliant circuit with a series of great corners and undulations that just gave it that extra challenge, and it was relatively quick too. It still is a great circuit and I loved racing there.

I was probably lonely at the time even with all those stunning Brazilian women nearby, and rang Beverley back in London and asked her to marry me. She said yes, and that started a whirlwind of activity for my return. I never thought this would be the third thing to change, but it was.

We got married in a church in Chiswick on St Patrick's Day. The old man stood in some dog shit or something and couldn't stop laughing in the church. I turned around and gave him a dirty look. We had an Aston Martin DB6 wedding car that I had bought for Bob Jane, but we got some use out of it before putting it on a boat for him. Then it was off to Malta for our honeymoon. Then back to the serious work. I had a career to build.

My Brabham had previously been raced by a New Zealander named Allan McCully, who coincidentally joined AIRO with a Lotus 69. We had a trailer on the back of the truck and we went across the Channel, first for the three of us to race at Paul Ricard and then down to Monaco, where there were 70 cars trying for the 20-car grid.

I qualified sixth for my heat, the quickest of the three AIRO cars, and was running well when Tony Brise spun in front of me then backed onto the track to get going again at the Station Hairpin. I had to stop to miss him. I stalled the car and needed a push start – without that little incident I would have made the final easily. Brian didn't qualify for the heats, while Allan made it into the final where he finished fifth after the heavens opened.

I also got my first taste of corruption that weekend. There was a lot of talk about the Alpine that Patrick Depailler used to win the race, but the scrutineers didn't want to check it out while they pored all over the Lotus and Ensign cars that finished second and third. Both cars were cleared.

Mo Nunn, who owned Ensign, asked for the Renault engine in the Alpine to be vacuum-tested, but they managed to break the tester. George Robinson offered up his, but then the police got involved and said it would cost the equivalent of £90 to get it tested – which we, as AIRO, paid. Then they did the test in secret with only the Alpine team allowed to witness it. Of course it was cleared. It was very distasteful, but more of this was to come in my career.

*

I had a pretty good season in that Brabham and tested for March at Silverstone during the year. March had just started in Formula One, but it also had a really good Formula Three team, which had won one of the British Formula Three championships with Roger Williamson in 1971 and then would go on to dominate the class for a few years from 1973. Williamson was killed in only his second Formula One race in 1973 driving a March at Zandvoort. That crash was pretty significant at the time because there was such a shitfight afterwards. Roger was unhurt from the crash but died after the car caught fire and the marshals weren't able to help because they didn't have the equipment. David Purley, who I would have a brief brush with early in my own Formula One career, stopped his own car during the race and tried to get Roger out with the marshals watching him – he won a humanitarian award for his actions.

The March was a beautiful, simple, agile little car. The only trouble was I couldn't afford one. I couldn't really afford to go out and drive ten-tenths in one either, in case I smashed it up. But, being a heedless bastard, I didn't think of that and every time I hit the track I gave it my all. One of the tests was a sort of open day to look over the new March cars and I had been invited.

I was surrounded, literally, by rich kids who'd driven up in their brand-new Porsches and who had sponsorship cheques dripping from the back pockets and were whipping around photos of their little pad in Surrey they'd hired at some exorbitant price for 'the season'. It was enough to make anyone sick, these kids walking in and ordering brand new cars, brand new engines and then saying, 'Christ! I nearly forgot a transporter! Can you tell me where I can find a new transporter?'

I knew half of them couldn't drive out of sight on a dark night, and I couldn't help the anger and the envy. Now I realise that they thought pretty much as I thought: that they were going to go out and race and brain everybody in sight. I don't think many people go into motor racing knowing they can't drive and will never make it; some just take longer than others to get that unhappy message. And among them are probably some with huge potential who drop out at the slightest little setback; life hasn't hardened them up enough as it had me.

I did a couple of races with March but I didn't get the full-time drive even though I had some good results. In my first drive in the March I qualified fifth and was then caught up in an incident on the first lap that took out the first four cars in the field. The next week I scored a second in one of the British Formula Three Championship races at Mallory Park.

After I missed out on the March drive, George helped me to get a works Formula Three drive for the rest of the 1972 season with GRD, Group Racing Developments, which had formed with a lot of staff from Lotus, who had closed the customer side of its business. I had a brand new chassis and George supplied the Vegantune engines.

It was good for me, I enjoyed it. They allowed me to prepare the car and I did it at home, in my garage – well, Jim Hardiman did really. He was also doing a bit of racing in England in a Hillman Imp. Eventually GRD got their own transporter and started looking after the car and getting it ready.

I was on a £2000 a year retainer as a works driver, which wasn't enough to live on but all my racing was covered. So I topped up my wage with a few little extras. If someone wanted to buy a new Formula Three car they could have me go down to Snetterton where we tested, and spend the afternoon in it, setting it up for them. This suited me, I was learning while getting miles under my belt – and getting paid.

In all those laps I started to learn how to drive to a time, which is what Otto Stone was trying to teach me in the go-kart. All I had to do was drive fast enough to win. If I was opening a gap without stressing the car, that was all I needed to do. I also tried to be serious by keeping a record of things like gear ratios and the like that we used and what it did for the car.

If I wanted a longer third or a shorter fourth, I knew how to graph it, but it was Jim who would actually change them. If I took the back of the gearbox to pieces, Christ knows what would happen. 'What's happened to that other gear?'

I did my first race for GRD in the Formula Three race at the British Grand Prix in July and finished sixth, which was a pretty good place to put on a reasonably good show. There were lots of races for that class in England at the time, so I got in quite a few races between then and the end of the year.

We had some reliability issues, which wasn't making me easy to be around, especially at Thruxton Park when something broke and sent me into the ditch at Club on the warm-up lap and people were saying I crashed. But when the car ran, we were competitive.

Over the winter I joined the GRD team run by Scottish industrialist Denys Dobbie (DART – Dobbie Automobile Racing Team) and ran the 373 chassis. Every year there's one or two like him: they have a little surplus money and they think motor racing ought to be fun. Dobbie announced that he was going to sponsor three cars for GRD: a sportscar for John Miles, a Formula Two car for Dave Walker and a Formula Three car for me. My first year was to be in Formula Three, my second in Formula Two and my third in Formula One! I signed the contract and thought, 'Well, this is it! I've done it at last, someone had made a plan for me and all I have to do is my job!'

My first race for DART was at Brands Hatch in March 1973 for the Lombard North British Formula Three Championship, which was one of the three British titles available in Formula Three, but not the most important one. Two weeks later I won at Silverstone, again in that series, and I was off and running. On the Friday of that race weekend, the old man died, just short of his fiftieth birthday.

Dad had been getting progressively worse, and after he had a stroke we had to put him in a nursing home. Beverley did a wonderful job looking after him for many months, but it just kept getting worse. We got to the stage where we had to put plastic up the walls and in his bedroom because he was so incontinent, and to her credit she used to shave him and look after him while I was doing my thing, but it became too much.

I was away when he died. After the news came through, Mike Warner, who owned GRD, said, 'Alan, if you don't want to race, we understand.'

But there was no way I was not going to race. The old man wouldn't have been happy if I pulled out of a race just because he had died. For my win at Silverstone I got a big laurel wreath, which I put in his coffin before it was sent back to Australia.

He was quite unique, my old man, illustrated by the fact that he wanted to be buried in a lead-lined coffin with a phone. The lead lining because he didn't want to be eaten by worms and the phone was so he could make a call just in case they got it wrong and he wasn't dead after all. He got his lead-lined coffin, because you couldn't fly a body on a plane unless the coffin had lining to stop any leakage. But no phone.

Unfortunately I didn't come back to Australia for the funeral because I couldn't afford it, but I did my own little farewell to him. He's buried at Springvale Cemetery in Melbourne, right opposite the Sandown car racing track, which is fitting.

I loved him dearly and I was so lucky to have him with me in England those last couple of years, even if he was hard work. One time he hopped in the car and took off to Belgium because he wanted to ship a car back to Australia and they wouldn't do it without him present. I got a phone call from the Belgian police who thought he was drunk, because of his slurring. But the mere fact that he got in a car and went over there in that condition, gives you an idea of the bloody pigheadedness of the man.

After that win I felt like it was all starting to come together. There were three different Formula Three Championships in England at the time, the other lesser series was known as Forward

46

Thrust Championship and the main one was the John Player British Formula Three Championship. I started winning in the other two series as well.

I only did six of the 13 rounds in the Forward Thrust series and still finished seventh. I missed a few of the Lombard rounds too and finished fifth there. It could have been better, I got a one-minute penalty at Castle Combe for jumping the start, which I didn't, and that dropped me from first to 17th.

We focused on the important series, the John Player. The first round was at Silverstone and I had a sticking throttle that took me out of second in my heat, but I still qualified for the final because of my lap times. I fought my way to ninth by the end of the race, and that was a good recovery.

The next week it was wet at Oulton Park – it was England after all – and I got a second there before winning the round a week later at Mallory Park. Now I had wins in all three series and I felt like I was a serious contender.

Strangely, the championship had a round at Zandvoort, a sensational track in Holland. I qualified second quickest to a Japanese driver called Masami Kuwashima, who I was having some great battles with. There's a big right-hander going on to the front straight, and he told me that he was leaving it in a higher gear, but taking it flat, which made the car a lot more settled. I was in a lower gear and the car was unsettled, so I tried Masami's tip in the warm-up and I was instantly quicker. I went on to win the race – with Masami in second.

If I was ever in any doubt, I really learned that weekend not to volunteer anything to your enemy. I'd spend the rest of my life bullshitting people at race tracks, I'd never give up anything to anyone, I didn't spend two days working out all my gear ratios just to hand them over to an opponent. If I was Masami, I would have said I was taking an even lower gear. But he told me something that helped me win that race, at his expense.

More importantly, I returned to England with the championship lead. But by this stage the March 733 was the car to have and Tony Brise had switched from the GRD to that mid-season and started to get the results. A couple more DNFs didn't help me, but some good results and more wins sent the title down to the wire at Brands Hatch in October, with me heading in with a five-point lead over Jacques Laffite – or Jackie the Foot as I called him. Because it was a double-points race, there were mathematically a few drivers with a chance to win.

I led with 109 points in my GRD and Jackie the Foot (Martini Mk12) was second on 104 and it was then a gap back to Russell Wood (March 733) on 89 points, and if it was a standard points race the last driver with a chance. But it wasn't, and that meant Tony Brise (March 733) on 83 points and my mate Masami (March 733) on 76 were also in there.

I wasn't great with playing numbers, but this was perhaps a race to have them in my head. First or second place meant no-one could beat me – even Laffite if he won and I was second – and from there it tumbled down. If Wood won, fourth was enough for me to win on countback. If Brise won, fifth was enough and then if Masami won, seventh would do. If anyone else was winning, they'd have to calculate that in the pits and work out how to let me know . . . but my plan was to win and that would make it easy.

I went out to practice in the morning, and my engine blew up. That forced us into the situation I hate: a big panic and a change of engine over lunch. Nothing should be done in a hurry in racing, except the drive itself; for everything else, you need calm. They got the engine in, just in time, and I gave it a quick try: the bloody thing wouldn't fire properly, or was running on one too few cylinders. I knew I was in for a tough race.

Part-way through the race I was fifth, in front of Laffite while Masami had retired and Tony was leading. Fifth, which was enough to win the championship – and as low as I could afford to drop.

Sitting just behind me was Larry Perkins, another Aussie, who wore glasses as thick as Coca-Cola bottle bottoms. As we went down into Hawthorn, Larry tried to pass me on the outside; I moved over to take up my line, and the next thing I know, we rubbed wheels and I see Larry's Brabham spinning down the straight. I wasted no sympathy on him. I just thought, 'Thank God for that, I'm still in fifth, I should be OK.'

I expected to come around on the next lap and see ambulances all over the place, but when I came around, the track was clear: not a sign of Larry and I wondered where the hell he'd finished up, because he must have hit something. No such luck! Lo and behold, I looked in my mirror and there was this white Brabham coming back at me. 'Oh no! Don't! Please don't!' Here I am with a handful of laps to go and a buggered engine, all I had to do was not drop a spot and the championship was mine – but if he passes me, that's it, no championship.

Well, the engine grew progressively worse, he passed me, and I lost the championship to Tony Brise.

Disappointed is not the word; I was shattered. I headed straight for the bar after the race and there I heard someone say Perkins was going to enter a protest against me for dangerous driving. Larry at that stage was the new boy in Europe and he was writing for the newspapers back home. He said fellow Aussie Tim Schenken was over the hill – but Perkins wasn't fit to clean Schenken's boots, in my opinion. He wrote that this was my third year in Formula Three and he didn't see me progressing much beyond this point. You could say we never struck up a close relationship.

Anyway, when he walked into the bar, I went up to him and said I'd heard he intended to protest me for dangerous driving. In the middle of his answer, he said he hoped he would never have the displeasure of racing against me again. He did have the misfortune to drive against me again too, but he never worried me. He actually made it into Formula One but never got anywhere . . . not even a single point, which I like to remind him of whenever we see each other.

With Jones' Law, which you'll hear of more than once, something like double points was always going to hurt me, and it did. I lost the championship, but I gained valuable experience.

Just as I had spent a lot of time talking with George Robinson, I used to spend time walking around the pits and paddock areas networking and selling Alan Jones, and I was pretty good at saying the right thing. Like when I was testing for March, I'd always say to the designer Robin Herd (who was the H in March), 'This car is fantastic, if it goes as good as it looks . . .' It comes back to me being a salesman – I knew you had to tell people what they wanted to hear to get what you want.

It's a cruel fact of life. I wasn't selling mini-vans, I was selling myself and this winter I was going to need to do a pretty good job.

3

Formula Atlantic Year

THE 1973–74 WINTER after my first full Formula Three season was like every other winter until I joined Frank Williams; cold, long and unsettling. I spent it by the telephone waiting for it to ring and wondering why it wasn't. I thought I'd done well enough to be picked up by some team for a works or a drive, but it was as though once the season was over, I faded from sight.

I was a race-winning Formula Three driver and near as dammit the British Formula Three Champion. During the season I'd had the usual expressions of interest; in fact I'd been courted. But this was just about the nastiest winter of all. I no sooner got a drive teed up than it fell through and that process started with GRD and DART and my promised Formula Two drive.

The writing was on the board during 1973. The sportscar and Formula Two teams weren't competitive and Denys had pulled back his efforts and investment to concentrate on me. What is it they say about motor racing – the best way to make a small fortune is to start with a big one. That was Denys' story, and both he and GRD were pulling out. I thought I knew what was happening, and then it was all gone.

The fact is, I had to stick it out. I wasn't a playboy. I've never known playboys that were all that good, with the possible exception of James Hunt. Niki Lauda was a wheeler and dealer and still is, but he lived in a basement flat in Earl's Court and he didn't go around flaunting himself all over town. Like me, he took his racing seriously. Having to wheel and deal hardens your character. Playboys can go out and just buy what they want – but they generally don't make it. When the shit hits the fan they struggle. If things don't go their way, they call it a day.

For me, it was either throw in the towel and go back to Australia and become a car salesman or have enough strength and conviction to fight for what I wanted. I was determined to get into Formula One and, this time, I wasn't going home a failure. It wasn't as though the whole Australian public was waiting with bated breath to see if I made it or not, but my friends sure were.

I'd seen my old man in his disappointments. He said he'd made his decision not to race in Europe and he didn't regret it. Most of the time, I believed him. But sometimes I think that when my father stood there and said he wished he'd done Europe, which he said as often as he said he didn't regret not having done it, in his heart of hearts he knew he didn't really have the hunger.

My old man was distracted because he wanted to be distracted. He was distracted because he never had to answer to a boss or a sponsor; he was his own boss, he was his own sponsor. That makes it all different. If I were a trillionaire and had my own Formula One team, I too would have been answerable to nobody and I probably wouldn't have got anywhere either. As it was, I had to make the best of everything that came my way.

I recognise that I'm an egotist's son and that I'm an egotist myself and that everyone I know in motor racing is no less of an egotist than I am. I raced for my own satisfaction. I enjoyed the accolades, but that's not what it was about for me. So when it wasn't happening, I imagine I was unbearable.

When I began in Formula Three and I had my first works drive and the transporters rolled up, the motorhome and all the gear, I thought, 'Christ! All this is here for me!' I was more worried about that than I was about the race. I thought, 'If I don't win, all this effort's going to have been wasted!' I had to change my thinking. Yes it was there for me, but I was there for a reason. If I gave it my all and we didn't win, there was nothing more I could do. I had to keep my focus, put the shit to the side and do my job. The old man was distracted. I wasn't going to be.

To help with the finances a bit, Bev and I started running a bed and breakfast to supplement my income. We rented a four- or five-bedroom house, and people would ask, 'Why do you want four or five bedrooms?' My answer was something along the lines of 'I'm from a very big pastoral company and twice a year the whole family comes over and we'd like them to have their own bedrooms.'

As soon as we got the house we went down to the military disposal shop, got some bunk beds and put them in the rooms and opened up for business. We'd head down to Earl's Court to try and get some guests and we'd charge something like five quid a day. It wasn't a lot of money. But when there is about six in each room it adds up.

My job was to get up in the morning and cook breakfast – the full British thing with baked beans, bacon and eggs. It worked well for us: Bev was in charge of housekeeping and I was the breakfast cook and done by nine, which meant my day was free. If I wanted to go to Silverstone or if I wanted to go visit March, or whatever I had to do for my racing career, I had the time. We did that for a year or so and did quite well out of it.

After I'd been running around and trying to get drives and talking to people, I'd come home and we had our own little room away from the guests where we could have time to ourselves. Bev was as invested in the process as me; at least that's what she said in the divorce papers.

She didn't like coming to the races much, so even when I was earning good money in Formula One she often stayed home. She didn't like the hustle and bustle and the running around getting on and off planes. Screaming down to a track somewhere in the middle of nowhere, parking the car outside the circuit and straight out after the race, rushing through the crowd to get to the parked car just to get to the airport.

When 1974 was starting, I had nothing going for me and I was getting desperate. I went up to a race meeting at Silverstone and ran into Bev Bond, who I had briefly raced against in 1971. He told me of a man named Mike Sullivan he knew down Cirencester way, who had a Formula Atlantic and was looking for someone to drive it. 'It's a March and it's got a Ryan Faulkner body on it. He's got a transporter.'

I wasted no time at all and called him up right away.

He was one of those men who come on strong right away over the blower, very straightforward and assured. 'Look,' he said, 'I want you to know we're not mucking about here, we're going to do this properly!' He'd barely hung up before I was down there.

The trouble is, you meet all sorts in this game. I pulled up in his street and there was this Nestle chocolate van outside his place. Something that looked like an open-wheeler was poking out the back of it. I knew I'd been put deep in it right away. The Nestle van was his transporter and that car inside like a slab of beef was his great new challenger in the 1974 Atlantic series.

I weighed up the alternative, which was nothing, wasted no time over it, and said, 'All right, I'll drive for you, but first I've got to go and do a test drive at Snetterton.' He agreed, looking as though he were doing me a favour. When we got down to the circuit we pulled the car out, set it down on the ground and it was plain to see there wasn't one wheel pointing in the right direction. I tried to look very cool and business-like and I said the wheels being all awry was no problem; we could get that fixed. I would drive for him in the Martini International at Silverstone if he'd get his car fixed by March.

He took the car to March and they answered back quick-smart: the sensible thing for us to do was throw that car away like a used Kleenex and buy a new one, because we weren't going to get that one fixed up for less than five grand. So I talked to Robin Herd myself and I told him to forget the rest, just to get the wheels on straight and I'd have a go. I think that shows just how bad that winter was.

Meanwhile, Mr Nestle Van was giving me a hard time about how I was test mad and asking for too much. I suppose he'd been brought up in the old school or flown Spitfires put together with chewing gum. It wasn't looking good. I remembered meeting Baron Beck at Brands the year before, and he'd offered to sponsor me in Formula Two. I called him again this time looking for that little bit extra to get us on the grid properly, well as properly as we could given the circumstances, and he agreed.

I took the car to Silverstone and qualified sixth quickest, with Bev Bond on pole. When the race started, Bev flew off at the first corner, Tony Brise blew an engine, Dave Morgan went wide and damaged his nose cone, while I hung in there and won the race. Fantastic! I gave Mr Nestle Van a job-list of what I wanted done before the next race at Oulton Park, but when I got up there, the car was still in the transporter and what was more, it had never been out of the transporter; absolutely nothing had been done – it hadn't even been washed.

They had put it in the van after the race and probably celebrated down the pub for the two weeks between races.

'Do we do this right?' I asked him. 'Because if you don't get this car right, I'm not going to race for you. If you don't give this a hundred per cent as I am, I'm not going to drive it. You've got to show me you're as keen as I am.'

I wasn't asking him to spend a whole lot of money; it was mostly minor, mechanical things. But there are lots of fly-by-nighters at that level of racing; they don't really have the cash or the guts to do a job properly. I knew we'd been lucky to win that race at Silverstone. I'd made a great impression in a car that was a shitbox. If I went on driving that car, things could only get worse; people would forget Silverstone and my name would be mud.

From which I concluded that I should get out while the going was good. And I did.

I went round to all the people who had good cars at Silverstone and told them why I was withdrawing from the race: because my owner had done nothing to the car, and I was in racing to get results and not just to ponce about. I'm professional, and if they are not going to be professional, I don't want to drive for them.

I hopped in my car and I drove back to London. Sure enough, I got a phone call about four or five days later from Harry Stiller, who was running Bev Bond in the Formula Atlantic. The car was the latest March with a good engine and had all the support needed to do well.

'Alan, would you like to come up to Silverstone and give us a hand?' he asked. 'Bev just can't seem to get his head around the car and he complains of terminal understeer all the time.'

Even before I had said yes I was formulating a plan. I immediately jumped on the phone to Robin Herd and called on the favours earned from my testing work with March.

'Robin can you do me a favour?' Bicester, where they made Marches, was only half an hour from Silverstone. 'Harry Stiller has asked me to come and drive Bev's March. Could you give me an hour of your time, come up and help me sort it out, please?' He said, 'Yeah, no worries.'

We spent most of the morning burning up a set of front tyres trying to dial out the understeer, and between the two of us we sorted it and I went a second under the lap record. Before the day was done I'd taken another half a second off it too.

Old Harry was over the moon about it and waving contracts all over the place. Bev Bond was to be team manager, I was to drive

57

for Harry the rest of the year and Mr Nestle Van and his unpaid bills was to be left to his own devices. And serve him right. I'd found not only a real man and a proper team, but a friend.

Mallory Park was a couple of weeks later and I debuted for Custom Made/Harry Stiller Racing and finished third. That was round 8 of a 14-round championship and all I had to my name was the one lucky win. My relationship with Harry and that team just clicked, and I was away.

I scored pole and won the curtain-raiser to the British Grand Prix at Brands Hatch, as good a time and place as any to perform like that. My qualifying time would have put me on the back row of the grid for the grand prix, which was pretty good for a little Formula Atlantic car with its 1.6 litre engine. And I won the race by the length of the straight.

Harry was jumping up and down with that win. Our main sponsor was Custom Made, who made double-glazed windows, and we had support from one of Harry's business partners named Rob Walker, who also used to sponsor Stirling Moss. I got to know Rob quite well through that period. He was a lovely old man and his wife used to always bake chocolate brownies – good brownies too.

Every race we did in that March we broke a record; it was just a bloody quick car. It had big tyres, wings and a BDA engine with I don't know how many horsepower, but it was a great car. I loved driving it.

I did only seven races with the team in that car and we had two wins, a second, a third and a fourth, along with a couple of retirements. The retirements were probably a result of Bev being overworked. He was doubling as chief mechanic and team manager, and our reliability left something to be desired. That was demonstrated by my gearstick coming out in my hand three races in a row.

My other win in that series was at Oulton Park in the wet. The paddock area was quite literally a paddock. There is a picture of us getting ready to go out onto the track with me sitting on slicks behind Toby Brise on wets – my biggest challenge was just getting out of the bog. I dominated the race on a drying track before it rained again near the end, which made the final laps a bit hairy, but it worked OK in the end.

While the car was going, it was the quickest thing on the circuit, bar none. We may not have won the championship – New Zealander John Nicholson did that with consistency and a full season – but we'd impressed all the right people. I also did a few rounds of the Southern Organs Formula Atlantic Championship, and while I was running I was the leading competitor. I lost that series by two points to Jim Crawford, who had 10 points up when I started.

We'd also pretty much raced everywhere in Britain and Ireland with that car, so I was continuing to build my bank of knowledge on the tracks I would need in the future, as well as a couple that were just plain old interesting. Phoenix Park in Ireland was one of those. It was located in the middle of Dublin in what I am told is the largest enclosed urban park in Europe, and a typical old hay-bales type of track that was a lot of fun.

Fun was what Harry had planned for 1975 too – as well as being serious. We were going Formula 5000 and finally I could have a relaxing winter and Christmas. I had a drive for the next season, I had a wage from my racing and we were earning quite well from the boarding house. Everything was looking rosy.

We'd run a couple of Formula 5000 races at the end of the season and I really enjoyed those cars. My old mate Brian McGuire was racing them, so it was good to spend some time with him again, because our racing paths were taking us in different directions.

Then quite a bit after the season had finished and we were bunkered down for winter, Harry rang and said, 'I'm going to America, the English tax guys are after me.' I went, 'Fuck, here we go again.' He was a bit of a wheeler dealer, which I could appreciate; he was a car dealer and he owned an amusement park in one of the seaside resorts in England. He was a bit of a character and he used to race himself in the 1960s. I got on extraordinarily well with him, but it seems the tax man didn't.

So there I was again going through another winter of discontent.

About three weeks later I got another phone call from Harry . . . 'Fuck it, I'm staying and we're going to go Formula One.'

4

Formula One Debut

THAT PHONE CALL from Harry had me both shocked and surprised, and my up-and-down winter continued its ride. Only this time I was on the up part.

'Look,' he said, 'I'm as tired of pissing about as you are, so I've done a deal with Hesketh. You're going to race a Formula One Hesketh.' I couldn't believe it. A few months ago I was going to race a very good semi-works Formula 5000 car, then for two months I'd been unemployed and wondering if I would ever race again, and now I'd got a drive in a bloody Formula One car. Miraculous!

The Hesketh was the original 308 updated to the same spec as the car James Hunt was going to run in the 1975 championship – the 308B. James had finished the 1974 season quite strongly in the car, starting the US Grand Prix at the end of the season from the front row and finishing on the podium. It was state of the art, designed by Harvey Postlethwaite – the designer who first used the anhedral high-nose design in the 1990s that is now commonplace – and built in a factory at the back of Lord Alexander Hesketh's family home . . . and when I say home, I mean mansion.

Easton Neston it was called, and I'll never forget driving up to it the first time – it was an impressive place, centuries old. When I drove up to the Hesketh headquarters and went up this huge driveway and into the workshop, it was like going into another world.

Strangely, I didn't actually penetrate the great house until 1979, when I was driving for Williams and Bev and I stayed there during the British Grand Prix. We arrived at about eight o'clock, parked the car and went in to see where everyone was. They were all sitting at this fifty-foot long dining table with servants lurking about and Alexander ebullient as ever. I sat down and, after about twenty minutes of chat, I said I'd better go out to the car and bring in my gear. When I got out there, the car had been stripped. I thought someone had stolen all my stuff. But when we were shown to our room, there it was, all unpacked and laid out on the bed, the toilet stuff in the bathroom. Every evening we dressed for dinner, while eight or ten miles down the road were the fumes and the screaming noise of Silverstone. It was a little weird.

Everything in the garage was in its place; the factory was immaculate like a scrubbed surgery. It was another world from the grotty garages I had previously worked in. It sure didn't look the way it did in *Rush*, where it looked as if they had just kicked the horses out. Now this was much more me. My car was up on blocks, all the tools and the floor were spotless, and they even had a little box for me to stand on to climb into the car. When I was being fitted into the car, if I wanted a quarter-inch off here or the steering wheel lifted a bit, it was all, 'Yes Alan, no problem.' My first Formula One seat-fitting – I'd died and gone to heaven.

The mantle of the superstar was falling on me, with everyone very attentive and highly professional. It's all very well for people outside to look down on Lord Hesketh and call him a buffoon who just stumbled into motor racing; from the inside, when it came down to the nitty-gritty of the business, they were very professional. Bubbles Horsley was running the team – a former driver, who was capable of getting the very best out of James Hunt. In that respect it was a very good team. And I always got on well with Alexander. He treated me fairly and everyone made me feel very welcome.

The whole scene was an eye-opener. I had no idea whether all Formula One teams were like Alexander's or whether I'd landed up in some extraordinarily exotic outfit. But it's not in my nature to be thrown by externals: I didn't bother with the social scene; I just did my job. Alexander lived the life of the lord he was, all champagne and pheasants. Helicopters in and out of the track, fabulous parties and lots of fun. It would have been easy to be distracted by the lifestyle that was opening up to me, and sometimes I was, but I was pretty focused.

For me, this was the other extreme of life. I had been scratching to earn a living while pursuing my dream, whereas if I had just stayed in Australia selling cars I would have been doing quite well. Trying to build a racing career in England was not so easy, but here I was.

James Hunt – or Master James as Alexander referred to him – lived the lifestyle of the rebellious public schoolboy that he was. His wife, Susie, was beautiful and just added to the glamour. She ended up leaving him for Richard Burton. At the track he was focused, but away from it he was something else. He was quick and aggressive. Some thought he was dangerous and he had a lot of crashes to his name – the drivers referred to him as Hunt the Shunt.

We weren't ready for the start of the season, which is hardly surprising given it started in January in Argentina and Harry had only just worked out how to pacify the tax man. The next two races were also out of Europe, in Brazil and South Africa, so we targeted the 1975 BRDC International Trophy at Silverstone for my Formula One debut.

James was now in his third season of Formula One and he was making a name for himself in addition to his dangerous reputation. I got to know him quite well during that first half of 1975 and he was a great bloke. He put his Hesketh on pole and I qualified in eighth, which meant I was sitting next to John Watson on the grid and ahead of Mario Andretti.

I ended the race in seventh, which was a great result to start the next phase of my career.

Before joining Hesketh, Harvey Postlethwaite – or Doc as he was called – had worked for March. The Hesketh 308 from 1974 was a fairly conventional racing car derived from the March 731, which the team initially raced. Doc didn't have full control at March, but he did at Hesketh, so he worked on what he saw as the weaknesses of the 731 and eventually the 308 was the quicker car.

For 1975, the Hesketh 308B was developed with rubber front suspension. Doc wanted to make the front suspension lighter, so he started working on the idea of rubber springs based on the concepts used for supporting buildings in earthquake zones. He started playing with the design in 1974 and had it ready for the 1975 season. There was a bit more to the 308B than just the suspension, and all the little tweaks made it a good race car . . . not that I cared that much at the time. It was a Formula One car and it had my name on it.

Two weeks later we were in Spain at the Montjuïc street circuit in the hilly area of Barcelona just off the main strip, for my Formula One championship debut. It was a great track for a street circuit, flowing and picturesque with nice undulations. Not that I was taking much of it in; I was there to race and it copped my full focus. My first race there would be the track's last, thanks to the disaster that awaited.

But before I got to race, there was politics. I tried to stay away from the argument that was happening between the drivers and the race organisers. I remember the drama clearly: all of us sitting in the Grand Prix Drivers' Association trailer arguing about safety. What was this? A debating club? It's extraordinary the heat that can be generated at those meetings, and let me tell you now, the politics of the sport was right up there. There were always people at both extremes, and only a few in the middle. If anything, I sympathised with the get-on-with-the-race group. I knew I wasn't in Barcelona for the Spanish Grand Prix to sit in a motor-home and argue about Armco and fencing. Now I might be a bit more conscious of that, but back then I was thinking only about my own little world.

I was staying at one of hotels with most of the drivers, it was square with a huge air vent down the middle of it that all the windows opened onto. Mario Andretti and his wife were staying either directly above or right below me, and I was lying in bed one night and all I could hear was a broad American accent, 'Mario, Mario, I've got diarrhoea.' If I could hear, so could others, and I felt like shouting out, 'Shhh, everyone can hear you.' But I was the new boy, so I just laughed to myself.

I qualified right down the back of the field and completed only three laps, taking some consolation that they were three really good laps. Emerson Fittipaldi had a dummy spit and pulled out of the race after completing the required three laps in qualifying, which showed the politics hadn't stopped. The race started with a crash in the first corner that took out Niki Lauda and Patrick Depailler, while others were damaged like Andretti, Clay Regazzoni and Vittorio Brambilla. Wilson Fittipaldi and Arturo Merzario pulled out in protest of the barriers, and that all meant I made up a lot of spots . . .

Then Jody Scheckter blew the engine in his Tyrrell and I crashed out with Mark Donohue on the oil that was left. But this race turned into disaster about 20 laps later. Rolf Stommelen was driving for the Embassy Hill team being run by former world champion Graham Hill, and the rear wing flew off his car approaching the Stadium jump. The car flicked into one of the dodgy fences and bounced across the track, where it was glanced by the Brabham of Carlos Pace and became airborne, hitting a lamp post and destroying a barrier on the far side of the road and flying into the crowd.

The race kept running for a few laps because Stommelen's car had taken out TV and phone cables and reports of the crash didn't make it back to the pits. It was red-flagged on lap 29 and that is when the news started to filter through.

Five spectators were killed. Rolf broke a leg, a wrist and a few ribs. That was the last time we raced at that track, and it made for a very sombre mood later. It didn't bother me too much though, which may sound callous now, but they were going to races to watch us get killed and it was a very dangerous sport back then. Yes, you feel sorry for spectators who get killed, but that's about it for me.

The other notable aspect of the race is that it's the only Formula One event where a woman has earned points. Lella Lombardi came sixth for March – but only half points were awarded, so she got just half a point.

*

When I came up into Formula One, the big names were people like Emerson Fittipaldi, Ronnie Peterson, Niki Lauda and James Hunt, particularly James, who seemed to like living his life bathed in brilliant publicity. It was something I would have to get used to, though I was just a beginner and nobody paid all that much attention to me yet. It was still an odd sensation to see my name and picture in the papers: even when I couldn't understand what they were saying about me in the countries where English wasn't the language.

For me though, it was all about the racing. I was there among the biggest names in the sport, and already I was sizing them up as the people I had to beat. If I could get in front of them, that was just another brownie point for me. You get no help from other drivers when you start out in Formula One, and nor would I expect it.

There were two types of drivers: the ones who made you feel welcome, and the ones who snubbed you. I was a new boy, and tradition dictates that you snub new boys. It was like going to a new school; you have to force your way in.

In Spain some drivers came up and said hello and made me feel welcome; others walked right past me as though I wasn't there. Emerson was always polite; Carlos Reutemann was one of the friendly ones, ironic given how things panned out. Jochen Mass was one of the nicest – but then he's just a supremely nice man. Too nice to be a racing driver, some said, though that's not my opinion. He was driving just as hard as the rest of us, but never had a first-class team. He did win my debut grand prix though, his only win in Formula One.

A number of drivers were just neutral: they did their own thing and left me alone to get on with mine. Tom Pryce was nice, but very shy. As for the ones who snubbed me in 1975: they were the ones who were going out of their way to be nice in 1978 and 1979 when I started winning. And when it came to the end of 1979 and they felt I had some say in who my teammate would be for 1980, they were more than just ordinarily friendly.

I can understand why they don't help you out. I would not myself presume to go up to a new driver and give him advice. He might be a better driver than I am. It would be different if he were a younger teammate: Clay Regazzoni and Carlos Reutemann were both helpful to me at Williams, as I was to them. We'd swap information. We were driving very similar cars; we could legitimately help each other. But basically I'm very reluctant to tell anyone anything. You never know: the man you help today could be your enemy tomorrow. I have my own career to think about. Why should I help some newcomer to blow me off?

*

My second grand prix for Hesketh was at Monaco, which was a bit of an eye-opener in a Formula One car. It is such a mongrel of a place, not suited to Formula One at all. If in 1975 you had proposed to start up a race there, the people running the sport would have laughed at you . . . but they *were* racing there; it had history on its side. I used to call it Posers' Paradise . . . still do in fact. It's beautiful to see all the lovely yachts, and all the exotic cars parked in Casino Square and all that crap, but as a racetrack it's hopeless.

Having said all of that, I really regret not having won it. I led it by 20 seconds one year and had a fuel-starvation problem. Gilles Villeneuve passed me going up the pit straight with Murray Walker yelling out, 'Look at that magnificent passing manoeuvre.' That's my favourite place to pass, up the straight. That always gave me a bit of a giggle.

Anyway, there were only 18 starters allowed after the disaster in Barcelona, and I only just scraped in, last qualified. Graham Hill didn't qualify and some other hot-shots didn't either. With about 10 minutes to go in qualifying it looked like I was going to miss. We put on a set of new tyres and I went out on the track as hard as I knew how; and when the flag showed qualifying was over, I remember sitting in the pits waiting for the PA system to tell me if I'd made it. They read it out, starting at the front and after seventeen other names, I finally heard mine.

The celebrations in the Hesketh pits were as if qualifying were winning a grand prix. I was lying 10th in that race when a wheel came off.

At Zolder in Belgium for the next race, I again improved my qualifying but a crash with Jackie the Foot on the opening lap made that my shortest race yet in Formula One. I had qualified only two spots behind James and I was the new-found hero. Alexander was frothing at the mouth saying he would run two cars the next year for James and myself.

Well may he froth: Alexander was soon reclining in his motorhome strapped into all these tubes with an oxygen mask trying to come back to life after a monumental hangover. Meanwhile at the other end of the social scale a bloke called Tom Parks, who owned a restaurant, was cooking bacon and eggs for the mechanics. Whacky days.

Then we jetted off to Anderstorp in Sweden, which was a good little track set up on an airfield, where I got my first finish – 11th off 19th on the grid. But it was also my last race for Harry Stiller and Hesketh. It seems the tax man still wasn't being that friendly, and Harry was off to the States after all. I was devastated. It wasn't that he was out of money, he just didn't want to pay tax in pounds. Harry had put a fair amount of his own bread on the line and had to talk to a lot of people before he got me that drive with Hesketh. I wouldn't have got to where I did without him and George Robinson.

When Harry bailed out of England to sell cars in Los Angeles, he told me not to worry, he would fix an American Formula 5000 for me. While earlier in the year that would have all been great, I now had four grands prix under my belt and I'd been bitten by the bug. I thought I could make it in Formula One. In fact, I thought I could be world champion, and I didn't welcome the thought of quitting Formula One to go race in the unknown in the States.

He was a bloody character Harry. We had some great times together and he will always be the bloke that first put me in a

Formula One car. He is back in England living in Christchurch, Dorset with his wife, Annie. He's a life member of the BRDC, he won the British Formula Three Championship in 1966 and 67, and you'll often see him around the track. I heard recently he was trying to do some sort of deal with Bernie Ecclestone to get him to look after the British Grand Prix.

Harry represented everything that was great about the British people at that time and British motorsport in general. He didn't care if I wasn't British. When he decided his racing career was over and he was going to run a team, he just wanted the best driver he could find.

He obviously thought that I had the talent that warranted giving me a go, and so he did. There were a lot of English people like that and I'll be forever grateful to them.

Fate intervened, as it does. First, there was Rolf Stommelen's big accident in Barcelona; that put Rolf out of commission for a fair bit of the season. Then there was Graham Hill, who ran the Embassy Racing With Graham Hill team – everyone just called it Embassy Hill – for which Stommelen was driving. Hearing on the grapevine that old Harry was taking off to the States and that I might be without a drive, Graham asked me if I would take Rolf's place until he recovered. Yes thanks.

Graham had tried a couple of drivers during Rolf's layoff, including a fellow Australian named Vern Schuppan, who went on to win Le Mans, but he was still searching. From the outside it looked like a dream job, but it wasn't the happiest period of my life, even though I drove in four grands prix for Embassy and scored my first points. The Hesketh was a much better car than the Hill, but a drive is a drive.

71

Socially, butter wouldn't melt in Graham's mouth; he could charm snakes out of the trees. He was a superb diplomat and I learned a lot from him. I've seen him turn from a monster in a heated debriefing argument into a smiling, jovial snake-oil salesman: all it required was that someone from outside would walk in the door. The moment that person left, his smile would vanish and it would be back to business. A great showman, a great ambassador, but a wretched man to work for. Graham was one of the two most difficult people I ever drove for. Having been a world champion, he *knew* better than any driver how to set up a car. Deep down he just wanted to drive. He wouldn't listen to advice. He was stubborn and inflexible. As a result, every car I drove for Graham was different; no two were ever alike.

One race it would understeer like a pig, next it was taily and all over the place. It was almost impossible to handle, and when Stommelen did come back to the team, he had exactly the same trouble with the car and with Graham that I did; it ended in a flaming row and Rolf quit.

So I did my races with him at Zandvoort – where James Hunt scored Hesketh's first and only win – Paul Ricard, Silverstone and Nürburgring. It was good to debut there at Zandvoort, I knew that track. I'd won there in the Formula Three and learnt some tricks. They always had fantastic crowds there too. It is right by the sea and the wind comes off the water, blowing sand over the track, so it can be quite difficult and slippery in places – and different on each lap. But I knew the circuit. The race started in the wet, and although it wasn't my first time in an F1 car in the rain – it had rained at Monaco and Zolder – they were nasty cars in the rain with all that power.

I finished that race in 13th – which was only the second time in Formula One I had seen the flag.

At Paul Ricard I had a spin while dicing with Carlos and Ronnie and I finished in 16th, but it was great to be racing hard with some of the name drivers. To me, it felt like I was starting to settle into Formula One; it felt like I was making an impression.

Silverstone for the British Grand Prix was a very big weekend. Graham was a pretty big name in British motorsport and that weekend he announced he was retiring as a driver. Until the Australian Grand Prix came about, this was my home grand prix too, so it was always special to race there. Tenth wasn't too bad a finish at the time either, given the car, but it was a wet race and I've always been good in the rain. The race was actually cut short when the rain got really heavy and cars were firing off everywhere and there were only six cars still running when they red-flagged it. Of those I was third; if they'd let it run another lap I could have been on the podium.

The German Grand Prix was at the real Nürburgring, with its near 23-kilometre lap and 174 corners that made it near impossible to learn the track in your first outing. You had to drive on reflexes rather than memory. I hadn't been there before as a driver, and like a lot of people I went and hired a little BMW and started to learn the track.

In those days it was a few Deutschmark to do a lap. I had a stopwatch and I just did lap after lap, but you had to stop at the end of each lap to pay your money before you can go again. At the start line there's a whole lot of people, mainly young guys, that wanted to go around as passengers. One guy kept saying, 'Can I come? Can I ...'

'No mate, I don't even know where I'm going myself. I don't want to have a passenger with me.'

I was trying to pinpoint various geographical points to help me and I really didn't want any distractions. There's sections with blind corners and rises, and you need to find landmarks – a tree or a church or whatever – just to get a bit of a guide.

It is the sort of track where you can never do enough laps, which is what I was doing. Anyway, after about the 10th lap or something I pulled up to pay my money again, and there he was again, banging on my window, 'Can I come with you? Can I come with you?'

I gave in this time. 'All right, jump in.' Sure as eggs, halfway around I've lost it and gone into the Armco and pushed the side of the car in and broken the windscreen. My passenger was screaming and the last thing I remember is him jumping out and running off into the distance. The car was rooted, it was crabbing with the front left-hand wheel tucked under it. 'Bloody hell, it's a hire car – what do I do here?'

Around the track there's breaks in the Armco where the marshals have these little chalets. I pushed it into a gap and the idea was to wait until dusk when the circuit was nearly closed, and then try and get out of there. Mark Donohue, who was obviously a stranger to the Nürburgring as well, was doing laps, as was James Hunt. They pulled up and said, 'Are you okay, AJ?' I said, 'Yeah, no dramas.'

They escorted me out at dusk with this thing crabbing like you wouldn't believe. I drove it about 20 kilometres down the road and then rang the hire car company and said I swerved to miss a deer – 'and the car is not in a very good state'. They came and exchanged cars and off I went with the replacement. At the time I was panicking a bit, but now it's quite funny – especially with that bloke pestering me.

Quite a few teams were struggling after Silverstone, because the storm that hit late in the race made the conditions treacherous, and a lot of cars were badly damaged. A couple of cars didn't make it to Germany at all.

It was a real weekend for upsets and upstarts at Nürburgring. Again I qualified nowhere, which I wasn't really enjoying. To say the race was only 14 laps is to perhaps misrepresent it. What the lap distance meant was that if you had trouble somewhere, it could take a very long time to get back to the pits. And so it was . . .

Carlos Reutemann ended up winning the race – his first win of the season – and amazingly Jackie the Foot, Jacques Laffite, was second for Williams. It was his first time in the points and his performance from near me on the grid shocked plenty in the paddock. Only 10 cars finished the race, and I was in fifth – my best ever result and two championship points.

I can tell you, after a grand prix at Nürburgring you come away with a stronger sphincter valve, which I was going to need for the flight home. I flew back to England with Graham. It was a hair-raising flight – he wasn't the most attentive pilot I've ever been with. He sort of wandered a bit. 'Graham, there's a plane in front of us.'

'Oh, okay, thank you.'

Anyway, we got back to England, went and had a pint of beer just near where he kept his plane north of London and then I went home. It was a relatively successful outcome because Embassy Hill got a couple of points, and so he was happy, and felt like I was up and running, although even then I knew it was about to end – Rolf was fit, so that was it for me.

It was also it for my debut season in Formula One. I had points on the board and no drive lined up for the next season. In spite of that car and the problems, I scored more points for the Hill team than anyone had before, or since, and Graham asked me to come back and test their new car at Ricard although he changed his mind which turned out to be okay.

Only a few weeks after that he took Tony Brise down to Ricard for testing instead of me. Graham flew them and four other team members back to London's Elstree Airfield. But they never made it home, crashing in a fog while trying to land. It could easily have been me I suppose.

I wasn't surprised Graham died in a plane crash. I'm not saying anything about the cause of the crash, but he was a shit pilot. As a pilot he didn't concentrate. Numerous times with him I feared for my life. Keeping in mind he was a complete legend in England, you couldn't say anything about him for fear of being run out of the country.

I found out about the crash while Bev and I were hosting an early Christmas party and John Hogan, who was pretty much in charge of the Marlboro money at that stage, rang and delivered the news. So much for the party . . . Graham, Tony and the four engineers all died. He was landing in fog after being advised to use a different airport. Typical Graham, 'No, I should be right, I've done this a hundred times,' and he's flown straight into the side of a hill at a golf course.

But Graham gave me a drive and I'm very grateful for that and I'd like to think I repaid it, because I gave him his highest ever finish as a team owner. At Embassy Hill if you could keep Graham away you could get somewhere. And don't forget, he was twice World Champion as a driver.

*

1975 was coming to a close and, once again, I had nothing lined up for the next season. I did a few Formula 5000 meetings for RAM Racing in a March with a 3.4L V6 engine and scored a couple of podium finishes and some wins. The team was owned by a couple of mates of mine, John Macdonald and Mike Ralph (remember about working the paddock?), and they eventually made it into Formula One as well. Even though I enjoyed the Formula 5000 cars, and winning, it all seemed hollow to me. It was just filling space until the next Formula One opportunity arose.

I had the odd telephone call, I had promises, and I had hints, but nothing solid. I had a midnight call from Louis Stanley, a real waffler if ever there was one, who used to run the BRM team and was now running his own offshoot, Stanley BRM.

There are some cars you don't want to drive and some people you don't want to drive for: Louis and his team covered both of those. His car came to be known as the Stanley Steamer because on track it behaved just like an old-fashioned tea-kettle. He gave me the business as he always did, about how wonderful his car was, how wonderful he was, how wonderful his organisation was. I just didn't believe him; not about himself, not about his car.

The next to call was John Surtees. He said, a bit loftily I thought, that he was trying out a few new boys and would I care to come down and test his car. 'Fucking test drive?' I felt like saying, but beggars can't be choosers.

I went down to Goodwood, a track I knew quite well from all those laps with March, and put in some pretty competitive times. John took me to the coffee shop and offered me a drive for the '76 season.

It was the best offer available and it was Formula One, so I said 'yes' on the spot. If I thought Graham Hill was bad to drive for, I was about to find out he had a competitor.

The whirlwind began. 'We're going down to South Africa to do a week's testing in the new car, the TS19,' he said. 'I'll take you down there and you can get to know the car.'

So I fronted up to Heathrow a few days later. We were sitting in the lounge when he pulled out a contract for me to sign. I tried to fob him off, 'John, I'd really like my solicitor to have a look at this before I sign it. Nothing personal, but that's what I should do.' It was a one-year deal with an option that he could exercise.

'I'm not taking you all the way to South Africa and spending all this money without making sure that I've got an investment.'

I thought, 'Shit, hang on. This is not looking good.' In typical fashion though, my mind was saying be careful, while my hand was saying 'Bugger it, I'll do it and worry about it later' while signing the paperwork.

Then he said, 'I've booked us a spare seat between us.' We were flying economy, and I should have known then what I was getting myself in for.

We hopped on the plane and there was a lady sitting in the middle seat – the plane was full and they put someone in there.

John carried on as only he could, and eventually we took our seats with the lady in there with us, although we shuffled around and she had the window, which left me next to John.

She started talking to me. 'What are you doing?' 'I'm going down to South Africa to . . .' and he started jabbing me in the ribs, 'Don't say anything, she could be a plant.'

I thought, 'What? Who would want to plant somebody on an aeroplane to find out about John Surtees' new car?' He'd never won a grand prix – did he think Ferrari had put somebody on the plane as a plant to find out what was going on with his new wonder car? My doubts were growing fast; I may have just signed for a lunatic.

It's a long flight, so she put the blanket on and it got a bit interesting – but Surtees was still stressing and jabbing me in the ribs. The odds of getting lucky on a plane are very long – and I've got to be sitting next to bloody Surtees when it does. Bloody typical! That stymied me. I didn't even have a drink because I wanted to create the right impression. I didn't want him to think, 'AJ's on the juice.' What a fucking flight.

In South Africa we headed out to Kyalami and I got to meet Brett Lunger, my American teammate who had brought Chesterfield sponsorship to the team. Because he was paying, the first car built was his – and it was the only one that was taken to South Africa. So he did most of the testing, and the fabricated rear uprights kept cracking and breaking. So they'd take bits down to the local engineering shop to have them re-welded.

So I spent most of that week on an off-road bike going up to the nearby snake farm. I didn't get near the car until the Friday. I think John must have suddenly thought, 'Oh, shit, I'd better put

AJ in the car and give him a few laps.' This was the bloke that said, 'I'm not spending all this money and investing all this time unless you sign the bloody contract.'

Anyway, I finally got some laps – six I think – before the uprights cracked again. That was it; that was my test in South Africa. A complete waste of time.

I had my worries about the team and John, but I knew I could outdrive my teammate and maybe we could get some results and the car would be OK if they could make it last. Despite my concerns, I had a drive in Formula One, there was no tax man coming for the team owner, and maybe I could relax this Christmas.

5

I Was There . . . But I Didn't Want to Be

As is so often the case at the beginning of a career in Formula One, getting a drive at all is hard enough, and almost always complicated by the involved deals that are required to make that bit of magic possible. That was doubly true in the case of John Surtees.

Surtees had just enough money, but it came from Brett Lunger, who was Bert Plunger to me. Plunger had all sorts of money behind him, being one of the heirs to the DuPont fortune in the States. He had connections too – which was OK when it was helping me.

He had, in fact, taken over my Hesketh for the final three races of 1975, and now he was my teammate. Because he was the money-man he was to get his car first, and everything else, and I would get mine as soon as it was built.

1976 wasn't a happy season for me, though it could have been.

The TS19 was a pretty good little car to drive and it had a lot of potential. Neither car was ready for the season-opener in Brazil in late January, but Plunger raced in South Africa a month later, qualifying 20th and finishing 11th.

I had to wait another week for my first race for Surtees at the Brands Hatch Race of Champions event. I arrived at the track and walked around everywhere looking for our transporter; it hadn't arrived, which was a worry. Here I am with helmet and race suit ready to race, and I have no team and no car. It did eventually arrive, just before the first practice session, and there was my first real exposure to the frenzy I came to associate with John's running of the team. The mechanics were working on the car in the back of the transporter getting it ready to run. In some ways it was funny, in others scary.

I had to take the car out literally untried. It was brand spanking new, but luckily, because it was a wet, greasy sort of day, preparing the chassis didn't count for much; it was a matter of having some track knowledge and just having a go.

We had already caused quite a stir that weekend. The London Rubber Company was our major sponsor and we were running Durex branding on the cars. England wasn't very enlightened back then, and the idea of the BBC covering an event with a condom-maker prominently displayed on a car was just not going to happen. At that stage in England, they weren't even allowed to run sponsor logos on football shirts in televised games, so we were really pushing some boundaries.

There was a lot of debate going on. The BBC demanded we take the signs off the cars, and John was rightly refusing to do so. Not every Formula One race was being telecast back then, so the fact this non-championship race was on the agenda was pretty significant, and the effect of the Durex backing even more so. John wouldn't back down and the BBC packed up and went home. I think they didn't cover a race all season because of the word 'Durex' on the car.

I qualified sixth quickest as the lone Surtees. David Purley, the driver who tried to rescue Roger Williamson from his burning car in 1973, was down to drive the other car, but it just wasn't ready, which was good because it meant I had the full attention of the team . . . and it didn't have much attention to give.

The race started in the wet and eventually dried and the cards fell my way early. Tyrrell had a trick at Brands, particularly when it was cold, where they used to put lots of toe-in to generate a lot of heat in the tyres and get a bit more grip. Jody Scheckter had used that trick to comfortably qualify on pole and he flew off into the distance at the start of the race and then flew off the track. When that happened I was leading, and I was in front of James Hunt for most of the race, with the car getting better and better as the track dried out. James finally overtook me to win the race, but I finished second and everyone was running around saying our car was obviously going to be the car for the season. Except that we went to Long Beach and only just scraped onto the grid.

I had a very fraught time driving for Big John. He was like Graham Hill in that he thought he knew everything there was to know about racing; he presumed that because I was relatively new to the championship, I knew nothing. Every time I changed gears in that car I scraped the skin off my knuckles. I asked John to put a bubble on the side of the cockpit. He wouldn't do it: he thought it would look funny if there wasn't a bubble on the other side of the cockpit. It just wouldn't look symmetrical. Damn symmetry, I thought; I'd rather be able to change my gears and not come away bleeding.

John was something else. He would take our car down to Goodwood and test it without any bloody wings. All right, except for the fact that if you take the wings off, you've got to change the spring rates to compensate for the loss of the extra downforce. But John would go down and take the car around in a leisurely one minute and 12 seconds and pronounce it 'beautiful'. I'd go down there and take it around in three seconds quicker and it would be a shambles. Any time you take a car out as though you were taking the kids out for a drive, it's likely to feel marvellously good; it's only when you put the real stresses on that the car begins to hurt.

I couldn't understand why you would bother testing the car without wings. He said it was to get a feel for the actual geometry, the mechanical grip. I said, 'But once you put the wings on you're going to generate "X" thousand pounds of downforce and that'll push the car down and give you a completely false reading of what you've had when driving the car without any wings.'

It was just a nightmare.

It took us four months to develop a nose on the car that would generate more downforce. It had a full nose on it like a sportscar, as opposed to a skinny nose with wings like most of the rest. On the full nose you have a splitter, which comes out from underneath the nose, and the further out you bring that, in theory, the more downforce you should create at the front. Then at the side of the full nose it had aluminium fences that came up the sides, which also made more downforce.

And so we'd go through this bloody pantomime at every grand prix. He'd unload the car from the transporter. The front splitter would be in, the fences at the side of the nose would be down and I'd get this bloody crap about how there were some new tyres that would probably suit the car better, blah, blah, blah. Then of course after the first 10 minutes or so, we'd start to undo his theories.

'What's it doing?' 'It's understeering.' 'OK, just put the splitter out a little bit at the front and put the dams up.'

Ten minutes later. 'What's it doing?' 'It's a bit better, but it's still understeering.' 'OK, put the front splitter out a bit more.' By the end of this dance, we'd end up with the front splitter and the dams exactly where they were after the last race. I mean, it was just like a comedy.

We always had to go through the rigmarole of John insisting on his opinions; sometimes it was as though we were re-inventing the wheel. It was a shame, because as I said it was a sound little car, the right shape and very quick in a straight line. If Patrick Head, the designer at Williams, had got his hands on that car, it would have been a world championship car. It had the right stuff.

Then there was the bubble. I was wearing out a set of gloves and still taking the skin off my knuckles. Still he wouldn't give me a bubble. It took a major incident in Germany – the 10th round – to get him to make the change. I was having a nice dice with Vittorio Brambilla – the Monza Gorilla – who was in a March. There's a lot of gear changes on that track, and I was struggling to get it into gear and it was damaging the gearbox.

Early in the race I missed a gear going over the Adenauer Bridge and I wound up with the nose of the car in the gutter and Vittoria went off with me. I got going again, running about ninth or 10th and literally had to do the last two laps without being able to get into third or fourth gears. After the race, I screamed and yelled at John and showed him my hand which was scraped raw through my gloves.

'You put a fucking bubble in this thing otherwise I'm not driving it. I'll end up writing your car off because I can't change gears properly.' He said, 'We'll do that in next year's design, but we'll do it in such a way we do the other side so it's symmetrical.' I said, 'Fuck symmetrical, I want to change gears.' This is the sort of bullshit you had to go through with him.

Anyway, we went from Brands Hatch to Long Beach in the US and I scraped onto the 20-car grid in 19th and, as I said, that was a big comedown for us as a team, especially given the Plunger didn't even make the grid. That track was a great little street circuit and it had a unique character.

The Spanish Grand Prix had moved to Jarama for 1976 after the disaster the previous year at Montjuïc, and while we still qualified well down the order we were more competitive in the race, although Brett again missed the cut. This was the race where Tyrrell ran the six-wheeled car for the first time and James won the race with McLaren, was disqualified and then eventually reinstated after an argument over whether tyres expand when they get hot. The politics of the sport baffled me then as much as it does now.

My next race was something different. I had a relationship with Teddy Yip, because I knew him from running in the Macau Grand Prix on my way home each year. I got on well with him, and as it turns out he was looking for a driver for the SCCA/USAC Formula 5000 Championship in the States. There was only one round I couldn't do because of a Formula One clash, but otherwise I was in. It was running here that I formed a good relationship with Jackie Oliver, who was running in the series for Shadow.

Teddy's Lola was a good car and the team, which was being run by Sid Taylor, posed a stark contrast to what I was dealing with in Europe. Rather than chasing the quicker cars with a more nimble V6 as with my previous Formula 5000 outings, they opted for a Chevy with V8 grunt, and it was a different beast altogether. I settled in really quickly. In Pocono for my first race, held on the one weekend free between Spain and Belgium, I qualified third and finished a lap down in seventh after some dramas.

Sid was a real character. I liked working with him and he kept popping up in my career for a while. He always wore maroon patent leather shoes. Once in the States we went to a pizza restaurant for dinner. When the waitress brought the pizza out, she asked if he wanted it cut into four slices or six. He answered in his strong Irish accent, 'Jesus, four, I couldn't eat six.' He was fun to be around.

No sooner was that race done than I had to get from the wilds of Pennsylvania to New York then England and then off to Belgium. Remember, this was in the days before lie-down beds on planes. I had set myself a pretty gruelling schedule.

Belgium was funny. John had the motorhome parked, literally, next to the track going into turn 1. Brett came up to John in the transporter, and with all due respect, lovely guy, but a typical American running around feeling his pulse and going through the theory of everything rather than just getting on with it, and he said, 'John, I know I can go a second quicker.' Surtees looked at him and said, 'Well, if you brake 50 metres later into this bloody corner that'll help.' I just burst out laughing.

It must have worked though, he finally made the grid in 26th and I was 16th. As a team, we worked pretty hard to get the car right, and in the race it all seemed to fall into place nicely, as I climbed up to fifth with a few retirements helping me. It was my second set of points in Formula One and Surtees' first in nearly two seasons, so that was a big deal for all of us.

The glory was short-lived, because Monaco, as ever, was there to dent an ego. A crash on the second lap gave me an early shower.

Both cars finished in Sweden, where the six-wheeler Tyrrell won its only race, and then at Paul Ricard I retired with suspension failure. I jumped a spot at Brands Hatch after the race as the little war between Ferrari and McLaren kept rolling on with protests, this time Ferrari winning and James being disqualified. So I jumped up to another fifth-placed finish while Brett didn't make the chequered flag.

By now I had won my first Formula 5000 race in the States, well Canada really, at Mosport Park but it was in that series. It was an almost perfect weekend, I just missed pole and then went on to win the race by a second or two from Jackie Oliver. Brian Redman, who won the first round, was down in eighth, so already, just two rounds in I knew I was in the championship mix.

I backed up that win with another at Watkins Glen just after the British Grand Prix. Qualifying didn't go so well as I adjusted to the March 76A I was given that weekend, but I came second in my heat which improved my grid position and then I just had to take over the running in the main race from Al Unser, and I won the race from him by quite a margin and was leading the championship – that series rewarded winning well in terms of points. Plunger was in that race too.

And that brought us to the German Grand Prix, the last at the old Nürburgring. Niki Lauda had been trying to get all the drivers to boycott the race because he felt it was unsafe, but that was never going to work with people like me wanting to race. So we set about practice and qualifying, me learning a little more each lap. I qualified 14th (Brett was 24th), which was not a bad result considering how many laps you can actually run and the little games I had to play with John to get the car sorted.

The race started on a wet track that was going to dry, so with a seven-minute lap you had to work out how big a gamble you were willing to take. It is not like a normal track: firstly, the track doesn't dry quickly because you simply don't have cars going over the same piece of tarmac regularly enough, and if you have the wrong tyres on it is a long time before you can fix the error. Jochen Mass was the only driver in the field brave enough to run slicks at the start and that proved to be the right decision for speed, and by the second lap pretty much everyone had stopped and he led the race.

On the second lap, Niki crashed his Ferrari just before the Bergwerk curve. He hit the wall quite hard and bounced back onto the track with his car burning – there was a bloke in the crowd who filmed it all on his little hand-held camera, and you can find it on YouTube. His car came to rest in the middle of the track on fire when Brett came around the corner and hit Niki's car.

As with a lot of that track, it can take a bit of time to get help, so Brett and Harald Ertl, who also hit Niki's car, were trying to get him out of the burning car. As we all know, Niki was badly burnt, lost half his ear, and his lungs were never the same. But he was soon back racing. The race was stopped after just two laps and then it started again for the second part after Niki had been taken away to hospital.

In the 14 laps that made up what they called Race 2, I skinned my knuckles to what felt like bone for a 10th-placed finish, and that is when I cracked the shits with John. I was there to race, not look after the aesthetics of his car, and if he put a bubble in it so I could change gears I could do that a lot better. We had a good argument and I got my bubble – which you could barely see.

Back to the US again for the Formula 5000 at Mid-Ohio Raceway, a great track but again in the middle of nowhere. I qualified for the final back in a newer Lola than earlier in the season, but didn't start the race. Jackie joined me in the lead of the championship, with Brian Redman and Al Unser closing in.

Back at the Austrian Grand Prix I didn't finish, but I got eighth at Zandvoort a couple of weeks later, which was the only clash for the season with what I was doing in the States. Interestingly Brett decided to do the race in the States over the Dutch Grand Prix, and ultimately missing that race cost me that title.

Monza wasn't much fun and I was a lap down, we just didn't have speed in qualifying, because we weren't preparing the car properly. We had to deal with John and his ways, and I was not really enjoying myself all that much. To top it off, I didn't think that either the team or I could get anywhere the way it was structured, so by then – which was September – I was already trying to think of a way out.

The whole thing was demotivating and making me angry. I knew every time I turned up at a grand prix when they unloaded the car the splitters were going to be reset and we'd have to do it all again. We wasted practice sessions on this; no wonder we were getting nowhere.

I knew I was better than what I was showing. I know Brett wasn't a superstar, but he was missing the cut in qualifying and I was making the grid, so if you measure yourself by your teammate I was doing OK. He had a nice pulse, or I assume he did because he was always taking it, but he really wasn't a yardstick to measure myself by.

It's an old saying, but the first person you've got to beat is your teammate. Simple as that. You've got to establish superiority in the team, because then if you want any alterations or any modifications they're more inclined to do it for you than for him. You're further up the grid, you've got the better results, you're going the quickest . . . so let's look after you. Anyway, Brett had worked out he wasn't a Formula One driver and we had a range of other drivers come in and out of the team – each I assume with a bit of money, which again reinforced my feeling I didn't want to stay.

The Canadian Grand Prix ended up being just more of the same, as was the US Grand Prix at Watkins Glen the next week and that took us to Japan.

I stayed in the States and went to the final round of the Formula 5000 Championship. I needed to win the race to have a chance at the championship. I didn't win the race; in fact all I could manage was fourth, with all my main title rivals in front of me. Brian Redman ended up winning the series from Unser, Oliver and then me . . . if I had won the race I would have beaten Brian.

The problem for me though was that John had an option on my contract for 1977 and had until something like midnight on the Thursday before we started practice in Canada – the last day of September – to exercise it. In Canada I was hiding in my room so I didn't have to sign that bloody option.

Eventually I thought, 'Ah bugger it, this is ridiculous. I'm going down for a hamburger.' Well, the lift door opens, and Surtees is standing there, holding the option.

There was no way I was going to sign that option. If the only way I could race Formula One in 1977 was with Surtees, then I would find something else to do.

I wanted more. I was there to do a job, not just to tool around playing games with an ex-driver who couldn't let go.

I have the greatest of admiration for John's achievements as a racer, and Graham Hill's too. Both were World Champions, Graham twice in cars and John in cars and bikes (four times). He is still the only person to have done both. Big John went for two years without losing a motorcycle race. He started in two classes of bike racing, he was bloody good and even today must rate as one of the greatest on two wheels.

But that doesn't mean they were suited to running a race team. As soon as I started driving for John I realised why the results weren't coming. People like Mike Hailwood and John Watson had driven for him and none of them got results. Another Aussie and one of life's gentlemen, Tim Schenken, also drove for him.

I was told the story after I started about a test session at Paul Ricard. John had to go back to London on business and while he was away Hailwood made up some aluminium plates to put on the front of the car to stop the 'Surtees understeer' as we called it – it seems it was always a factor.

'Well, John, I think I've just found half a second,' Hailwood announced, when John got back. To which Surtees said, 'I don't care, I didn't OK those modifications,' and made him take them off. Megalomaniac.

There were several occasions where I could've just told John to go and jump in the lake, many, many occasions. But you had to wait until an offer came around for a better team and I did have that bloody option for the second year to deal with.

*

The final race of the Formula One season was the first ever Japanese Grand Prix, at Fuji, and it was wet, which always suited me. It had its moments. James and Niki, who was back racing but hardly recovered, were fighting it out for the title. The conditions were so bad that Niki pulled out of the race after the second lap – he was one of four drivers to simply decide it was too dangerous. That meant James had to finish in fourth or higher to win the title. I was running fourth late in the race and closing in on what I hoped would be my first podium, a position I held for precisely one corner.

James had to change tyres while leading near the end of the race – which is how I got to third – and then he started to get back all the spots he needed. Unfortunately that included me. There was nothing I could do to stop him when he was on fresh tyres and mine had had it. James knew he had to finish fourth or better, but he didn't know where he was in the race, so he was driving as hard as he could. He didn't need to take the risk of catching and passing me to win the title, but he thought he needed to. So he did.

They pretty much wiped me out of the *Rush* movie, because my old car had been crashed just before filming began and they couldn't show it. So if you've watched the movie, it was actually me that James passed to take third, not Clay Regazzoni.

The weather was really bad, it was almost dark, but that didn't bother me. When you're in a shitheap you've got nothing to lose, so it's head-down, bum-up, and go for it. I put that car where it shouldn't have been. I'm sure if it was dry it would have been 12th or something, not looking at a podium. Because it was wet, you take a few little chances and stick your neck out. I may very well have got third had it not been for James. The opening laps of the race in the rain I was just passing people; in the latter part of the race I was just looking after tyres, although I still had as much speed as anyone but James.

Niki never spoke to me for years after that because he was absolutely convinced I pulled over and let James go through, because I was good mates with James. I kept saying to Niki, 'No way.' Did he really think I would surrender my first podium? Niki was calling me the 'champion maker', which was shit. James passed me, simple. I would have loved to have been on the podium.

Fourth was a bloody good result for that car and in those conditions. It did surprise me that Niki pulled out; I wouldn't have if I'd been a chance for World Champion. I wasn't and I didn't. I've got respect for him for having the strength and courage to make that decision, but I lost a little bit of respect for him as a racing driver. I get back to what my old man always used to say: motor racing is only as dangerous as you want to make it, you only have to drive as fast as the conditions allow for your car on that day, and hopefully it's faster than the others.

Niki didn't have to do much, all he needed was a point or two and he would have won the championship. He didn't have to win the race. He may have only had to trundle around, keep it on the island, and he could have been world champion again. One thing is for sure, as soon as he pulled in the pits he left it wide open for James.

It was a big gamble to take. I appreciate the fact that he had half his face burnt off and that maybe he had some issues with tear ducts, and that probably made him think a little bit more than what he would normally have done. I just think that if you're a racing driver, you're a racing driver. The Ronnie Petersons of this world just get in and go.

Crashes can either sharpen you up or blunten you. I think you need to have some kind of sense of your mortality otherwise you can be very dangerous. I remember Ayrton Senna got to the stage where he saw God going through the tunnel at Monaco, or some bloody nonsense. I think you do have to have a little bit of fear. Invariably I'd say you'd have two really good scares a season, and if I had mine at the beginning of the season I was happy because I got them over and done with.

I always used to make sure that I had insurance and that I had all the best safety equipment I could afford. I took all the necessary precautions at the beginning of the year, then I went for it. That's all you can do. Otherwise go and be an accountant.

With Niki, I just couldn't work out why he made that decision. As I said, it was entirely up to him, and I respect his courage that he did it, especially driving for a team like Ferrari. I don't think the team with all its Italian bravado would have been that impressed.

I didn't think about it for too long though, I had my own mess to sort out. Even though I had a good season, it could have been

95

better, but without signing that piece of paper I was out of a drive for 1977.

Knowing I was now free for 1977, Teddy Yip asked me if I wanted to run an IndyCar. I figured I had nothing to lose, so he took me out to this place called Ontario Motor Speedway, which is an exact replica of Indy and nowhere near Ontario in Canada; it was in the City of Ontario in Los Angeles. They had a McLaren of Bill Simpson's – he made safety equipment for racing. I drove it and I hated it. I've never spent so much time in a pair of overalls and so little time on the track. A bloody aeroplane would fly over and they'd stop practice because of the shadow it cast. A little bit of wind and racing or practice was stopped. I just didn't like it.

Then I started taking lines. I started going up on the right-hand side of the track and cut down to go through the corner. At one stage I cut off AJ Foyt and he came up to me and said, 'Boy, we don't take lines, we just go around.' I thought, 'Oh OK, good.'

McLaren may have won Indy that year, but I'm pretty sure it wasn't with the car I was driving. In fact, Steve Krisiloff drove the car as well, and he said, 'AJ, if it's any consolation it's the biggest bag of shit I've ever driven.'

Dan Gurney tried to convince me to drive one of his cars, he said it would be a lot better. But no matter how hard I tried, I just wasn't into it. I just didn't like the cars and didn't like the ovals. I didn't like the fact that I could be in sixth position, minding my own business, and old mate that's winning or coming second, loses it, goes up and hits the wall, comes back down the track and either you're hit by a gearbox or a flying wheel. Or if you swerved to miss him, because they're rear-engine cars it becomes a pendulum and you go in to the wall yourself. It's tantamount to rollerball and it wasn't for me, but I went and had a look.

In the end I said to Teddy I just didn't want to do it. I didn't like it and I figured if I was going to be unhappy racing I may as well be unhappy in Formula One, and I bailed. Before I could even sit there in my own misery, Teddy said let's go to Vegas for the weekend, and that is as good a place as I know to forget anything.

Eventually I made it back to Australia and then I thought, 'I don't know what I'm going to do.'

Niki Lauda

I never really had a lot to do with Niki Lauda, but I admire much of what he did even if I did think he was soft at Fuji.

I never did entertain Niki's argument that I let James Hunt through at Fuji, and I don't think he liked that. Even though he was fairly charismatic we had a period like the cold war. James used to socialise with him a reasonable amount, and he kept saying, 'Niki's a good bloke, give him a go . . .' but I didn't.

Niki used to like the odd fag and a drink from time to time, but he was very clever, and wanted people to think he was articulate – which he was. But he was very pig-headed in a Germanic way. We mended our bridges over time, and I quite enjoy what time I get with him now.

I remember I was coming back from London one year, and I got on the plane and this very unmistakable voice came on and said, 'Good morning, ladies and gentlemen.' It was Niki. I asked the hostess to go up to the pilot – who she would not confirm was Niki – and say that Alan Jones is here and says hello. She came straight back – Niki had invited me up to see him and I spent most of the flight with him in the cockpit.

While his airline is no longer in business, it was a big deal for a while. When one of his planes crashed and killed more than 200 people in Thailand back in 1991, it was his tenaciousness that finally got Boeing to accept the blame and completely exonerate Lauda Air. They had to modify the fault out of their planes. That's the sort of guy he is. He was part of the investigation and just would not give up.

He's reasonably heartless, he is very Germanic, he's

strong-headed and single-minded, ruthless and intelligent. He was not as robotic as *Rush* made him out to be, but that film did show his courage well. From what I know, all that stuff in the movie where they were sticking things down his throat and clearing it out all happened as shown. That was amazing, I'm not sure I could have done it.

The fact that he made the comeback so quickly and went to Monza was just amazing bravery. I hold Niki in very high esteem despite my doubts over Japan, I really do. He's one of the greats.

6

Me and My Shadow

So THERE I was having an Australian summer that I really didn't want. Strangely, given my intense dislike of the cold, I craved to be back in Europe in the middle of winter. It was frustrating: just as I was getting momentum again, it had all stopped.

I knew my next step in Formula One had to be a serious one. I had to pick right. I couldn't afford to drive for another lunatic, but also, I couldn't be too fussy.

While in Australia I ran in a thing called the Rothmans International Series in a Formula 5000 car under the Theodore Racing banner for Teddy Yip. The series ran on four weekends in February, starting with the Australian Grand Prix at Oran Park, which I won but was pushed back to fourth when they said I jumped the start. The glory days of the sport in Australia were well over – there were no superstars coming down for the races like when Dad was running, so I had to battle a bunch of locals and a few Aussies who were doing well overseas, but not in Formula One, since that season had begun, as I was all too aware.

Surfers Paradise, which was a great little track not far from where I now live, was no better for me and I finished fifth. At Sandown only five cars finished, and I wasn't one of them. Which brought us to the Adelaide International – and let me tell you there wasn't much that was international about that joint.

But everything clicked that weekend and I won the race from pole in an older Lola T332 that the team had. I lapped the field, which was satisfying, but on 27 February that series was done and I had nothing lined up.

Into March, it all changed. Lady luck played a shocking hand to one driver – and she was being very kind to me.

Tom Pryce was a driver in a similar place to me. A Welshman, he was also working his way up and had done OK in winning the 1975 Brands Hatch Race of Champions, and in 1977 was driving for Shadow. The first two races of the season were nothing for him, or his teammate Renzo Zorzi, who was responsible for some of the money coming in the door for the team.

The third race of the season was at Kyalami. Zorzi had fuel problems and pulled over. Two marshals ran across the track. One made it. The next one, a teenager carrying a fire extinguisher, didn't. Just as he was crossing, teammate Tom Pryce came over the hill at 270km/h. He clipped the marshal – he was thrown in the air like a rag doll and his injuries were so bad he could not be properly identified. His fire extinguisher hit Pryce in the helmet. He was virtually decapitated and died instantaneously. It was gruesome.

I got a phone call from Jackie Oliver, who was running the team, and he asked if I wanted to take Tom's place in the team. Silly question. It was a pretty good car, or so it seemed on the outside. Renzo, who made Brett look like a superstar, had picked up points in the new DN8. The only problem was Surtees and that bloody option on my contract that he wanted to exercise.

But what many in the paddock knew, and I didn't, was that while John fancied himself as a lawyer, he was no more than a bush lawyer. Jackie said he'd handle it, and lo and behold the contract had enough holes for Jackie to drive two DN8s through. He got me out of the contract and into the Shadow team.

There was a break before the next round. I flew from Melbourne to Heathrow, where we met up. I signed a contract with them, went up to Northampton, where the factory was, for a seat-fitting. Then we got ready for the United States Grand Prix West at Long Beach. I had a half day's testing in the car at a track called Willow Springs, a hundred miles or so out of Los Angeles, and then it was on to the streets of Long Beach.

This felt right. When I raced for Graham Hill or John Surtees, I felt I was just doing a job. I was glad when I'd finished my daily chores, whether it was practising, testing or racing. At Shadow it felt different, and in hindsight it was clearly a turning point for my career.

Joining Shadow was a revelation. They didn't have quite enough money, but they had a racer's edge. Don Nichols owned the team. Now he was an odd, shadowy figure; a strange, lanky, bearded American who'd spent years in Asia in the 50s and 60s doing none of us knew what. His job in military intelligence inspired the team's name and logo, a spy-like figure lurking in the shadows.

Alan Rees, the team manager, was one of the best in the business and, as a team, Shadow was very professional. Having a good team manager can change your whole outlook on racing. He breaks down the isolation you feel out there, alone in your car; he makes you feel that you belong to something bigger than yourself. Every good team manager is a man who can read a driver's mind – and respond with sympathy. He understands his driver's needs, he senses dissatisfaction, he is aware of the whole man, not just the employee who sits in the car and drives it.

He is also as fiercely competitive as the man he is managing. If he gets a whisper that somewhere there's a good set of wet tyres hidden away, he gets his hands on them before anyone else has wind of it. A team manager is a facilitator. His job is to extract the best from the material – human and mechanical – at hand. Often, that isn't a matter of spending money, it's a question of having brains, judgement and organisation. Fundamentally, he needs to be a good shrink.

Alan Rees brought me out of the endless dissatisfaction I'd felt working with Hill and Surtees. The one word that describes 1975 and 1976 is frustration – let's make it two words, frustration and anger. There's nothing pleasant in knowing that you're driving among the wankers who would have difficulty getting a Formula One drive if they weren't bringing in money. I don't like having the finger pointed at me and people saying, 'Oh, he doesn't count for much; he only qualified 15th.'

My year with Shadow was much less frustrating. Mostly because I knew there wasn't much we could do short of a new car. The one we had was overweight and very slow in a straight line and nowhere near as competitive as I thought. Nichols and his team

103

were in deep financial trouble and I considered myself lucky, at that stage, to have a good, steady drive. To drive a consistent loser is in some ways better than driving a potentially quick car being ruined by mismanagement, which was what I had at Surtees.

And there was a process of constant improvement too within the financial constraints. During the season Tony Southgate came to the team, and altered the bodywork on the car. He made it a lot thinner and a bit more streamlined. It started out the year as quite a bulky old thing, and ended the year nice and trim – a bit like me actually.

A season with Shadow kept me in play. Either at the end of the year Shadow would get a new competitive car or somebody would spot me and ask me to drive for a better team. Around the business, people know when it's your car that's at fault and not you. I think I was rated at Shadow by what I could do within the limitations of the machinery at my disposal. 'Look at old Jonesie,' someone would say, 'he's doing well in that old shitbox of his, isn't he!' After all, there's always next year, so my task was to wring what I could out of it and get noticed.

There's no shortage of drivers, but if you're good, you'll be spotted. Motor racing doesn't have the equivalent of the great poet dying starving in a garret because no one knows he's great.

So I went from sitting in Australia and pondering what the hell I was going to do, to joining a team where I was finally happy.

We stayed on the *Queen Mary* for that race at Long Beach. We could walk to the track from the ship and I liked that. For many years the team was UOP Shadow, which stood for United Oil Products, but my car was sponsored by Villiger cigars – and Henry Villiger was a very nice guy.

As I said, it was a much happier atmosphere and I was pleased I backed away from the Surtees deal for 1977. If I asked for a change to a car, they just did it, as opposed to questioning you. I was now able to qualify mid-field rather than the back of the grid, which was amazing given the Surtees was so much a better car.

Long Beach was a pretty sombre affair in many ways. To make matters worse, Tom Pryce's death had been followed by a plane crash that took the life of Brazilian driver Carlos Pace.

I qualified in 14th but failed to finish the race, getting to half distance before the gearbox let go. Mario Andretti won – which the Americans loved – in the Lotus 78 wing car, which was the first win for a ground-effects car and the start of an era that would agree with me.

Spain was a month later, which gave us a bit of time to get ready for the European summer. Not that we got too far with it: we qualified in the same spot again and I crashed out during the race. Renzo was the slowest driver in the field and was the first car lapped by Mario on the way to another win for Lotus, and at the next round Renzo was somehow replaced by Riccardo Patrese.

Monaco, as I have said, is both a place I love and hate. You know when you have done well there that you are at the top of your game. It is a tough little track. Our speed was comparatively a little better, and we were knocking on the door of the top 10 in qualifying, and then in the race the cards fell nicely and I ended up in sixth, my first points for Shadow.

I've now got the right horse, well a semi-right horse, and I knew this was just the start of it. I was always very much one race at a time, so it was only when Monaco was done that I turned my attention to the next, the Belgian Grand Prix at Zolder.

105

I only qualified 17th, but the race started wet and that was good for us. It dried out during the race and we had to change to slicks, but we made good ground and claimed fifth spot. Plenty of people fell off the track that day, and I have always prided myself on my wet-weather driving. I stayed out of trouble and kept it running and was faster than most. The Shadow was also good in the wet; anything that caused the others to slow was going to help when we weren't dropping at the same rate.

I didn't socialise much at the track so I didn't know if people were talking about me, I hoped they were, but I had no idea. I thought with that car, that we as a team were doing really well, and I was driving as well as I ever had.

The Swede Gunnar Nilsson won his only ever grand prix in Belgium driving the second Lotus 78, and that made the future of the sport clear to me: ground effects. Lotus with Mario would win a lot of races in 1977, but with a shocking run of reliability they didn't win the title. Niki did that with consistency.

The big straights of Anderstorp just didn't suit our car, and the grunt of the Matra engine in the Ligier driven by my old mate Jackie the Foot won the race when Mario had engine trouble. In some ways I was envious about the position of the French, not that I ever wanted to be French mind you, but they backed their own, like Ligier backed Laffite. I was beating him in the smaller classes, but Australian businesses just wouldn't get behind me, so I had to do it the hard way.

His win, I believe, was the first time a French driver had won a grand prix in a French car with a French engine and a French sponsor. That's a lot of frog's legs. Early in the race, I was running with him, but our little Shadow just wasn't in the same league as the Ligier in a straight line, and he picked off the cars at the end in a way we just couldn't have done. At least they didn't have the French national anthem to play, not having expected he would win . . .

They did have it ready at Dijon in eastern France, not that they needed it. Jacques finished two laps off the leaders with Andretti winning again. I lost another gearbox.

Silverstone was a real power, top-speed circuit back then and I dropped a couple of spots from my regular 10th in qualifying. The race was nothing special except that I finished seventh, one spot off some extra points. James won that race, which made for a great atmosphere with the British fans.

There was no respite from the top-speed tracks with the German Grand Prix moving to Hockenheim. You needed a good chassis to conquer the stadium section, but the rest of the track was essentially a drag strip. Seventeenth was a shocking qualifying effort and I crashed out on the opening lap.

Thankfully Austria was a little twistier and wet. They had slowed the track down a lot since the death of Mark Donohue there a couple of years before, but it was a tough few laps at the start regardless. I qualified 14th and sat next to Vittorio Brambilla on the grid on slick tyres.

It was damp at the start of the race and the old girl was pretty good in the wet, being reasonably softly sprung and heavy. It was just a bit more forgiving than a lot of cars in those conditions. Andretti in the Lotus was great up the front with that ground-effects car. After a few laps I passed Niki to get into the top 10, and some of the cars that started on wet-weather tyres had to stop, so I moved up a few more spots.

Mario's car broke down and James was leading and then I was in fourth. I felt like I could do so much with the car that day, I picked off Hans Stuck and then Jody Scheckter pretty easily which put me into second. The track was damp, so if you went off line it was pretty treacherous, but we seemed to have so much grip.

With 12 laps to run, I passed James sitting by the side of the road with a blown engine. The next lap around, the pitboard said P1: I was leading my first grand prix and the track was now pretty much bone dry. I was just waiting for someone to catch me, but I was able to extend the lead by a little bit each lap. In those conditions you have to do just enough. I went back to my early days testing for GRD at Snetterton: if you're doing a certain time in those conditions and you're increasing your lead, even if it's only a fraction of a second, you don't need to try any harder. Don't try any less. Just drive it to that pace and you'll win. And that's what I did.

I started hearing noises, I started to feel everything in those 12 laps leading. I'd had late-race failures in that car before, so it was a very nervous time. I was able to run away from them all to win by more than 20 seconds from Niki at his home grand prix. It wasn't a popular win, since Niki had never won at home, and like Jackie the Foot a few weeks before it was so unexpected they didn't have the Australian national anthem to play.

Some drunk in the crowd with a trumpet played 'Happy Birthday' and I couldn't have cared less. I'd just won my first grand prix from 14th on the grid, one of the lowest qualifying positions ever for a race winner. The emotions after that win were strange – mainly an overriding sense of relief. You've spent all those years in shitheaps and with poor management and now you're in a semi-shitheap with some good people, and you've won Shadow's first – and as it turned out only – grand prix. And they've had some bloody good drivers.

The whole team was over the moon. We had a big night after that – the Shadow boys really lived it up. All those mechanics work their guts out, they're unsung heroes and the win meant as much to them as it did to me.

Beverley was with me at that race, which was unusual. We'd just picked up a new Mercedes in Stuttgart and driven it to Zeltweg for the race, and I remember saying to her after the race that it didn't matter what happened from there, I had just won a grand prix.

Then, of course, two days or so later when the alcohol wears off, the hunger kicks in and you want more. If I can win one, I can win two . . . and so on. In my mind, I had proven a point. That car wasn't good enough to win a race, but in really tough conditions that is exactly what I did.

I used to go reasonably hard after every grand prix, because I used to abstain from alcohol in the lead-up to a race. I wasn't a big drinker, I used to allow myself a pint of beer every night when I was at home when I'd go to my local. During the race weekend I wouldn't drink at all, but then on Sunday night I had to replenish my lost fluids from the race. That was my excuse.

I got to the stage where the people who were running the motorhome used to put the cans of Foster's in the fridge or the freezer at the right time, even allowing for me to go onto the podium, so it was just the right temperature. By the time I got back to the motorhome I was so dehydrated that it virtually hurt going down – and it meant that I was pissed on one small can.

It was great. I wish I could simulate that all the time.

I was staying at a pensione because there were no real hotels near that circuit, and had the obligatory Wiener schnitzel and copious amounts of white wine.

About that Mercedes. At that stage in my career, I was earning about 100 grand a year, which was enough for me to buy a £50,000 house in England and also the Merc. A guy named Gerd Kramer was in charge of VIP deliveries for Mercedes-Benz and we got on really well. I had to order my car through him. As ever, I had my own name for him, which was Dirty Gerdy . . . I'm not sure the Germans understood, but I got away with it.

The deal was you could order a new Mercedes and they would give you 20 per cent discount off the factory price – not the retail price – less stamp duty and sales tax. When you bought the car, you drove it to the border, handed in this form and then about a week later you got your sales tax and duty back. It worked out a bloody cheap car.

The only stipulation was you weren't allowed to sell them within 10 months, which I found out about because I sold one pretty much straight away one time, and I got into a bit of trouble over it. So normally you'd keep them for 10 months and then offload it in the UK or bring it back to Australia.

The German Grand Prix was also near the Mercedes factory and Sindelfingen, where Hugo Boss clothing is made, was also close by. So I'd fly into Stuttgart, pick up my new car, drive up to the Boss factory, load up with a full boot of shirts and sports coats and trousers and Christ knows what else, go back and stay at Gerd's place that night and then drive up to Hockenheim for the German Grand Prix, and then after that drive back to England and have all the pants altered and everything. Beautiful.

At the Boss factory for the first time, I met Jochen Holy, who owned Boss. I picked out a few clothes because I thought I was paying for it and didn't want too big of a bill. Boss was and still is expensive, so I was being very cautious. When I got up to Jochen's office he said, 'No, that's compliments of us.' I thought, 'Shit. Thank you. Any chance of going back in the factory?'

So I got Gerd to get me some Boss stickers for my helmet and I think I got a patch for my race suit as well. When Jochen walked down the grid at the start of the grand prix he saw me with the Boss stickers on, and from that time on I didn't have to pay for Boss gear while he was there. He was that rapt that I didn't just take the clothes, that I went to the trouble of sourcing some badges and putting them on. He eventually sold the business – and that arrangement was ruined. Jones' Law.

After the win Don Nichols said he wanted me to go with him to the States and try the Can-Am car. I said, 'I don't know whether I want to do that.' To which he replied, 'Oh you fuckin idiot, I'll pay you.' I think he paid me something like 25 grand a race.

In typical Jones' fashion, I said, 'Yep right. What flight am I on?' He also flew me first class, which was pretty impressive and left me wondering how long that had been going on, and why wasn't I in there all the time. I had a big bowl of pears floating in champagne. Amazing. No beds or anything back then, but it was pretty slick. I now had every intention of always turning to the pointy end when I got on a plane.

My first Can-Am race was in the Shadow DN4B at Mosport Park in Canada. I'll never forget it, the nose was scraping on the ground. It was a monster. It had a 5-litre Dodge engine in it and they were talking big numbers when referring to horsepower. It had a wing on it the size of a large dining table. It was black and a very aggressive looking thing.

In all, I did three Can-Am races that season. I put that thing on the front row at Riverside in October right next to Patrick Tambay, who was leading the series and racing for Carl Haas. After that Carl offered me a drive for the 1978 season. I was keen, because that was the car and the team.

I'm not belittling Patrick, but I used to say to Carl, 'Jeez, this is C&C, cruise and collect.' He had really good mechanics, he was the North American distributor for Lola and also for Hewland with the gearboxes, so his cars wanted for nothing. The two mechanics were fantastic. And the guy that was sort of working with him was Jim Hall, who was pretty famous stateside.

Anyway, I did have to go back and drive Formula One first and finish the season, now as a race-winner. I had engine dramas in Holland just after getting back from Mosport Park and didn't finish, which was almost as humbling after the win as was my 16th qualifying spot.

But there was bad news when I got home.

My old buddy Brian McGuire had been killed.

He was testing at Brands Hatch when a fulcrum pin came out of the brake pedal, so when he went to brake the pedal just fell away. The car clipped the inside curve, I think it was at Stirlings Bend at Brands Hatch, and that launched it over the fence. He landed upside down at the marshal's post – the crash killed a marshal as well.

Brian was my best mate. We'd grown up together. Brian was my best friend, from way back in the days when his father was the spare parts manager at Dad's Holden dealership in Essendon.

We grew up together. He was a year older than me, but it didn't matter. We'd go to Dad's Holden dealership and get up in the spare parts loft and eat fish and chips. Our families went on holidays together. Our parents pulled us together, and from there it was all about motor racing and our dreams. We knew each other for a long, long time.

We went to England with a shared dream, selling the minivans to fuel that dream. We'd both had a crack at Formula One. We were as thick as thieves – which maybe we were. He only got the one race and didn't qualify, but I am sure he could have done more had he not been killed that day.

I eventually concentrated more on racing than he did, while he stuck with the vans and built up a really good business. When I got my contract with GRD and gave up on the vans, we drifted apart a little and then even more when I started in Formula One. But he was the kind of mate that was always a mate, you don't have to spend a lot of time with someone like that.

The van business was doing well, and he bought a Williams FW04, and then another, giving him two cars to play with. He won a round of the Shellsport International Series at Thruxton Park and then entered in the 1977 British Grand Prix. He didn't make the grid though, and a month later he was dead.

When he died he was driving that Williams FW04 that he had modified and called McGuire BM1. We'd spoken about the need to prepare that sort of car properly. I remember during one of our chats in the pub, warning him to be careful with a Formula One car. The cars that I was driving at the time were being pulled apart after every single race, crack tested, and meticulously put back together again. Brian couldn't afford to do that. He was basically in a Formula One car, even though it was maybe two or three seasons old. Who knows, had he done that would the pin have broken? He had so much more to do. He was killed in a practice session he didn't need to run, but he just loved driving and loved racing.

Brian had talent as a driver and he was keen, but you can't be a businessman and/or caravan dealer for four or five days of the week and then a racing driver on the weekend. It doesn't work. He couldn't afford to concentrate on it 100 per cent because he had to rely on the business to fund the racing.

I look back on this a bit to work out if I was luckier than him – you know, getting the right break – but I don't think it was luck. I walked away from the business to give my racing 100 per cent, and he couldn't or didn't.

I didn't look on it at all as Brian getting killed motor racing; it was just Brian getting killed. It would have been the same if someone had called up and said Brian had been electrocuted. The fact was that Brian was dead. I was upset by his death, but not by the way he was killed.

There's no question his death hurt.

At that time in car racing, death was always a factor. Losing a good friend didn't change the way I viewed my sport. I dealt with it and prepared for Monza. That's what I had to do, simple as that.

I qualified no better than I had in Holland, but the car was good in the race and I fought my way into third, which was a very satisfying result.

In those days I raced better than I qualified because I just couldn't get the outright speed from some of those cars. Over the two-hour period of a race I could get the best out of whatever car I had, and that meant if it lasted I would climb up the order . . . the only question was how far. Making the podium at Monza was a great experience, especially being up there with a Ferrari driver.

I had four races on consecutive weekends in North America, starting with the Can-Am car at Sears Point in a new Shadow DN6 and finishing with the same car at Riverside. The first of the grands prix was at Watkins Glen where it was wet, which normally would have made me smile, but I crashed out after only three laps. I got fourth in Canada a week later which was a really good result after my best-ever qualifying, a really nice seventh on the grid.

So after the Can-Am race at Riverside, my racing year finished in Japan with another fourth place. What was funny that day was that James won the race, and he and Carlos Reutemann, who was second, left the track before the podium presentation. If it meant so little to them, I could have got up there for my fourth place, which did mean something to me.

Better still, I had finished the championship season in seventh spot and had 22 of Shadow's 23 points for the season. I felt it was a pretty good season in what was really not that great a car.

Fortunately for me, others thought so too. Assuming they kept the Can-Am Series on separate weekends to the grands prix, I had that lined up, but in Formula One I was still talking to people. Frank Williams was first into serious discussions, then it was Ferrari.

7

Ferrari Driver / The Turning Point

THE PHONE RANG one day back in London and it was Luca di Montezemolo, then the manager of the Scuderia Ferrari, its Formula One team. He asked me if I wanted to come down to Italy and talk about driving for Ferrari. I think you know the answer.

He said, 'We must keep this very secret because we don't want people to know.' That is – he didn't want the nineteen other drivers he was talking to to find out. 'You will meet Mr Ferrari,' he told me, 'and he will ask you a series of questions, starting with why you want to drive for him. You will need to have your answer ready.' Personally, I thought it was pretty obvious what my answer would be.

The whole world knew Ferrari was looking for a new driver to replace Niki, who was leaving to join Brabham, so when I arrived at Milan airport people were looking at me and pointing. At that stage the championship was still running, but Niki was looking good and eventually did win it.

Knowing they wanted it secret, I was all prepared for some cloak-and-dagger stuff – remember, I was a Shadow driver. I walked into the airport hall – and there was a driver waiting for me in blue overalls with a sign over his head saying 'Alan Jones'. He led me to a Ferrari outside with Prova number plates – which meant it was some sort of experimental model. This was the Italian way of keeping something secret!

There are two things about Italy that make it such a great place. One is that Formula One is a national pastime; two, nothing stirs their hearts more than Ferrari. People were whispering as I passed them. Driving for Ferrari was important to the nation – which only made my desire for this drive grow.

So I've jumped into the passenger seat of the Ferrari and he's taken off like a rocket, passing trams and trains on the wrong side. I am not a good passenger at the best of times, but I was quite looking forward to actually meeting Mr Ferrari and in the end I said, 'Mate, slow down.'

You could just hear him thinking, 'What is this fucking Australian doing here? Like I should be going to talk about a test drive. I'll show him I can drive.'

Amazingly, we did make it to Maranello, which is normally a good two-and-a-half hour drive, in what felt like ninety minutes. At the factory I was met by Piero Lardi, who I didn't realise then was Ferrari's illegitimate son to an actress named Lina Lardi. He was driving a little Fiat so I just thought he was some shitkicker from the factory there to entertain me for a bit. Turns out he was Ferrari's only son, the other having died long ago. So when the old man died, Piero inherited 10 per cent – which was worth US $1.1 billion when the company went public in 2015.

Anyway, Piero took me for a tour and it blew me away. Once I saw all their facilities, I just couldn't believe that they didn't win every race: with their own foundry, their own private circuit, their megabucks. It was so different from the teams I had been with that were just scratching around trying to get enough new bits to go racing.

Yes, I did want this drive.

From there we went over the road to the private track, Fiorano, to meet the Old Man. We went in through the security gates and up to his casa. There were big double doors, and I was left there waiting outside for a bit. In the end the doors opened and he was sitting behind his desk with all the mementos on the wall, and dramatically lit, like a movie. To me, he was this god-like figure known as Enzo Ferrari. My first impression was how very pale he looked. 'He's dead,' I thought. 'They've propped him up and they've got a recording of his voice coming from behind a curtain.' If I hadn't known he was Enzo Ferrari, I don't think I would have been greatly impressed.

He was friendly enough in the ten minutes we spent together, but the only question of his I remember was, 'Why do you want to drive for Ferrari?'

'Please sir, I'd like to be World Champion, that's why.' May as well get to the point.

After I had my ten minutes with him, we went for a look at Fiorano. I mean Ferrari had its own test track! I knew it, but I couldn't get over it. At that stage they were the only Formula One team that had anything like telemetry – remote monitoring of all performance data – in as far as they had lights at the beginning of the corner, the middle of the corner, and the exit. They could measure when they made a change on the car whether it changed the speed on entering, leaving or going through the corner. Again, I thought, 'How do they ever get beaten?'

All they had to do to win was bring every driver down there for a look and they'd be psyched out.

'So, Alan, if you get the drive, would you be prepared to live in Italy?' I wasn't sure if Piero was just making idle chat and if it was important to answer him at all. I felt like saying, 'Listen, I'll live at the North Pole if I can race for a team like this.' I was a little more straight with my response.

My last visit was to the accounting department where we discussed the terms of a contract and so on and they gave me a contract to sign, which I did. Then they told me, 'We must warn you that we are looking to hire a North American driver because it helps our sales in North America. We are talking to Mr Andretti. But if we can't get Mr Andretti, you will be our driver.'

'OK, I understand.'

So now all I had to do was wait. And wait I did. When I picked up a copy of *Motoring News* and the headline on the front cover read 'Andretti Re-signs to Lotus', I thought, 'Yes, I'm a Ferrari driver.' I went back home and started packing, well, mentally at least. A couple of days went by. I didn't hear from them, and I started to wonder.

I eventually rang them to see when I was expected in Italy. The response was sharp. 'Well, you know how we told you we wanted a North American driver?'

'Yes.'

'Well, we have signed Mr Villeneuve.'

'But, hang on, you told me that if Mr Andretti didn't sign . . .'

'Yes, but we also told you we wanted a North American driver.'

I said, 'Well, what do I do with my contract?' I think the response was as clear as 'I'd stuff it up your backside'. I wish I still had that contract!

Gilles actually ran the last two races of the season with Ferrari. I knew I had to work out something from my other options. Don Nichols was keen to keep me at Shadow, and I would do that if I didn't get something better. I liked it there, but we weren't going to beat Ferrari in a fair fight. If I didn't know that before, I did now.

The conversations between Don and myself had reached the point where I had to tell him, 'Never mind arguing about how much money I'm going to get next year. How about paying me what you owe me from this year?'

The other serious option was Williams. My chats with Frank Williams were hush-hush too, because he was talking to others, like Gunnar Nilsson, and he wanted to be in control. He also knew I'd been in discussions with Ferrari, and he said to me, 'If you can drive for Ferrari, I think you should, because I can't offer you that sort of drive at the moment; but if it all falls through, come back to me.'

Frank had plans. They'd been a struggling team up to this point, but he had a plan that I liked, and he was right, he wasn't Ferrari. No-one was. As soon as Ferrari told me that they'd signed Villeneuve, I was on the phone to him – not that I told him I'd missed out there. We arranged to meet on the side of the motorway so he could take me up to the factory at Didcot. It's one of those typical small English villages near Oxford, only this one had an industrial area and a power plant. We used to call it Dead Cat.

Frank took me on a tour and then I met the team's designer, Patrick Head, who showed me the FW06, which was the first car that Patrick and Frank built together. It was a pretty little car, very straightforward with Cosworth power. But the thing that impressed me more than anything was that it had Saudia written all over it. At that point petro-dollars were swilling all around Europe, and anything Saudi was the flavour of the month – they were the boys with the money.

The plan for 1978 was to run as a one-car team and then in 1979 add an extra car. We were all about the same age, and I really got on well with Patrick. He impressed me like you wouldn't believe. He was very down to earth. It felt right – we could be honest with each other and get this thing moving. His ego was under control, even if mine wasn't.

When we were looking at the drawings I did the old, 'Ah, it's beautiful. Jesus, I reckon this thing could win races.' I could see Patrick's chest getting bigger. Then I left and went home with my fingers crossed . . . I had a good feeling and I wanted to get that drive.

I don't know whether it was days or weeks, but Frank rang and said, 'Do you want to come up and talk terms?' So I did, and I was a Williams driver for 1978 and beyond. It felt right. By signing Villeneuve, Ferrari had done me the biggest favour of my life.

AJ by Frank Williams, 1981

The first thing I had on my mind when I formed Williams Grand Prix Engineering was to find a good professional driver. We weren't over-ambitious; we couldn't afford to be. We didn't go after Niki Lauda or Jody Scheckter: they were beyond our reach, both financially and in terms of their status in what we conceived of as a small, highly-professional team.

We wanted work rather than glamour; we wanted the sort of pro who, if the car finished races, would bring us results. AJ was on the list; so were Gunnar Nilsson and Jochen Mass. All three of them good, solid drivers.

It was no piece of exceptional judgement or foresight or intuition on my part. AJ knows perfectly well I didn't rate him that highly when he joined us; I acknowledge that we were lucky he became available at just the right moment. But I had no idea he would be as good as he is. His brief from me was simple: 'Don't crash our cars, for we can't afford that many spares; finish in the points and work hard to help us develop our new car.'

I admit, too, that I had almost no picture of his character when he joined us: I'd neither really spoken to him, beyond saying hello, nor spent any time with him. It wasn't until September of 1977, when we started negotiating with him, that I got a picture of his true character: he was as thorough in that as he has been in everything else. And as honest.

I wasn't at his first race in Argentina, but at the second, in Brazil, he was already eighth on the grid. I was both surprised and pleased by that. But it was at Long Beach that I first saw how ultra-competitive he was. He'd had a bad practice and was 17th on the grid, but when the race started, he passed car after car.

I remember turning to Patrick and saying, 'I don't mind if we don't finish; I've had my money's worth, because he's not just a good driver, he's an exciting driver.' And I hadn't been excited by a driver's performance in many years. He could have won that race if his car hadn't broken down. But I found out then what he has since confirmed time and time again: that he's the sort of driver who puts in the fast laps you need. He responds best when he's really got to hang it out.

It soon became obvious that AJ would be a frontrunner and that we'd got more than we bargained for. Being the good businessman he is, AJ realised that too: at the end of the season, he put his price up. I won't say I didn't mind paying more, but I will say he's been worth every penny.

As the team has matured, so has AJ; he's always been a stable driver but he has become quicker and better; it isn't merely that he has more experience, it's also that his mental attitude is much more suited to the task at hand and his intelligence begins to prevail over his instincts. There isn't time in running a team, raising its money, overseeing a manufacturing force and maintaining contact with our sponsors, for AJ and I to socialise that much. I enjoy seeing him and he's always good for laughs. Being in America a while improved his one-liners and he's a funny man anyway; but also a private one, which is perhaps why he hasn't yet hit the public consciousness the way James Hunt did.

I soon enough found out I had the best driver in the world, the most complete, the most competitive and the most meticulous. He also has this natural force when it comes to driving: he's on the mark from the start, he's single-minded about being best. He doesn't waste our time and I think our job is not to waste his.

Frank Williams, 1981

8

1977 Williams Grand Prix Engineering

IN 1977, FRANK was still one of the game's all-time least successful constructors. Everyone told me I was crazy and taking a big step backwards. I brushed them aside – there's no point in asking yourself, 'Have I made the right decision?' You make the decision and then do everything you can to make *sure* it's the right one.

Frank knew what he had planned. He knew he could not afford a Niki or Jody, so he had to look for an emerging driver that could grow with the team. I am so happy he felt I was that driver.

Frank's track record wasn't fantastic, but I thought, new car, new team, lots of money from the Saudis – which they didn't actually have yet – and this could be really good. It was a one-car team, so all the attention would be on me. There weren't many other options anyway. Fate brought us together.

My mate Charlie Crichton-Stuart was involved with the team

as well – he was the one with the initial link to the Saudi royal family that Frank had to convince to put up the money. They had plenty of it, but it wasn't an easy task, and he decided to take a gamble . . . not that I knew that at the time. I still think to this day that we ran the first two races of the season on Frank's credit cards.

The good thing for me was that I was now, for the first time, in a very good place. Williams suited me, and I think I suited it. I liked Frank, and I had complete confidence in Patrick Head as a designer. Both designer and driver have to have faith in each other. Patrick had to have faith in the information I gave him, and I knew that when Patrick designed a car, he designed one that was both very quick and as safe as he could make it. He didn't skimp on my life. If he could make a car stronger, even if it added a little weight, he'd do so. If he built a new car and I went out testing in it, I knew it wasn't going to break on me.

One of the good things about staying some time with the same team is that you have time to build up that sort of faith. Even from the start though, I could tell Patrick what he needed to know in the fewest possible words, and all he wanted to know was what it was doing – not what I thought it needed. If I spoke of a mid-corner understeer on turn 10, he'd have an idea. If I told him I wanted the X springs in it, he'd have no idea. He was the engineer and I was the driver; we knew our roles and we suited each other.

1978 started for us with a lot of promise. I felt confident with the car and the direction we were headed. Of course, I knew nothing of budget constraints and I had no idea things were so tight. Frank didn't even come to the first race in Argentina, where we had overheating problems, and I retired. In Brazil we qualified well at the flat but bumpy Jacarepaguá circuit, and that started a little battle between us and the other non-Goodyear contracted teams.

Goodyear had an extra set of tyres it gave to the best qualifying non-contracted team. The big teams like Lotus and McLaren were sorted, because they were contracted and got free tyres, but for Williams, Arrows, Shadow and the like, this was a big thing. Goodyear had dominated the tyre war for years, but this year Michelin joined the sport, so the battle to be the dominant tyre manufacturer was on – and this was one of Goodyear's tricks to try to stay in front.

In Brazil we qualified eighth, but Emerson Fittipaldi just beat me for the tyres. We had a few dramas in the race and made it home five laps off the leaders, with valuable lessons learnt. Then we had a month off; well, a month off racing at any rate.

A lot of teams didn't have their new cars ready for the South American races in January, as was the case most years, so South Africa in March was often the place for change. Ferrari and Brabham had new cars, and like us they had not yet moved into ground-effects. Brabham would try a fan later in the year to suck the car down onto the track, while Ferrari was more concerned with trying to get the car to work with Michelin tyres.

So some people went to South Africa filled with hope; I went there with a cold and felt lousy. I qualified poorly but I got a good start and then it was head down and bum up. I finished fourth, which gave Frank three points. It was the team's first points, so everyone was super happy.

Frank had been around a while, but this was his first season with his own car. Up until 1978 he'd been playing with cars from companies like De Tomaso and Iso, who made road cars, and March, who made racing cars. Deep down he knew that playing with others' cars was just a starting point; the plan had always been to create Williams Grand Prix Engineering. That is, to do what we were doing in 1978.

Lotus was winning everything with its ground-effects cars, and Patrick was already planning his first car of that type, but we weren't going to see it in 1978. But the FW06 was a great little car to drive. We should have won a race in that car, but we didn't because reliability was the issue. At last Frank finally tied up the Saudi deal and we then had enough money to fix our issues.

After South Africa it was Long Beach, and that track just suited me. It was a street circuit, technically in Los Angeles, but another world away in personality to the streets of Monaco. I qualified eighth – good enough to get those extra tyres. I got a good start and was sitting sixth by the end of the first lap. As the race progressed people did silly things – Gilles was in the lead and hit a slower car while trying to put a lap on him in a twisty part of the track. I got to second and challenged Carlos Reutemann for the lead. I was having a big dice with him and we were to-ing and fro-ing when my front wing collapsed – it was scraping on the ground. Everyone thought that that was the reason I dropped back from Reutemann – they didn't know I had an electrical problem as well, which was intermittently cutting the fuel supply to the engine. Inevitably I dropped back, and ended up seventh. Carlos had a spin late in the race – without those reliability problems I could have won that.

It was a bitter pill to swallow, but it was also spirit-lifting.

Remember, we were battling for the lead when the problem hit. We knew we had a good car, we just had to get it to hold together. I got the fastest lap of the race, which proved our speed.

The night after that race I ended up by buying a house next to Bill Simpson in Palos Verdes, down Long Beach way. I got to the stage where I wanted to get out of England because of the weather – it was getting me down. I had to be one flight away in case I got a phone call saying, 'We want you to come over next Wednesday and test,' so that put Australia out of the equation, but this I could do.

It should have been on the east coast of America, Miami maybe, which would have been more practical, but I liked Palos Verdes. I used to stay with Bill at his house, and you'd get up for breakfast and he'd say, 'See that house down there? I could have bought it for X amount, and it just sold for Y amount.' I told him to give me a bell the next time one came up nearby.

It just happened that I was there at the time, and he said if I didn't buy it, he would. So I did, and we even shared a driveway. The night after the grand prix at Long Beach we decided to have a party at Bill's, and he invited all the Toyota people back, and I invited a lot of the young Arabs that were at the race, the young princes who were doing their schooling in California. They used to have briefcases where they could pick up the phone and ring Mum and Dad in Saudi Arabia. In 1978 that was very cool.

I invited Frank, but he didn't want to come – until he found out the princes were going to be there. Ever the businessman, he was in. He wasn't good in those environments, he never drank and never smoked. So he was sitting on the couch twiddling his thumbs, and looking at his watch and hopping up and down, and he was just about to leave when all the limos started pulling up with the princes.

Frank sat back down on the couch at a thousand miles an hour. At that party one of the Saudis said to me, 'Alan, could I see you somewhere private?' I thought, 'Fuck, what's this?' Anyway, I took him into the garage. He handed me an envelope and he said, 'This is just a small token of our appreciation for the way you drove today showing Saudi technology.' I don't know how my driving showed Saudi technology, but he was happy and I wasn't going to spoil the moment.

I said, 'There's no need for that,' but the envelope went straight in my pocket and I went to the bedroom to open it up. Ten grand US, cash, which in 1978 wasn't bad. He became my very new best friend.

That wasn't the last time something like that happened; the Saudis were very generous people. There was one time that Charlie Crichton-Stuart called me and said we needed to go and meet the crown prince of whoever, at some hotel in Monaco where they had the whole floor booked. At three every day they'd sit down and smoke those bloody pipes.

So at this one I was sitting there with them and the guy sitting next to me had a really nice Chopard watch that had an Albilad logo sticker on the face, one of our sponsors. Because I am a bit of a watch perv, I said, 'Oh, that's nice.' He took it off and handed it to me.

When I went to hand it back to him, the crown prince saw and said, 'No, no. No, no. This is yours now.' I said, 'No, I just want to get a look at it.'

'No, this is the Saudi way. This is yours. Don't worry. He gets a better one now.'

And then lo and behold on top of that, the envelope comes out again. I'm thinking, I really like these guys. I ended up with a Chopard watch and 10 grand in an envelope for being away from home for a day or two. It was a pretty good way to earn a living. It almost made me like Monaco.

Frank was good with all this, I'm sure he was getting some big envelopes at the same time. He had to work a bit harder for it though. He'd fly down to Riyadh and he'd sit in a waiting room in an office six or seven hours until he got to see the bloke that he went there for. Generous yes, but they didn't mind making you wait. That way you'd know who's boss. Frank would just sit there until he got to see who he'd come to see. As I said, he was very determined.

Frank deserves everything he's got. He was the best bloke I ever drove for; a really nice guy. We very rarely had cross words, a couple of things, but nothing really terrible. He knew how to get the best out of me without threats or whatever. He just knew how to press my buttons. Then Charlie was there to back up and press the other button. Charlie was, 'Come on, Champ, we can do this . . .'

Charlie was a nephew to the Earl of Dumfries and cousin to Johnny Dumfries, who later raced for Lotus. Johnny was my gopher. We used to go, 'Johnny, go and get me a Coke, will you?' Which was pretty funny when you realise his full name is John Colum Crichton-Stuart, 7th Marquess of Bute.

When Charlie died they buried him in the family plot on the Isle of Bute, and we went over to the family house and it was all marble on marble on marble. They took old Charlie down the road with the hearse with the bagpipes. That's a funeral.

Charlie used to tell me stories about how he'd go over there and just leave his clothes outside the bedroom and the next morning they'd all be pressed and ironed. It was real *Upstairs Downstairs* stuff. Johnny was a sensational bloke, you would never pick him for what he was. He had no airs or graces, just a pair of ripped jeans and a T-shirt.

Anyway, we were now at the stage where the Saudi money was coming on and our expectations were rising. Monaco, as I've said, is not a track I really liked, but again we had enough speed to qualify inside the top 10, then an oil leak one-third into the race got me an early Foster's. The next eight races were really hard. We showed some speed, but we were just unreliable. We finished in Belgium and Spain and I got points in France, and the rest were retirements.

We were learning lessons with each one though, and Patrick was fixing them as we went. I had to remember, it was a small fledgling team and we had to grow together. We quickly learned that prevention's better than cure, and we then became one of the most reliable cars, because they were very strict with their crack testing. Hell, we even got to the point where they used to change steering wheels if they thought they had too many laps on them, which is why the allegations over Senna's crash – about changes to the steering column made before the accident that killed him when driving for Williams in 1994 – were just ridiculous.

Sometimes the car was poor in qualifying, like 18th in Spain, and then it would hold together in the race. If I qualified well, like ninth in Sweden or sixth at Brands Hatch, the car would fail in racing. Jones' Law.

So from Monaco we went to Zolder for a 10th place, then Jarama for eighth, which could have been so much better if I had qualified well. I had a seized front wheelbearing in Sweden, which resulted in a retirement after some off-track adventures. In the race we were miles off the pace being set by Andretti's Lotus and Lauda's Brabham, but were running fourth for most of it and that could have been a podium when Mario retired.

That was the one and only race for the Brabham fan car, and I must say it worked well. The fan was at the back of the car and it sucked the air out from under it to create similar downforce to the ground-effects Lotus cars. It raced under protest in Sweden and the fan was eventually rated as a moving aerodynamic device – not the cooling device it was claimed to be – which meant it was banned. But gee, it had some grip. I think everyone knew they were going to have to master ground effects if they were going to beat Lotus.

The French Grand Prix was nothing special except for the points. I qualified 14th and raced well for fifth. I qualified sixth for the British Grand Prix and was running second when a drive-shaft broke and gave me another one of those what-if moments. I was trailing Jody at the time and he retired a few laps later as well, so again . . .

At Hockenheim we were going pretty well, sixth again on the grid and did enough in the race for Niki to come up to Frank and say, 'Your car's really going well today.' He'd never pay a compliment, so that was a pretty big thing for us. In the race I had a good battle with him and passed him around the outside into the first chicane – I think that made him stand up and pay attention. We DNFed again though, this time with fuel vaporisation problems.

I crashed out in the changing conditions that were experienced in Austria, which turned out to be Ronnie Peterson's last win. In

Holland it was a throttle problem that sidelined me, so at least we were finding new things to fix.

Monza was up next and I qualified sixth again, which put me on the grid beside Ronnie, who was one of the few guys I got on reasonably well with. He was a lovely guy, unbelievably quick. He didn't know why he was quick, it was just natural talent, fantastic car control.

We took off from the third row and I got a better start and got in front of him, but the cars on the back of the grid had not yet gridded up when they started the race, and they got great starts which made for a lot of congestion into turn 1. Riccardo Patrese wasn't quite at the back, but he got a great run nonetheless and had to go off the track to try and clear some cars, coming back onto the track he hit James who then took out Ronnie. Not that I knew much of this because I never looked in my mirrors except to find a way to block someone.

By the time we came around the Parabolica for the next lap there was a plume of black smoke and red flags. That was never a good sign. Even today red flags from startline crashes are never a good thing, in those days it was even worse. Fire was something we all feared – and we feared little.

It wasn't just the fire, those aluminium cars didn't have the protection they've got today. Ronnie's car was torn in two as it exploded in flames and he had shattered his legs. The race was stopped, and Frank just came up and said, 'Ronnie's had a reasonable shunt and it'll be about 15 or 20 minutes until they clear all the debris and get going again.' I just said, 'Right, no worries.' We eventually got going after another red flag for an incident on the warm-up laps and to this day I can't even remember where I finished. I now know it was 13th, but it was a big blur to me.

Amazingly, despite the fire, Ronnie wasn't even burned, the only injury he had was the broken leg. Neurosurgeon Professor Sid Watkins was now travelling to every race, as he pretty much did for the next three decades, and he was more worried about Vittorio Brambilla, who had been hit on the head by a wheel when he slammed into the side of the Lotus, than Ronnie. I think in many ways that crash was the turning point in Formula One safety. Watching some of the footage now, it seems almost farcical to see the drivers like James climbing into the flames to pull Ronnie out of his car.

There were other drivers arguing with people at the scene because there were 11 cars involved and plenty of drivers near it all. The crowd was out on the track and the police were holding them back, Clay Regazzoni was shouting at Sid and Bernie Ecclestone and whoever else he could see who was in some position of power.

With the Armco crumbling from the impact of a lost wheel on the next warm-up lap, perhaps things did need to change.

After the race I went back to the hotel. When I got up the next morning Frank said, 'Alan, I've got some bad news for you. Ronnie died last night.' I couldn't believe it. Because we just thought that he'd screwed his legs. Under no circumstances did we think he'd sustained injuries that would be fatal. Apparently he'd damaged his leg so badly, seven fractures in one and three in the other, that some of the fat from his legs got into his bloodstream and made it into his heart and kidneys. That's what killed him. I felt numb.

It is a strange thing. You never relate it back to yourself. I mean, I was on the grid beside him. I don't know whether it was just my self-protection mechanism, but I shrugged it off. I felt sorry for Barbara, his wife, and young daughter Nina, and I felt sorry for Ronnie, obviously, but as to me – I shrugged it off. The reality for me and all the other drivers was that three weeks later we would be racing again in Watkins Glen. You couldn't sit around and dwell on stuff like that.

At Watkins Glen Mario's Lotus was again really fast in qualifying and we thought he would be tough to beat, but on the Sunday he struggled a little and it was the Ferraris with that magnificent flat 12 engine that had the speed. The Ferraris of Carlos and Gilles were running away with it when I passed Mario, the new World Champion, for third, which became second when Gilles' car failed.

That weekend, our adopted son Christian was born – on 27 September 1978 – in London and he was given to Beverley within seconds of the birth. We had our first child. I was probably mortified by the carry-on back at the motel with all the baby stuff, but it didn't take long for me to appreciate life as a father.

Frank had now decided to be a two-car team for 1979 and he signed Clay Regazzoni, although he almost asked my permission to do so. I told him I had no problem with him signing anyone. 'Sign whoever you like. We've got to race against him anyway so go ahead and sign Superman if you want.'

From my side of it, I'd signed a one-year deal which had an option that Frank was exercising and I had negotiated a pay rise. I was happy with both parts of that. I felt like we were really getting somewhere. I liked Frank and Patrick and we worked really well together. With plans for a ground-effects car next year I knew we could win races. We just had to work out the little niggles.

The season ended with unfulfilled promise in Canada. We had

good speed and I was heading Gilles for most of the race when a slow puncture started to affect my lap times. I was running second to Jean-Pierre Jarier in a Lotus and we were running a quarter of a lap behind him when I let Gilles past for what would become the lead when Jarier pulled out. It was Gilles' first win and it was in my Ferrari!

Strangely though, I was happy with where I had ended up. I was a Williams driver, and for me that was better than being a driver for Ferrari.

Sid Watkins

Sid Watkins, the travelling F1 doctor, was a lovely man, a true gentleman and so caring for us drivers. I think you'd have to be a very strange person not to get on well with Sid. I'd hate to think where driver safety would be without him.

I remember being in Spain and Beverley had a fit and I went down to Sid's room at something like one in the morning – no dramas he just jumped up, came up to our room, sorted out Bev and headed back to his room as if it was nothing.

Fortunately he never had to look after my broken body, since I never really hurt myself in a Formula One car. At one stage I did have a doctor at the tracks that I shared with Emerson Fittipaldi and a couple of other drivers. I always remember saying to this doc, what happens if we have a big shunt and three of your drivers are involved, who are you going to go to first?

He was Portuguese and he charged like a wounded bull to come to each grand prix. He had a nice little life. He'd come to the grand prix and he'd always have the right passes and he just swanned around. Then I realised, Sid's here, why am I paying him, so I stopped. Sid was better than him too, and he was great at working out who was in greatest need and he dealt with drivers on a risk basis.

Sid's job was really to suss out where the hospitals were, which particular hospital was good for what particular injury. He would make a decision on the spot and he'd send you to the nearest appropriate hospital.

Belgian Cyclepaths

I was leaving Zolder one night and we had to go through a check-point to get out. There was a bike rider in the middle of the road holding up the cars, rather than moving to the side a little and letting us all pass . . . so I gave him a little beep on the horn that said, 'Can you move over?' And he gave me the bird. I was still in race mode, so I've rammed him up the arse and he ended up on the bonnet of the car.

My old mate Charlie was with me and he said, 'Fuck, champ, careful.' And I'm saying, 'No, fuck him, Charlie.' I kept going and drove back to the motel with him on the bonnet. Which he wasn't impressed with. I could hear him screaming and carrying on and his bike was back there all mangled. He wouldn't get out of the way and he's taking up a whole queue for one bicycle, so when he gave me the finger I thought that was clearly an indication that he wanted to be on the bonnet.

Anyway, the coppers came and they let me off. I think they saw the funny side of it but of course couldn't admit it. I was all contrite and concerned while they were interviewing me, but seriously I couldn't give a fuck about the bird-flipping bicyclist.

There was an advantage to being an Aussie in Europe back then. You could plead ignorance – or stupidity – and they would believe you.

9

Macau

FOR MANY YEARS I went home to Australia for the European winter via the Macau Grand Prix. Macau is a bit like Monaco, in that it is a stupid place for a car race. It was challenging, that's for sure. When you have a hairpin bend that is so tight and narrow you nearly have to do a three-point turn you know it is getting silly.

But the big difference was the cars and the people. This grand prix, I think, has pretty much always been run in the slower and smaller Formula Pacific and then Formula Three cars that I essentially cut my teeth on in the UK. It was run by Teddy Yip, a sensational bloke and a multi-squillionaire from Hong Kong, and he was the one who had me racing there.

So he started paying for my flights home as long as I would run the race, which I did for many years. I never won it, but I did get pole a couple of times and was leading when the car died on me.

I think it was in 1978 when Bob Harper, a big Ford dealer in Macau and China, had three Chevrons in his team for Keke Rosberg, Derek Daly and Riccardo Patrese. The cars were all lined up in the pits and there was a row of new tyres on the wall behind them. When I saw the cars lined up and those tyres, it shifted my mindset. I wasn't sure we had any new tyres and I was pretty certain we didn't have any qualifying tyres.

So I asked Sid Taylor, who was looking after the team, if we had any. He said, 'My word, we have,' and showed me a set or two of purple-tinged tyres. When tyres have been used, they get that look, so I knew straight away.

'Sid, they've been used.' He said, 'They're fucking good these. Don't worry about them. They were on pole last year.'

'Are you serious?'

I went and grabbed Teddy. 'Teddy, come here a second. I want to show you something. These are my qualifiers.' Then we jumped in the car and went to look at Bob's, and because Bob Harper was his nemesis I knew where this was going. I showed him the three brand new Chevrons all lined up and all the brand new tyres.

Of course, being Asian, for Teddy that was a major loss of face and Sid was in a bit of trouble. He went, 'I'll kill you. I'll fucking cut your balls out. I'll have you floating in the harbour.' Teddy, settle down. Then he got his head into what we needed. 'Right. I want nine sets of qualifiers . . .' I said, 'Teddy, we only really need one or two.' 'No, no, we need six.'

In the end, we had a wall of tyres flown in overnight from England. We used to prepare the cars in Teddy's garage, which was on the track but not near the pits. If we didn't get the equipment out each day before they put the Armco up in front of the garage, we had some issues.

Down in the pits I looked up the next morning and there was an army of blokes headed our way, each carrying a tyre. There must have been about 50 of them, so I've gone from one set of purple qualifiers to about 600 tyres overnight. What am I going to do now? Thank Christ, I put it on pole after that. I led the first lap, but a combination of a fuel cut-out and concrete dust in the track ended my day early.

We had a bit of a party in my room at the hotel that night. We all used to stay at the Hotel Lisboa and we all got a bit carried away, as you do when you're that age. It was loud. There was a bang on the wall from next door. It made no difference; we abused them and kept going.

Then Jones' Law came into it. At the very moment I stepped out of my room, the bloke that was banging on the wall stepped out of his room. It was Dan Gurney, who'd tried to get me to drive his cars in the States. Oops. 'Hi, Mr Gurney. I'm sorry if Keke made all those noises last night.' Dan, by the way, is responsible for drivers spraying champagne on the podium – he did it after winning Le Mans in 1967, and everyone has done it since. Well, I was an exception, which I'll come to later.

I loved racing in Macau for all the reasons I hated Monaco. To this day, I still love Hong Kong and pretty much everywhere in Asia. I like the food and I like the people and the frenetic atmosphere and pace. You get the hydrofoil over to Macau from Hong Kong, which Teddy owned in partnership with Stanley Ho, who you know is not exactly a pauper.

Then you'd check into the Hotel Lisboa, which I think Teddy

half owned as well, so you got a fantastic room. We'd go downstairs and there'd be this pretty ordinary dining room with Formica tables and everything, but the food was just absolutely exquisite. You know, you'd just have a ball.

Teddy used to have a garden party on the Thursday night. He had a sentry post outside his house with a guard in it, to keep the riff raff out. He was mad, but he was just an absolute character. It was just a great weekend. Then on Sunday night, every year there'd be a major party going on somewhere, often in my room. That's when I think Beverley made the mistake of flying straight to Australia and not coming to Macau. She shouldn't have left me by myself in Macau; she's got no one to blame but herself.

On the Monday, you'd inevitably get up with a shocking hangover and I'd start winding my way back to Australia, where I'd stay for as long as I could . . . maybe three or four weeks.

Frank eventually asked me to stop running in Macau, so 1978 was my last one. Frank figured he was investing a lot of money in me and he didn't want me taking unnecessary risks. So over time, all the extras disappeared from my schedule.

I respected Frank for his approach – and it worked both ways. After a major crash in testing in 1980, we worked together on getting a test driver rather than risk me. I was, of course, more interested in spending time watching Christian grow up, while Frank was totally focused on me as an investment. Now I'm not saying the other bloke was expendable, but why pay a bloke a million dollars and send him out to test something? Better him than me.

10

Can-Am / Cruise and Collect

I MAY NOT have liked oval-track racing, but I did love racing in the States. I had success there in Formula One, which obviously helped, but there was more to it than that. The tracks I loved to race on were long and fast, with sweeping corners, and there were plenty of those throughout North America. When they built a road course, they built a real race track.

The Americans were also friendly, cooperative and open – and they had proper hamburgers and cold beer. The English used to boil meat and put it between two stale buns and call it a hamburger. Or you'd ask for a cold Coke and they'd just pull it straight off the shelf, and you'd say, 'No, I want a cold one,' and he'd say, 'It is cold, guv.'

The Yanks did things more like the Aussie way – they had ice and the beer was cold. I felt a lot more at home there than I did in England. I liked racing there – and the weather was better too.

In 1977 I did those two Can-Am races for Shadow and I really liked the cars. They weren't the knuckle-dragging beasts from the early 1970s, but rather they were essentially Formula 5000 cars with sportscar bodies. With 5-litre engines they weren't lacking in the grunt department, and they were a lot of fun to drive and really quick. My 1978 season with Carl Haas Racing really started at the final round of the '77 season when I qualified in the new Shadow beside Patrick Tambay (who was winning the championship for Haas) on the front row of the grid. I led the race until the car broke, but it was enough to make sure that Carl knew I was the man to have when Patrick had to give up Can-Am for his Formula One drive with McLaren.

I signed up for 1978 with Haas before I had anything locked away in Formula One, so when I signed with Williams obviously Formula One was my main priority, but I still wanted to honour my contract with Carl. I did all the races bar one, where there was a clash with a grand prix, and it made for a busy year. I rarely had my bum out of a car, and that was perfect. You don't get better watching, you only get better from doing . . . and I was doing.

But the travel was draining; jetting across the Atlantic so often was not as easy or as glamorous as it sounds. Although it did get a bit easier as the year went on when the boss of First National City (now Citibank), who sponsored both the car and the championship, put me on the Concorde for the flights. It wasn't just quicker, it was better.

The food in the Concorde lounges was pretty special, and at Heathrow they had free international phone calls, so I'd camp outside the door waiting for it to open like it was a Harrods sale so I could get all my phone calls done for nix. Still lurking inside this jet-setting Formula One driver was the struggling hustler who'd cooked breakfast for his tenants in the Ealing boarding house.

The Carl A. Haas Racing Team Lola was designated as a T333CS and there were plenty of that model lining up for the season, along with the 332 from the previous season and a few other types of car like Shadow, Spyder, Prophet, Chevron and even an Elfin from Australia. Given my Lola was based on the Formula 5000 car, it had a central driving position which I quite liked, and with all the extra bodywork and that huge rear wing it had tremendous downforce. It was quite enjoyable to drive. Carl was the US importer for Lola, and the kit to turn a car from a standard T333C – or a T332C for that matter – into a CS was designed by his team and sold to all the other teams: it was the only way to race a Lola in the series.

For those that love to talk about racing car chassis, the Prophet and the Spyder were modified Lola 332CS cars, so I suppose they thought the best way to beat the 'factory' team was to make the old car better than the new and rebadge it. The T333CS evolved during the season as well, because these guys were throwing out a pretty serious challenge and Carl was as competitive as me and didn't want to lose to them.

The tracks we raced on were so good for those cars. Road America, Watkins Glen, Mid-Ohio and Mont-Tremblant were all bloody interesting tracks. Most of the tracks were in really nice parts of the world too, and even though Mid-Ohio was in the middle of nowhere, it was a really nice middle of nowhere.

At that time in America, public toilets didn't have doors, which I found really hard to deal with. I was dying for a crap at

Mid-Ohio once, and I didn't want to go to one of those toilets. I had an hour or so before a practice session, so I jumped in the hire car and headed off to the motel to do my business in private. I was screaming down the motorway and I could see the cop car coming the other way, and then I saw him put his lights on and do a U-turn and chase me down. The first thing he notices are my overalls, then my accent, which usually got me mistaken for a Limey.

He said, 'You were speeding,' and I said, 'I didn't mean to, officer, but your crappers over here don't have any doors and I can't go without a door, so I'm going back to the motel to have a crap.'

God only knows what he thought, but he said, 'I'm on my way to an accident, you get going.' No warning, nothing, just that. I felt like saying, 'If you're on your way to an accident, why did you turn around?' But I think he just wanted to get back to the police station to tell the rest of them about this crazy Aussie racing driver he caught rushing to the toilet.

Anyway, the season began at Road Atlanta in May, a few months after we had started back in Formula One. I had tested there with the team before signing on to drive, so I kind of knew the track. We had a really good but small team and we lacked for nothing. This series was big time in the States, and there were some other really good teams there too, like VDS, Hogan Racing and Newman-Freeman Racing, which was Paul Newman's entrée into motor racing.

I was comfortably on pole from fellow Aussie Warwick – or War Wick – Brown in the VDS Lola and Elliott Forbes-Robinson in the Newman-Freeman Spyder. The race went smoothly and I went on to win, setting up an amazing season for me. It was clear we had a great car. I knew that both Warwick and Elliott would be tough competition, as would Al Holbert, who finished second in the first race.

Charlotte was up next, and they had this road-course track slapped in the middle of the oval with some of the banking also being used. The car was sensational here, and again I started from pole. But on lap six I had to pit with a flat tyre and that put me right down the back of the field. Elliott was way out in front and I had to try and chase him down in 40-odd laps. In the end, he had too much of a gap, but I climbed from essentially last place to finish 30 seconds behind him in second place.

If I didn't know before, I knew my one-liner about 'cruise and collect' was far from accurate. You can never take anything for granted in motorsport – there are so many mechanical items on a car and so many other drivers on the track that anything could happen. At least these races weren't on ovals, where the lottery came into play, but we were taking the races seriously, that's for sure.

Mid-Ohio was the third round, and after fine-tuning my toilet run, I had a trouble-free weekend and what turned out to be an easy win when all my main rivals had some sort of trouble. The 1972 champ George Follmer was second in a Prophet.

In the middle of the Canadian summer, we were up at the Mont-Tremblant track outside St Jovite which is now owned by Lawrence Stroll, the father of Lance Stroll, who debuted for Williams in 2017. This great track was tucked away high in a valley in the mountains and it hosted the first few Canadian grands prix. I started from pole but got tangled up with someone in the chicane and managed only 13th. Follmer won his only race for the season there.

Watkins Glen was another that didn't go to plan. Again I qualified on pole and led the opening laps before dropping 10 laps during the race. This was the halfway point of the season, I had pole and the fastest lap at each race and a combination of poor luck, mechanical issues and some of my own impatience was costing me.

There was only two weeks from there to Road America, which was essentially the home race for Haas, in Chicago. I'm pretty sure I wasn't in the best of moods when I turned up, I had just lost the British Grand Prix because of a gearbox problem when I had the race under control. I wasn't that quick on Friday practice and then the weather was shit for Saturday, so everyone thought Warwick would be on pole because of his Friday time. But I was in no mood for mucking around: head down and arse up, I went for it. I took a few risks and ended up by whacking it on pole by more than a second.

I won the race by a handful of seconds – but I felt like I was in full control. I carried that momentum through to Mosport Park in Canada for pole again by more than a second and won by half a lap. Warwick was second again to me, and he was just nipping away at me in the championship despite the fact that I was winning more races than him. I knew I was going to have to miss the Laguna Seca round because of a Formula One clash, so I needed a bank of points to play with.

Warwick's VDS Racing was owned by the van der Straten family, which essentially owned Stella Artois, and versions of the team are still running to this day, including the MotoGP team that Australian Jack Miller rides for. As a family, they love motorsport. The Count, as he was called, used to come along to all the races with his wife, who looked a bit like the old lady out of *Something About Mary*. They bought the test track that Jim Hall had built at Midland, Texas, drove the rattle snakes out and built a big house there ... so she could sunbake and smoke while they all went motor racing.

VDS had run Warwick in the Rothmans International Series earlier that year in Australia and won every race. It was a Formula 5000 Lola. They really did know what they were doing and they were keeping us on our toes.

The two wins in a row moved the title back into my control, but we knew Warwick and VDS would capitalise if we mucked up. It was important to finish well up the points at Grand Prix de Trois-Rivières in Quebec, a street circuit with all the risks of a street circuit. I had raced there before a few years earlier in a Formula Atlanta car, which was the first time I ever raced against Gilles Villeneuve. I raced for a guy called Fred Opert in a Chevron, and James Hunt was Gilles' teammate. It was James going back to Europe raving about Gilles that gave the little Canadian his break, but I nearly had a fight with James that weekend. He was in front of me at the start, but I got away better and I slipped in front of him at the first corner with a pretty aggressive move, which he didn't like. He spent the rest of the race behind me, and he had a go at me afterwards. 'AJ, you fucking cut me off,' or some bullshit and I said, 'No, I passed you.' I left it at that. But I learned about that track then, and like a lot of street circuits it was hard to pass anyone.

So with that in mind, I really wanted pole, and during qualifying one of the mechanics hung out a sign with 0.2 on it. I took that as being 0.2 of a second behind. So I got on it, put the eyes on just like I did at Road America and got pole by more than a second. They were a bit grumpy when I came back in. 'Fucking hell. We told you you were 0.2 of a second in front.' We had a laugh when we all twigged.

I got third in the race, which was enough I thought with Laguna Seca next. Even if Warwick won at Laguna Seca, which he didn't, I'd still have a good lead heading off to Riverside for the final. I'd seen a couple of titles slip out of my hands already and I was determined not to let that happen again. At Riverside I dominated qualifying and had pole again, so every race I started in that series I did from pole, which was satisfying. Then in the race I opened up a lead early and then just kept out of trouble to win by 30-odd seconds.

That gave me my first championship, which was a bloody good feeling. To win a substantial championship, an international one really with a quality field of drivers, meant a great deal to me. We had good equipment, but no more so than anyone else. We all pretty much had the same Chev engines with the same horse-power – we just did a better job overall, winning half the races in the series.

I think what I learned in the run to that championship helped me with Formula One, especially in 1980. When you're leading the title, you think to yourself, 'Well hang on, don't panic, you can do it.' And deep down you know you can, but you have to bury doubt. Until mathematically you can no longer be beaten, you can still lose, so you cannot ease up at all.

I didn't defend the championship in 1979 because Frank didn't want me to run in it any longer. I filled in for Jacky Ickx at Mid-Ohio when he had a clash with Le Mans and I managed another win, and then I ran the final race of that season only to crash out. But that was it for Can-Am, and I walked away from it with a championship, some great memories and friends and a love of America.

The Lifestyle

Life has always been pretty good for Formula One drivers, but there is a cost. We only did 16 races a year, instead of the 20 they do now, but even then you'd get sick of airports and hotels. And bloody Heathrow Airport – you could wait an hour for your luggage.

During the season at home, I used to allow myself a pint of English beer every night, that was it. On a Sunday night after a grand prix, I used to get on it a bit. Which didn't take much because I was dehydrated from the driving. I was probably pissed out of my brain on about two cans.

There were plenty of other opportunities for fun, and if you've watched the *Rush* movie, I was not into anything as outrageous as James Hunt. But I had my fun. You would meet the odd person, I suppose, that was fairly interested in the fact that you were a Formula One driver. Occasionally I'd share my knowledge with them . . . up in my room.

But even before that time in my life there were plenty of distractions. Carnaby Street when I first went to London was a pretty good place to be. You'd make a beeline down there wearing your horrible checked dacks and a striped shirt, which just screamed at each other. There were parties everywhere both down that way and at Earl's Court, where we lived. The Rhodesian Club was pretty good, but we quickly learned which clubs and pubs had the girls and that is where you'd find us.

When I started travelling for the races, Beverley often stayed back at 'headquarters' and left me to my own devices. I always figured she knew, so I felt no guilt spreading my knowledge. At the end of the day if something's presented to you on a plate there's no aggro. Takes a strong bloke to knock it back, but I never went out hunting.

I wasn't that bad though, it wasn't like I rooted my way around the world. Because I didn't, it was only half the world . . . no, I didn't really. I mean there was the odd indiscretion, but most guys were doing it. Bev was more than welcome to come to all the races. At no point did I say no I don't want you there. She chose to stay at home.

I was a mutt compared to James. He was up to no good every grand prix.

11

IROC and a Hard Place

WE KNEW WHAT we had to do in 1979, and it all revolved around the FW07 that Patrick Head was working on. This car was a big undertaking for what was then a small team. I had full faith in Patrick and his crew . . . we just had to get it finished and on the track.

I was happy with 1978, but now I wanted more. I had plans to defend my Can-Am Championship and a few other opportunities were coming up too, but I let most of them go.

I knew I was making a name too. I had been invited to run in the so-called 'International Race of Champions' in the States, which was a quirky little series with lots of money up for grabs. All the drivers were kitted out with supposedly identical Chevrolet Camaro Stock Cars. After my experience in the McLaren in 1976, I thought those big old Chevies, with the big roll-cages across them, were safe enough.

Anyway, they invited people from USAC Champ Car, NASCAR and Road Racing and I was there with Mario, Emerson and Niki – which wasn't bad company – as part of the road-racing team. It was being run by a guy called Les Richter, who was a hell of a nice guy, and he was the one who rang me to see if I wanted to do it. When they told me how much it paid, I was in.

So, the first race for the road racers was at California's Riverside Raceway in October and I got fourth, which qualified me to go on to North Carolina. I'll never forget the first time I drove out of the pits, I let the steering wheel go for a second just to tighten up my safety belts and the thing turned sharp left. I thought, 'Shit, there's something wrong with this.' The suspension's broken or something.

'Oh, no, it's jacked,' they said, 'Well, can you un-jack it?'

By jack they mean they put stiffer springs on one side of the car than the other to compensate for the banking because the G force pushes the car down, and the strongest springs on the outside stop that. On a road track, it also gives it a terrible bias to the left.

I came straight back in and got a lesson. First of all, there was a little bit of white tape on the top of the steering wheel, which I like to call a rudder indicator, and they said that was to let me know when the wheels were straight. I thought, 'Fuck, if you don't know that, there's something wrong.' But it was all done so that when driving on the banks your hands were at nine and three on the wheel.

Anyway, I worked my way through that car and the oddities of US racing to get fourth in both the qualifying race and the final with the NASCAR and CART racers added in to the field. Niki didn't even get a lap done and there are rumours about him blowing up the car so he didn't have to go back for the finals. He didn't want to get paid for the racing, he just wanted them to cover the costs of flying his Learjet to the States to get some new instruments done . . . that took precisely one weekend and he was back on the jet and home. If the rumours were right, I could see the logic behind his decision.

Silly me took it seriously and I ended up going down to race the final in March of 1979 – a few races into the Formula One season – on a banked oval at Atlanta. Before I went there for the final I had some warts on my dick surgically removed. If only I'd used the products of my former sponsor.

Anyway they wrapped the old fella in gauze and put a little knot on it and I thought it was all good. So I got down there and I hop in this car and the good old boys, which were the Allison brothers, took me under their wing because driving those things on an oval is a bit of a black art. I didn't realise that the guy behind you can make you understeer or oversteer depending on where he puts his car. There's various little tricks like that. I think it was Bobby who said, 'Come on boy. Come around with us and you can follow me around.'

I was getting the hang of it now and had set the second quickest time. Sportscar racer Peter Gregg, who was known as Peter Perfect, decided he'd join in the fun. On the track there were two cars behind me, the second car being Peter's. Suddenly Peter with a double tow pulled out from behind the car that was on my tail and went past both of us as we went into turn three. Which was where Peter lost it. He went broadside right along the middle of the track. The driver behind me chose to go below Peter; I tried to get above him, between Peter and the wall. If you lose it in oval racing, what you're meant to do is turn into the slide and spin your car into the infield, but Peter, being a road-racer like myself, did what I would have done in the same conditions to correct the slide: he corrected it and shot straight up into the wall.

I was doing about 170mph when I T-boned him, I went from his car into the wall and from the wall back into him, completely demolishing the Camaro. At first I thought I'd really hurt myself badly: I hit him so hard the Coke I'd drunk earlier exploded out of my body and soaked my race suit. Because I was strapped in and had my helmet on, I couldn't look down and all I could feel was wet against my body.

I'm thinking, 'Oh, shit. It's blood. Oh, fuck. This must be a big one.' Of course the marshals have come running up and then they take a step back. I thought, 'Oh, Christ. This must be bad, my guts are hanging out or something.' Then the major trauma unit came – because you know in America you can't call it an ambulance, that's not dramatic enough – and they finally extracted me from the car, and said, 'We'll take you down to the medical centre.'

So I've gone down to the medical centre, and all the good old boys have come down to see how I was, which in reality was pretty good – even the bow tied around my dick stayed in place.

I think in a big one like that, a driver always thinks the worst. After I'd hit him I went straight into the concrete wall and pushed the engine right up through the body of the car. I was completely winded; I couldn't breathe. Luckily, all I had was a very bad case of bruising, but for a few seconds I had a clear picture of myself being dragged out of the car and raced to hospital.

When I hit Peter, it was as though I'd come right out of my seat and been suspended against my safety belts. Later on it was as if someone had taken a tar brush and painted stripes on my body where the seat belts had been. I could barely move. But I thought, hold on here, if this happened in a big safe old Chevy Camaro, think what that shunt would have been like in a little fragile USAC car like I'd tried in 1976. It didn't take much to convince me, after that, that there was no way in the world I would go USAC racing on an oval again. Ever.

Even when a shunt seems inevitable, you fight it right up to the end: until it really is. When that moment comes, everything is happening so quickly that a driver doesn't really have much time to do anything, nor even think very much. I go into a state that is not really a daze so much as an acceptance of the inevitable. My thought is: 'It's going to happen; I've got to make sure I get out of this alive.'

At the moment of impact, everything is happening so quickly that you are simultaneously aware of its happening and of its inevitability. The G-forces throw a driver's hands all over the place. It's not as though he could react calmly and throw the car into neutral or shut off the master switch: not while he's banging into the wall. At that stage he is just being knocked about. He is a dead weight, a human dummy. His next reaction is when he finally comes to rest. His first thought is probably to check his body out in all its particulars: is it all there? Is anything radically wrong? Almost simultaneously he will turn off the master switch – because fire is what every driver dreads most – and the next thing he'll do, if he's not winded or unconscious or unable, is jump out of the car and get away from it as quickly as possible. The worst things occur when you stay in too long; and that only happens when you can't get out.

158

In that shunt with Peter, I was badly winded, I was confused, I didn't know what this liquid was and I really couldn't move. I could see the car was steaming and I was thinking, 'Let's hope this bleeder doesn't catch fire, because if it does, I don't know how quickly I can move.' And as I thought that, I was also hoping and praying the marshals would get to me quickly and get me out.

There are really three stages to a crash. In the first, you're still fighting for control, still trying to prevent the crash, even when you know your chances are minimal. That stage continues until you know it is going to happen and there's nothing at all you can do about it. At the impact, you don't think at all. Your mind is a blank. From that point until you come to a standstill is stage two: it happens so quickly and so violently there is time neither to think nor to do – you're in the lap of the gods. There are huge, loud noises, there are wrenches and twists, lurches, bangs, forces twisting you every which way: it's like being set upon by a gang of thugs in an alley. When you come to a stop finally, which is the third stage, you realise that you're still alive and functioning – and if you're not, you don't – and then your mind can start working again on what to do next.

I don't think there's a gap between conscious and unconscious thought during a shunt. It's largely a question of whether I have time to do any thinking of any kind at all, conscious or unconscious. Even your reflexes dry up. Once you accept that there's nothing your mind can do, that there are no longer any effective orders it can give, you ride it out.

Perhaps it's not that you lack the time to think. It may be that you don't want to think. Perhaps what a driver feels is resignation, or a refusal to acknowledge what is happening to him, or even outrage that it is. I do not sit there helplessly and think about anything outside the car. I'm not looking at my past life or thinking of my family or bills I've forgotten to pay. I know something is happening, but I don't actually think about anything. The body isn't paralysed; it isn't that you can't move or twitch. It's a form of knowing that nothing your body can do will help.

Meanwhile, however, you observe everything that is going on. Very acutely and almost abstractly. It is happening, and it is happening to you. When I T-boned Peter Gregg, I knew I was going to a split second before I actually did. I kept my eyes wide open and, after I hit him, I saw very clearly that my car was bouncing off him and heading straight for the wall. You don't think: you register a fact. The fact is in the form of a thought: 'Oh Christ! I'm going to have a big one, I'm going to hit the bloody wall!' I hit the wall and registered coming away from the wall and sliding down the embankment and into him again. At that point I knew that, as far as crunching into things went, the crash was finished. I'd been through the worst.

I was lucky that it happened during a practice session and that there were only three cars on the track. During a race, I would have sat there just as helplessly, but I would have registered another fact: that I was going to be hit; someone was going to whack into me. And then likely it would happen again.

What you do when you face a potential crash depends very much on its nature. I had a big one at Donington in 1980. I was testing some new radial tyres and the tread flew off one; one moment I was barrelling down the straight as fast as I could go, the next the car was turning left into the Armco and I went bouncing off it all the way down the straight. It was as if I was glued to the

Armco, and I couldn't get the car to steer at all; it kept pulling into the wall. I knew the car was badly damaged, but I concentrated on riding it out, taking my hands off the wheel so that if it wrenched very quickly, it wouldn't break my fingers.

It seemed a huge distance down the straight when the tread flew off, but by the time I'd decided what I would try to do, there wasn't any straight left. I had no brakes because my left wheel was down in front and my right wheel up in back. I was still going fast and coming up to the escape road. Great, I thought, I'll just slide up the escape road and come to a stop. Unfortunately, there was also a little ditch and then a succession of eight-foot tall concrete posts. It hit me that when I came to the end of the Armco, I was going to turn left and start mowing down the concrete posts.

I put my head down and mowed into the first three or four and the fifth one actually flipped up; it flicked the top of my dashboard and flew straight over my head. From the dashboard down on my car it's all skin and no open space, but for sure, if I hadn't ducked, that cement post would have taken my head off. When I got out of the car, the whole of its left side was ripped right off and the front had a huge dent where the post had end-over-ended and gone right over my cockpit. I was just lucky that day. And sometimes a simple reflex will save your life. I didn't think, 'Here's that post coming, now I'd better duck'; I just ducked.

To me, the worst shunts of all are when a throttle gets stuck open. Because when that happens, the shunt is almost bound to be a big one. You know what you have to do: you've got to declutch and blow your engine up – anything to get some of the speed off. If you can de-clutch, that stops your back wheels spinning. And if you've got time to do that, maybe you have time to flick the kill switch, too. But jamming on the brakes, which is what most of us would do instinctively, is of no use at all. The moment you brake, you lose your steering, and then you inevitably go head first into whatever you're trying to steer away from.

It happened to me at Zandvoort, in Holland, also in 1980. I was on a really quick lap and had just come out of the right-hander before the Hanserug, which I usually go into a little bit sideways, keeping my foot deep into it, braking at the last possible moment and then steering left to go up the hill. The trouble with corners like that, in which a driver will commit himself very deep, is that if anything goes wrong there is no time or space for him to either get around the corner or do anything to avoid a crash. That day, it was getting towards the close of practice and I went in very deep indeed. When I took my foot off the accelerator, it made no difference at all. The throttle was jammed wide open. What was the point of thinking about avoidance? I was in the fence before I could even consider evasive action. I gave that fence a proper whack.

But the strange thing is, the moment the car came to a rest, I didn't think what a lucky escape I'd had; I just thought, here it was, the last few minutes of practice and I'd messed up a good lap! My instinct was to jump out of the car and run back to the pits so I could go out in my spare.

Later, you might sit down and think about it. Then you say to yourself, what the hell am I doing running back to my car when I should be running away from it! But I get so worked up and so obsessively concerned with a result, with being well up on the grid, that I'll brush by people and ignore the danger and do absolutely anything to get that result. It's a form of blindness, and as long as a driver can keep his mind working that way, with only his place on the grid or in the race counting, he's all right. It's when he starts to sit down afterwards and think, 'Christ! I might have been killed!' that he ought to start thinking about giving the game up.

The worst crash I ever had was not on a racetrack. My friend Brian McGuire had bought a Ford Thunderbird and we were going to a party in Earl's Court. The T-Bird is just about as poor-handling a car as you can buy, so Brian should not have tried to out-corner a Lotus Elan. But he did and we just went straight into a brick wall, and from the brick wall, just as straight, into a tree. I took the door handle off with my ribs and went through the windscreen, busting my nose and shoulder.

All right, that time I knew I was seriously hurt. And if you've actually injured yourself, in a way that's easier. You know there's nothing you can do for yourself; you're totally in the hands of other people. So in Atlanta I just lay back and let them get on with it. I was in a sort of day-dreamy daze. They put needles in you, cut you out of the metal, and twist your body free from the wreckage. You just go along with whatever they're doing. You're a good boy, because it's their business to look after you now.

So it felt good to walk away from the medical centre. All the drivers had come to see if I was OK, and Les Richter turned up with the good news . . . they had a spare car for me to keep using. I think I audibly said 'Oh, fuck,' which is not good with the good old boys. These things were piles of shit even though the NASCAR boys were saying, 'Oh, aren't they honeys? They're so agile.' I'm thinking, 'If they call these things agile, their things must be like Kenworths to race.'

I really didn't want to do it again.

Then they said, 'Right, first of all we'll get you down the local gym. They've got a beautiful spa down there, and you can have a nice big spa.' Not with my dick wrapped in cotton wool and a bow on it, that would get them talking. So I managed to talk my way out of that and headed back to the hotel.

'Oh you Aussies are so tough.' If only they knew.

Back in the hotel I've got into bed and it looked like someone had had a paint brush and literally painted black stripes on me where the belts were. So that was all right, they were just bruises. Then the phone rings . . . 'How are you, Alan? I met you at Long Beach, and I hear you've just had a big wreck.' I could barely get a word in, to Cathy, or Mary, or whoever it was. I uttered acknowledgement of that and she said, 'Let me come up and look after you.'

Jones' Law kicked in, because even after I said I was OK and declined as politely as I could she had raced upstairs and knocked on the door. I thought it was someone from the hotel, so I opened the door and there she was. I rushed back and sort of jumped into bed, with the blankets up around my neck. She was giving me the big come on and I'm saying, 'No. Look, I'm happily married, I'm a Catholic . . .' The old fella stayed in his wrapping that night.

Anyway, I survived the night and went out to race on Sunday. They're all bloody banging door handles and carrying on, but mentally I was out of there. I stayed out of that fight and finished the race down in eighth, way out of danger.

That was my IROC experience and the last time I was ever going to race on an oval. Aside from a couple of Can-Am races in 1979 (for one win and a crash) and a one-off CART race at

Road America in 1985, that was pretty much it for me in terms of American racing.

I loved racing in America, I loved the fans, but I hated the ovals. I valued all my limbs and my life too much to race there full-time.

12

Williams 1979 / Emerging Contenders

When the season started in Buenos Aires, Argentina in January, we were still in the old car while plenty of others had jumped into new ground-effects cars and the season would be decided by when and how well each team introduced its new Lotus-busting cars. Lotus were the leaders of ground effects, and while Ligier and Tyrrell were really good at the start of the season, the rest of us would switch as the year progressed.

Some others had much-improved engines even if they didn't have new cars yet, so we just had to be patient, which is not a virtue of mine. We were miles off the pace. Jackie the Foot in a Ligier smashed the qualifying record as we qualified down in 15th.

There was a big crash on the first lap, which took a whole bunch of the quick qualifiers out of the race and it was red-flagged. I managed to pull up on the grid while others went into the pit lane, so I just sat there in my car as I liked to do until I realised the wait was going to be more than an hour. The second part of the race was nothing special for me and I finished a lap down on Jacques Laffite in ninth.

Two weeks later we were back at the Interlagos circuit in Brazil, which is a great track that I never went well at. No idea why; it should have suited me, but it didn't. Filling in time with the old car still, 13th on the grid turned into a DNF with fuel-pressure problems.

A month later we made it to South Africa after the battle between FOCA and FISA threatened the race for a while. Jean-Marie Balestre, the Frenchman who headed FISA, was rearing his ugly head and taking the focus off the racing and putting it firmly on himself. Ferrari had its new ground-effects car in South Africa and dominated the race with a one-two. Renault in its little way also showed turbo power was going to become a threat to all of us with a pole position, but as ever the engines weren't that strong and detonated in the races.

My weekend was a miserable 19th on the grid and a DNF when the rear suspension failed in the race, and to me it was simply a matter of when could I get into the new car. Unfortunately that answer was when the European season started for round 5 in Spain, but not after we bid farewell to the FW06 with a podium in Long Beach.

That was just one of those days, and it was the sort of track where I could muscle my way around the track. Tenth in qualifying was certainly OK compared with where we had been. There were three attempts to start the race, which is not good for a Formula One car. The Ferraris of Villeneuve and Jody Scheckter were in another league that day and they sprinted away for an easy one-two, but behind them it was on.

I showed enough patience to get the old girl into a good position, then I harried those in front and jumped at any gap. First it was Patrick Depailler, then Mario and then Jarier . . . and with less than 20 laps to run I had climbed to third. I stayed there comfortably clear of Mario, far enough behind Jody not to even dream of challenging for second.

Straight after this race we went to Ontario Motor Speedway to test the new FW07 for the first time. This day changed my world. I'd sat in the car before, but it had never turned a wheel.

I went out for those first few laps and I just couldn't believe it. I came back and said, 'Jesus, it's no wonder Andretti's winning these races. I tell you. It stuck like shit to a blanket.' The downforce was unbelievable. I was staggered at how deep I could go into the corners and how early I could get onto the power.

As a driver I needed to start reassessing a few things. Commitment into the corner was one, because this was so different – you could almost brake into the apex with the car, and then you're no sooner off the brakes and you're on it. I thought I had a weapon to unleash on the Formula One world when we got back to Europe.

I still to this day don't know if it was just a car that suited me and my aggressive driving style, or if it really was just that good a car. Perhaps it was both, but regardless I was now excited about the rest of the season, even if I was starting from well behind the pack. Jacques and Gilles both had two wins by that stage of the season and Gilles led with 20 points. I had four. Mind you, at this stage of the season my new teammate, Clay Regazzoni, had no points and I was out-qualifying and out-racing him, which was my first measurable.

I knew I could do it as a driver. We would have won races in the FW06 if those Lotuses hadn't have been around and we didn't have so many mechanical problems. But 07 was just such a good car I knew if we could make it last we could win some races. Sometimes you hop in a car and you just feel at home . . . this was one of those cars.

My first race in the 07 was at Jarama in Spain, but we weren't the only team with new cars to start the European part of the season. Lotus and Renault also had new cars and McLaren had made massive changes to its car after it was hopelessly off the pace.

It was a tough weekend with issues all over the place and my qualifying position was no better than I was getting in the old car, and then I had trouble with the gearbox in the race. Clay started one spot behind me on the grid and retired a few laps earlier than I did, so it wasn't the best way to debut a new car, especially compared with Lotus, who got both cars on the podium.

Zolder was better a couple of weeks later. I qualified fourth which was my best ever qualifying result. It was a strange field in some ways with people changing cars around all the time. Mario, for instance, went back to the old Lotus for this race. Jacques had pole with his teammate Depailler beside him. Nelson Piquet was in third and on the second row with me.

Laffite got away poorly and I jumped both him and Piquet off the start. The front row got away and Patrick and I went into first and second, with Jacques dropping down to fourth, he soon passed Nelson and closed in on me. With Jacques closing in on me, I needed to get past Patrick. I pulled beside him in front of the pits but just couldn't clear him going into Earste. I got onto the kerbs a bit on the outside and I left it open for Jacques, who went by and dropped me to third.

Jacques took the lead a few laps later and then I eventually got by Patrick. We were so quick when there was no traffic that I closed in on Jackie the Foot quite quickly. My tyres were in pretty good shape and I think the Ligiers were struggling. Jacques was struggling for grip and twitching. I think he missed a gear and that was enough for me and I swept by into the lead. The two Ligiers weren't helping each other and I pulled a really good lead.

I led for 16 laps and was extending the lead on each lap when some stupid little mechanical and electrical problem stopped the car on the exit to Bolderberg. Our team had sent a message that we were quick. It was a shame; that would have been Frank's first grand prix victory, without a doubt.

Remember, at this stage the team was really only a year old and was a minnow compared with teams like Lotus, Ferrari, Ligier and the like. After that day in Belgium it wasn't just the other teams we sent a message to – we sent one to ourselves as well . . . we knew we now had the equipment to do the job.

The 50th running of the Monaco Grand Prix was the next race. We qualified only ninth. I was second by mid-race when I clipped a wall and broke the steering. Clay was having a great run in the other car, and by the last lap he was challenging for the lead despite having a gearbox issue. Perhaps without that he could have passed Scheckter's Ferrari and won the race, but second was a great result for the team. After Monaco, James Hunt quit the sport. He was replaced by Keke Rosberg.

The Swedish Grand Prix was supposed to be next, but the organisers ran out of money. With Ronnie's death last season and local hero Gunnar Nilsson dead from cancer (there was a time trial event at Donington in his honour around that time, which I won), the Swedish appetite for our sport waned fast. So the French Grand Prix at Dijon was next. Patrick Depailler, meanwhile, had broken both his legs in a hang-gliding crash.

Because the gap between the two races was a good month, we went and did some testing at Dijon. Frank organised for Frank Ifield, the singer, to come down with us in a Beechcraft King Air plane hired for the trip. We came in over the road to land at the grass field, and the pilot put the bloody thing in reverse thrust before it even touched the ground. That's how short the runway was. I was too busy playing with my new Rolex at that stage to notice though. I was so happy I couldn't have given a rat's about anything else.

When race weekend came around, I reckon Renault had invested everything it had to win. The cars were rockets and Jean-Pierre Jabouille won the race from pole. He didn't have it all his way, my old mate Gilles Villeneuve heading him for most of the race. Gilles joined the two Renaults on the podium and I was fourth, more than 20 seconds away from the wheel-banging last lap by René Arnoux and Gilles.

It was the first win for a turbo-charged car in Formula One. Those Renaults were so fast in a straight line – it was just as well they were so unreliable.

After France, Patrick Head had found a little aluminium thing – I told you I wasn't technically minded – that he put at the back of the car. I could feel an immediate difference in the downforce, and it chopped 0.4 seconds off my lap time at Silverstone. Leading into the British Grand Prix at Silverstone, which in the absence of a race in Australia I rated as my home grand prix, we were quickest in testing.

I got my first pole position in Formula One by six-tenths of a second over Jabouille in a Renault. That kind of gap was pretty rare and it kind of came from nowhere. If we thought the FW07 was quick before, now it was a real weapon.

The Renaults at that stage were turning up the wick for qualifying and then winding it back to try and survive a race, which made the gap even more significant. They were amazingly quick in that qualifying trim, and on a fast track like Silverstone we had thought going in we had no chance for pole. At most tracks they would out-qualify us and have their own little battle for pole. Which never worried us, because we knew they'd have to come back to us in the races, and there are no points for pole.

For me getting my first pole was a strange feeling. By that stage, without wanting to sound big-headed, I was where I thought I should have been. I wasn't all that elated. I remember Frank saying to me, 'AJ, you don't seem very excited. You don't . . .' I said, 'Frank, it's because I should have had more of these.'

Any driver must believe that given the same equipment he can beat anybody else, otherwise why do it? I had that belief, but I always tried not to mouth off, not to show that belief as arrogance – because I don't like mouths. But deep down you know, and maybe within your family circles you'll talk, but that's all. These days a lot of sportsmen like to mouth off – like that tennis player Nick Kyrgios. They piss me off. I would be mortified if anyone ever thought of me like that.

Yet I was accused of arrogance. There used to be prizes given out by the French journalists – the Prix Orange and the Prix Citron. The Prix Orange was given to the driver that was the most cooperative with the press; the Prix Citron was for the one who wouldn't talk, wouldn't provide a headline, who left them with a sour taste. I was awarded the Prix Orange in 1979 and then the Citron in 1980. Problem was, I just didn't have the time in 1980. My attitude didn't change, but the amount of time I had at the track did.

I wasn't there for fun. I was there to win. I never used to take golf clubs or lounge around by the pool (I couldn't risk sunburn like I had in Brazil all those years ago). I was there to go motor racing.

My whole persona used to change from the minute I left the front door of my house. I turned into a racing driver – and a prick. I was in race mode until I got home Sunday or Monday. Then I'd go down to the pub and have a few beers with the boys. None of them were really into motorsport all that much, which suited me fine as it does today. They knew who I was, but I'd go down there and have a game of pool with them, have a few beers and preferably not talk about motorsport.

That was it. I used to separate my two lives, because as Alan Jones the racing driver, I really wasn't a nice person. I was there to do a job. I'd made the conscious decision to move from Australia 12,000 miles away, and I wasn't doing that for fun. I was there to get the job done. I was willing to do anything to anybody who got in the way.

So there I was in 1980 focusing on my racing and they fire stupid questions at me and get upset if I didn't sit with them for four hours. 'Look, mate, sorry, I haven't got time. You'll have to catch up later.' Then you become arrogant in their eyes.

I could not tolerate anybody that didn't know their subject either. Some journalists would ask you the most inane and stupid questions, and it was immediately obvious they knew nothing about motorsport; they were just simply given a job to come and interview you. I used to just wipe them. I was not arrogant, but I was intolerant.

We were fastest again in the warm-up, in my eyes everything was set for me to win the British GP. Even when I didn't get a good start and dropped to third, I still had the lead back by the end of the first lap. I passed both Clay and Jabouille in the one move at Stowe, which was a pretty good feeling. Jabouille stayed with me for a bit, then I started to pull away and built up a 20-second lead. Then the bloody heat exchanger cracked and I lost all my water and had to retire.

I was filthy, not just because it was going to be a grand prix win, but it would have been Williams' first grand prix win. That honour went to my teammate, Clay Regazzoni – and I was really happy for him, Frank and the team. But still, I jumped in my car and screamed back to London, with Beverley sitting in the passenger seat shitting herself. I didn't even wait around. I should have at least waited there to congratulate my teammate. I wasn't that sort of a person though; I was too competitive. They could all get fucked, I was going back to London. As far as I was concerned, the heat exchanger just shouldn't have cracked . . . I was foul.

It is great when the circuit gets to Europe because you pretty much get a race every fortnight. Hockenheim was a big power track, so even with our new-found speed we were not really likely to challenge the Renaults for pole, but I did get a front-row start that I turned into first place going into the first corner of the race and then I just led the entire race.

Late in the race I was losing a bit of speed from a slow puncture, but I had more than enough to stay in front of Clay, who was second. There was talk that he was told to stay in second, but I dispute that. If I was him and I had been told not to pass, I would have finished half a second behind me. That would have spelled out to the world that I could have done it. But when you're three seconds behind it's very debatable whether you got those orders or not.

Regazzoni, and later Reutemann, wasn't averse to saying that I got preferential treatment or better equipment, which was absolute crap, because Williams were in a position to give equal equipment to both drivers. When they can do that, I don't think any team favours one driver; it is just too hard to manage and too risky. Lewis Hamilton was talking about that in 2016, almost claiming his car was being made to fail while Nico Rosberg was allowed to go on and win . . . it was as much crap then as it was in the 70s. You don't spend hundreds of millions of dollars and employ thousands of people to sabotage your driver. The whole reason of running a two-car team is if one breaks down or has trouble, hopefully the other one will come through and win a grand prix for you.

Jabouille was my biggest threat that day. He had a lot of speed down the straights but he had to work hard to stay with me in the corners and into the stadium area early in the race he locked up and spun himself out of the race.

The German was my second grand prix victory, almost two years on from my first, and with a one-two I thought it was pretty clear we had a great car now and so long as it held together, we would be a contender every time we hit the track. I remember watching some of the footage after the race and hearing Murray Walker say when talking about one-two finishes that this was 'the first for Saudia Williams, but probably not the last'. I was hoping he was right.

I got to shake the champagne after my first grand prix win, but not for the rest of them. The bottle remained at my feet this time. I can't recall whether Frank specifically asked for us not to do it, but it was out of respect for our Muslim sponsors.

If we were lucky enough to win a grand prix it was almost compulsory viewing in Saudi Arabia that week, to show their people how technically fabulous they were. Never mind that they didn't know one end of a wrench from the other, but just poured the money in. Anyway, spraying alcohol all over the place was very naughty, because our sponsors supposedly didn't drink alcohol. Of course that wasn't the case, but we did need to show respect on the podium. We did things like shake orange juice, which was a piss-take on our part, but never any alcohol. We made up for it when the doors were closed . . .

In Austria I qualified second, this time to René Arnoux in his Renault. I thought I got a good start and was going to lead into the first corner when Gilles blasted past me in that Ferrari. He had plenty of straight-line speed, but my car was the better handling and by the start of the third lap I had the lead back – and I held it to the end. Back-to-back grand prix wins felt real good.

That weekend I was seeing my future. The Renaults with their turbo engines would always be hard to beat in qualifying, but then they'd dial it back to try to last the distance in the race. The

Ferrari and Alfa Romeo V12s were fast in a straight line, but the handling for each of Ferrari and Brabham was nowhere near ours. The FW07 was kind on its tyres and definitely had the edge in racing terms.

My win in Austria was by nearly 40 seconds over Gilles – and they had the Australian national anthem ready now. I was now fourth in the World Championship, but with the stupid points system for that year it was very unlikely that I could win the title . . . even if I won every race, which was my intention at that point. We could count our best four results from the first seven rounds – it was eight until Sweden pulled out – and then the best four from the final eight.

What that meant was that I had four points for my podium in Long Beach from the first half of the season and then could add only another 36 points if I won four races in the back half. I had already won two. I left Austria on 25 points chasing Jody on 38 points and the chances of him not getting another three points in the final three rounds was pretty slim.

Bloody René Arnoux beat me to pole at Zandvoort and I was again second, though I beat him off the start and had a good battle with Gilles for the lead. René crashed into Clay off the start and knocked one of his wheels off, so I think I was lucky to be clear of him that day. Early in the race I started to get gearbox problems and Gilles was able to go around the outside of me at Tarzan on lap 11.

It was a great battle up to that point, but Gilles, as ever, was going as hard as he could and eventually spun off the track and gave me back the lead, which I turned into my third win in a row. Jody was second after dropping to last, and that was enough to mean I could not win the championship, which was now a battle between him and Jacques Laffite, who hadn't won since the second round after we all developed better cars.

With three wins in a row, my head was at 42,000 feet now. Big-headed Alan Jones. You do start to feel bulletproof when you are on a roll like that. Firstly, you know you can do it, and secondly everyone else now knows too. Given the right car and the right opportunity, I knew I could win a lot more grands prix.

Some things still rankled though. Every time I out-qualified the Ferrari I'd drive down pit lane and give them a little wave, just so they knew. 'I'm the bloke you didn't sign, you dickheads.' Even though I was still shitty, it worked out much better for me that Ferrari didn't sign me.

In that era you would have cars more suited to one track than another – and on a power track we were not so good.

Enter Monza. I remember that race quite clearly because Frank was ropeable with me after I had a little incident that left me injured for the race.

I was driving down Chiswick High Road back in London and had a bit of an altercation with a van driver. We both got out of our vehicles. Turns out the other driver was a big black gentleman. When he uncoiled himself, he stood before me a man mountain and proceeded to bounce me up and down Chiswick High Road for about three minutes.

The bloke who was in the car with me locked the doors. Thanks a lot. Anyway, he broke my finger. So the next race was Monza and I had to race with two fingers bandaged up. When Frank asked what happened, stupidly, I told him. I had to have some injections in the finger to stop the pain, as I did in Canada too.

The funny thing was Beverley and I were looking at adopting a second child and I was on my way home to meet the lady from the adoption centre when this incident happened. She was there with Beverley when I opened the door with blood all over my ripped shirt.

Beverley looked at me with one of those looks, and dragged me upstairs. I thought I was about to get another hiding. We had a three-storey house and the main lounge room was on the middle and the bedrooms and bathrooms up top, so I had to go past the lounge to clean myself up. I was spotted, and the adoption lady asked what happened. Jones, king of bullshit, rolled out a good one. 'I've been hit by a motor scooter on a pedestrian crossing.'

She said, 'Oh my god, they're so irresponsible.'

I couldn't think of anything else. 'I won't be a moment,' I added. 'I'll just go clean myself up.' I went back down after I cleaned myself up. She thought I was very brave for continuing on with the meeting considering my injuries. Beverley was giving me dirty looks and threatening to kill me.

We never did adopt that second child.

Monza was a shit weekend, the bulletproof feeling had well and truly gone. At one stage I was wobbling around down the back of the field with ignition problems and I finished one lap down on Jody who won, and secured the championship. I was the fastest on the track though and without that niggle I could have beaten the Ferraris that day. Clay was much more competitive than me and finished third, which moved Williams into second on the Constructors' Championship.

Thankfully, Canada was better for me. This was the second race on the Circuit Île Notre-Dame, which is a great track on a man-made island in the middle of a river. It has places you can overtake, especially at the hairpin and other parts of it that are just great to race on. I grabbed pole from Gilles, who had massive support given he was a local and had won the previous year, and that set up a great race.

Before the start, Frank said to me, 'Don't do anything silly. Don't try and race too much too early, because you'll screw your tyres. Wait until your fuel load gets down and then have a go.' And to Gilles' credit, it wasn't me just sort of hanging back, I just couldn't pass the little bugger. I was trying since I'd forgotten most of what Frank said as soon as the race started, although I was trying to limit the wheelspin coming out of the hairpin.

We were nose to tail for about three-quarters of the race. Of course all the grandstand were on their feet cheering for him. Lap after lap I looked, but he was so hard to pass even when he didn't have much of a power advantage. On lap 51 I got a great run on him coming out of the chicane down the back of the track. He left the door open just a little and I went for it. I screamed down the inside and was completely beside him, which meant I had the corner, but we banged wheels, which was a bit silly on his part. He was on the outside and he could have had both of us off and neither of us would have won.

He didn't need to hit me. I had him well beaten in that corner. James Hunt, who had slipped into doing commentary for the BBC, was quite critical of him, but I didn't really care too much. I had the lead and was able to pull a small gap. James had driven for Wolf that year until he quit. From the commentary box he watched Jody Scheckter win the title for Ferrari – the drive that he had been offered, but knocked back. James' commentary was great – he didn't hold back. Just as well we were friends.

After I got into the lead I thought I'd be able to pull away, but I couldn't. Gilles stuck right on my gearbox until the end of the race. It didn't help when I had to lap his teammate, but that was all part of it. It was just a bloody good race. It was just two cars. You could have thrown a blanket over us for virtually the whole grand prix.

I finished one second in front of Gilles – and we were more than a minute clear of Clay in third. You can still watch the race on the internet – and it still looks good. The fans got their money's worth that day, even if they were pissed off that their man didn't win.

So there I was, I had four wins in the second half of the season, so no matter what happened at Watkins Glen for the final round, the silly scoring system meant no more points for me. I had pole position again, this time by more than a second from Nelson Piquet, and again I was beaten off the line by Gilles. That Ferrari was such a good starter. It was a wet race to start with and Gilles opened up a gap on me, but as it started to dry I was pulling him in at up to two seconds a lap – he was never good at looking after his tyres.

On lap 31 I went into the lead and then had that out to nearly four seconds when Gilles pitted for slicks. A couple of laps later when I had finally knocked the edges off the wet-weather tyres, I pitted. They had trouble with my right rear tyre, and while I was being waved away the mechanic back there was still trying to get it on. At the start of the back straight, it fell off and I was out of the race while leading.

Even with that I finished the season in third. If only we'd got the new car earlier, and if only we'd got on top of our reliability quicker, who knows what could have happened. As it turned out, the year was a battle of new ground-effects cars, of when they arrived and who mastered them quickest. Ligier was on top of the game for the first two races, with Jackie the Foot winning the first two races. Then Ferrari introduced its wing car and Gilles won two races from Jody, who then won two of the next three.

Patrick Depailler took a win in the Ligier and then broke his legs, Jean-Pierre Jabouille won for Renault in France and then it was us. The FW07 came for round 5, Patrick found a demon tweak for Britain three races later and then we were easily the best car on the track. I won four races from that point and Clay won in Britain, giving us five from seven and that could easily have been all seven.

Heading back to Australia for Christmas, I felt good, and not just because we flew home first class. We now had Christian and we had bought a modern house in Kew overlooking the old Skipping Girl Vinegar factory, so we had great views of Melbourne.

We had also bought a farm just outside Yea, but I quickly worked out I wasn't a farmer and put in a manager for that. I did buy the pub up there too though. I was much better at going to the pub after a day on the farm than I was on the farm itself. In hindsight, I was better on the customer side of the bar too.

I thought I'd remodel the pub. Influenced by being in Europe for so long, I started with black, red and white checked tablecloths. I put a veranda on it, painted it and put shutters on . . . I thought it was great. I was hoping to get the passing snow traffic in winter, let people come in and cook their own steaks.

Anyway the locals weren't happy. 'Are you turning this into a poofta's pub?'

'Fuck no,' I said, 'I'm just trying to turn it into a nice place everyone can enjoy.' I caught a bloke one night in a ute with a rope around one of the veranda stays trying to pull the bloody thing down. He was banned for life.

Then I started seeing dust that I never saw before I owned it, and that wasn't a good sign. I had a succession of idiots through there as managers – it was just a bloody nightmare. I couldn't wait to get out of it after a while.

On the farm I decided to breed Simmentals, which are cows from the Simme Valley in Switzerland. They're half a milking cow and half a beef cow. They're beautiful. They're really good cattle and I was breeding polls without horns. They were good because when you take them to the market in trucks, there were no horns to bruise each other with.

I bought a new Mercedes truck and had it all done up with Meraleste Pastoral Company on the side of it. I thought I was going to be the big pastoralist, pretty much as I had told people when scamming in my early days in England. I had a guy from Switzerland as my herd master, Fritz, who was a bit of a Simmental expert. He lived in one of the houses on the property, which was nearly 2500 acres, 80 kilometres northeast of Melbourne. The setting was great. I put in a tennis court and trees lining the driveway.

After Fritz had the cattle all settled in for me he headed back to Switzerland and I gave him a going-away party at the pub. We all went down there and when it was time to close I said, 'Right, close the doors. We're continuing on.' The manager came up and said I couldn't do that. 'It's time to close,' he said. I said, 'Look. It's my fucking pub. I'm staying here and this party's going on.'

He said it was his licence we were using, so I told him to fuck off and I sacked him on the spot. He got in the car and left. This was about midnight.

Then I thought, 'Okay, now what are you going to do, dickhead?' Someone had to open up the next day and someone had to stay with the takings. I got Beverley to go back to the farm and get a shotgun for me, and I stayed there with the bloody gun next to me, with the smell of cigarettes and beer that you get only in a country pub.

Then I had to go like buggery to get a new manager for the joint. Once again I had to pay for a spontaneous stupid act. I couldn't wait to get out of the bloody joint. Every boy's dream is to have a pub and a farm – and his second dream is to get rid of them. But, anyway, it's another box ticked.

Regardless of that, I was in a good place. The days of worrying over Christmas about what I was doing the next year were now well behind me. I was firmly ensconced at Williams and I knew we were building to something special. There were people sniffing around to see if I'd drive for them, but I was going nowhere in 1980. I was truly happy with Williams, and got on extremely well with Patrick, Frank, Charlie and everyone else too. My chief mechanic was an Australian named Wayne Eckersley, or 'Wayne the Pain' simply because it rhymed.

Strangely, even after the run we'd had I was looking at 1980 as just another year to race a car. 1980 was another 16 races and I wanted to win as many as I could. I never really thought, 'I'm going to win the 1980 World Championship.' I thought I was going to give it a fair old nudge, but the thing in Formula One is you never know who's got what.

Chapman could have had some super-duper bloody thing coming out of the garage at Lotus. Or Renault might have got some reliability. Anything could happen . . . and it is not easy to win that championship. 1980 was the 31st championship year, and up to then out of the hundreds who had tried only 17 had won titles and maybe only 50 or so had even won races.

Yes, I thought I had a chance, but to use an old cliché, it really was one race at a time.

James Hunt

James was a character, one of those guys that you never knew what he was going to do next. A really nice guy he was, very kind-hearted. James was one of the few drivers I actually liked. I respected him as a driver too. It should never be forgotten just how bloody good he was.

He didn't give a shit about anything. He'd go and buy a brand new Mercedes when he was living in Spain, and he had this whacking big Alsatian. He'd take him down to the beach, straight off the beach, sand and everything, into the back seat of the Merc. It was completely rooted after a month. He didn't care.

He also used to run up to some of the functions barefooted. He got off a plane once in Brazil and a bloke stood on his foot. He said, 'You fucking mongrel,' or something like that. It cost Marlboro a wing at the local hospital to get the incident all hushed up.

He used to call me 'Big Al'. 'Come on, Big Al, we'll go and do this and we'll do that.' But shit, could he get me into trouble . . . I blame him.

I went around to visit him one day when he was living in Wimbledon with his second wife, Sarah. I used to ride my bike up to see him on the pretence of training. I lived on a park and I used to ride quite a bit, so I didn't need that trip at all. But Wimbledon wasn't that far, so I'd ride up there for a beer or two. As ever, he was out the back with his budgerigars. He loved those birds, and because they were Australian he'd always say, 'Bunch of Aussies, Big Al.' I went out there and was on the hoochie coochie. He used to tell the wife he was going out to train the budgies and he'd get stuck into the hooch. I'm sure those budgies must have been high most of the time.

The things he used to get up to were just unbelievable. We went to the official opening of the brand new Nürburgring in 1984 and all the living world champions had been invited to race identical Mercedes 190e 2.3-16s. Which means James and I were in the field and so too was Ayrton Senna, since Mario and Emerson couldn't make it. Anyway, the race itself is quite famous. I was leading with seven laps remaining when the power steering broke and Senna went on to win. Senna's car is now in the Mercedes museum; I would have loved for it to be mine.

Anyway, Lufthansa was catering the event in a huge tent, and straight after the race it started pissing with rain and all the drivers went for cover. We started drinking, and soon we were placing bets on who could get back to the hotel first. We were racing hard, passing bloody trams on the wrong side and wheels on the grass and Christ knows what. I've no idea who won, and it's not really the point, is it. We got back there and James said, 'Big Al, come up to the room.'

When we got into his room, Sarah, his second wife, was in bed sick, not that it bothered James to invite someone in. We started on the beer and then after a couple he handed me a joint. I'd tried a bit of cocaine once and some other soft drugs too, and mari-juana actually did little for me . . . or so I thought. 'This is good stuff, Big Al, try it.'

I've had a taste of this thing and since I've got no idea what I'm doing and I'm a few beers into a big night, it didn't stop there. Anyway, obviously it's got the better of me. I said, James, I've got to go down for dinner and I headed off. Then James took me aside and said, 'Big Al, there's a waitress there and I've got a good shot with her. She's going to meet me in the car park. I've worded her up about you, when she comes over, can you give her the nod and tell her that I'm out in the car park?' I said, 'Yeah, no dramas.'

James' partners knew of his ways and no-one could ever change that about him. He was an upfront character and we were used to it. He's still one of the most celebrated personalities in the sport of Formula One.

I knew I was sitting at the table with the managing director from Mercedes-Benz Australia, and as I was heading there I couldn't stop laughing. I didn't know what was going on, and I was out of it. I thought, 'I know what I'll do. So they won't be able to see my face, I'll walk down the stairs backwards.' Well, that got everyone's attention.

Every word uttered at that table was hilarious. I laughed at everything. My sides were in knots. My face muscles hurt. Then I picked up the dinner menu and began shaking it up and down. All sense of control was lost by this stage.

Anyway, the waitress has come up and given me half a nod. I thought, 'Jesus, she fancies me,' completely forgetting that it was the deal with James. 'She's trying to pull me.' I started with the legendary Jones' charm. James was by now bobbing up and down in the car park, slinking between cars waiting for her to appear. At that point, all the directors of Mercedes-Benz started to arrive in their armoured cars with bodyguards – they were all security-conscious because one of their directors had been kidnapped previously and they weren't taking any chances. So they move in packs and had the guards on hand. Anyway, they fronted up to this hotel and there's this bloke bobbing up and down between the parked cars. One of the bodyguards has seen him and it was on.

Inside, I continued to eye off the waitress, thinking that I was in with a chance. Then I saw security from the entire venue rush out the door to meet up with the others responding to the threat. They chased this bloke for a good minute before crash-tackling him to the ground. They pinned him down and turned him over to find that they'd captured James Hunt, ex-Formula One driver. I think as soon as they discovered who he was they let him go. It was just a nightmare. I didn't get the waitress. Nor did James.

Later on, he abused the shit out of me. I stood my ground, telling him that he should never have influenced me to suck a big puff out of that joint.

My adventures with James also broke through the darkness that could descend after losing a race. I remember once going back on the plane to England with him when he was absolutely blind drunk. James made the plane his own by playing around on the public address system and hanging out with the pilot in the cockpit. It was a long flight and all I can remember is how he made the trip one heck of a good time. It felt like a party.

Meeting Alan Jones

One night at a party in London, I met Alan Jones the racing driver. That was a highlight for me. There were a lot of Aussies at this pub and I was talking to this bloke and he said, 'I race cars.' I said, 'Really? What's your name?'

He said, 'Alan Jones.'

'Really?' I just let him go, hoping to Christ that someone would tap him on the shoulder and say, 'Guess what.'

I had some fun with him for the rest of the night, introduced him to my mates.

13

My Favourite Thing About Winter Is When It Is Over

LIFE WAS PRETTY strange back at the end of 1979. My run in the second half of the season had put me firmly in the spotlight, which was both good and bad. It meant I was earning a lot of money and I certainly felt some of the pressure and expectation that was coming my way, but I was dealing with it.

Because the weather in California was so good, I stayed there for the break between seasons. Back in Australia I still wasn't really on the radar, so there wasn't much to do there for me, but we had a nice home in a place we liked. The Australian version of *60 Minutes* did a program on me around that time, entitled 'Alan Who?'

They flew over to California and did the interviews with me while I was learning to fly out of Torrance Airport. One of them very stupidly came up on the plane with me, a little Cessna 180.

We went for a burn around LA, came back and landed. Relatively safely. I eventually decided that fixed wing was a bit boring, so I got into helicopters and I really enjoyed them.

Anyway, the whole show was about how no-one back home knew who I was. In Europe it was a different story, and the US was somewhere in between. But the *60 Minutes* show also proved that things were changing back home; my winning streak was having an impact. Channel Nine – which ran *60 Minutes* – was starting to get into Formula One and people were paying attention.

I had a new turbo Porsche with California plates 'AJ Turbo', so there was a little bit of wanker in me, but it was still under control I thought. I had a boat that I kept at Marina Del Rey. I don't know why, because on the coast of California, particularly down around that area, there was nowhere to go. The only place to go was Catalina; the boat wasn't big enough to get to Mexico.

I started up a business with an old friend of mine who used to live in Melbourne and was now in Los Angeles, and we called it Grand Prix Sunroofs. We had a bunch of Mexicans working for us installing – as you may have guessed – sunroofs.

Kent was my mate's name, and he was fucking mad. Mad, mad, mad. Had an apartment on the footpath in Manhattan Beach, half an hour from Palos Verdes, and all the sheilas used to skate by. He'd get them up in the apartment pretty easily – it was as if he had a fishing rod. He was a complete lunatic. He's dead now. But, yeah, funny days.

After all those winters of discontent, I was now finally enjoying my time off. Life was good. Christian was still really a baby and Bev and I were enjoying that too.

I didn't realise it at the time, but I was not really enjoying aspects of the travel that came with my life and success. Over winter, we'd go testing at Paul Ricard and it was bloody cold. You couldn't go onto the track until about ten in the morning, because we had to wait until it dried. Then it used to get dark about four.

You'd then go back to the hotel, and they wouldn't serve dinner until eight. There would be no cable TV, so it would only be TV in a foreign language. I'm not all that clever, so I don't speak another language. I never used to read all that much either, so it was not like I cuddled up with a good book. I used to go for a walk. It was all very boring.

But the urge to not travel was starting to grow in me.

14

BMW Procar

I DON'T KNOW how the BMW M1 Procar series came about, and in my purely selfish fashion nor did I really care. It was good for me, and that was all that counted at the time.

For the series they built these supposedly identical cars and they sold some to privateers and then made half a dozen available to Formula One drivers that qualified in the top six. It ran as a support race to several of the European grands prix, with nine races in 1979 and then, for us, six of the nine races in the series for 1980. Luckily in those days I very rarely qualified out of the top six so I was pretty much always there for a run.

There was good money in it for us drivers, and there were prizes of cars for winning races and for certain spots in the championship. Everyone wondered why the team owners were allowing their drivers to participate, but it turned out that the team owners

Dad shaking hands with Otto Stone and the ever-present son, me, not too far from the action.

The start of the 1956 Australian Grand Prix at Albert Park. Dad is on the front row in the number 8 Maserati and that's me at the front of the Zephyr. (*Autopics*)

I'm not sure if it was genes more than environment. Dad was a great racing driver and I think he could have been among the best in the world, but for me it was those early years with the cars and race tracks that inspired me to go racing. (*Autopics*)

One of my earliest races in 1964 at Hume Weir in the Mini that Dad had built for me. It's a pity the picture isn't in colour because it looked a treat with its silver paint and black wheels. (*Autopics*)

I really enjoyed Formula Three – the cars were quick and great to drive. This is the DART GRD back in 1973 when I came second in the championship because they had double points in the final race.

Harry Stiller was one of the nicest blokes I drove for and I have a lot to thank him for. These early drives in the Formula Atlantic car paved the way for our entry into Formula One in 1975.

Driving a V6-powered car in Formula 5000 was a great learning experience. We were able to race and beat cars with much more power, although we didn't do the full series.

Part of my dream was to race in Formula One, and I made my debut with Custom Made/Harry Stiller Racing in 1975, sharing a team with James Hunt, which is where we developed such a strong friendship. Harry eventually decided to flee Great Britain to get away from the tax man, so the team didn't even survive the season. (*LAT Photographic*)

I joined Embassy Hill a few races after Harry fled, and while I got on well with Graham Hill the team wasn't very functional. I did get my first World Championship points so I felt I was getting somewhere. (*LAT Photographic*)

I didn't get into racing for the fame, but it certainly had some benefits. Talking to the Duke of Edinburgh before a grand prix was just one of those perks, although I was probably more anxious about getting into the car and going racing than talking to him. (*LAT Photographic*)

Graham Hill was a difficult man to drive for. I was so lucky not to be with the team when he crashed his plane and all onboard died – I could have been there. (*LAT Photographic*)

The Surtees TS19 had so much potential, but it all fell away because the team wasn't run very well. Look at the narrow cockpit – this is the car before they gave me the bubble in the side so I could change gears. It was a very frustrating season. (*LAT Photographic*)

Because I walked away from my contract with Surtees I had nothing on in Europe, so I did the Rothmans International Series in Australia during February with Teddy Yip's Theodore Racing. I won one of the four rounds and finished third on debut here at Oran Park for the Australian Grand Prix. (*Autopics*)

After getting back into Formula One with Shadow in 1977, I did some Can-Am races and won my first-ever title in the Haas-Hall Racing Lola in 1978 when I felt like I was untouchable. I called it cruise and collect, but it wasn't that easy. They were fabulous cars to drive and I loved racing in America.

My partnership with Williams almost didn't happen, but when it did I knew right away it was the best option for me. In my fourth race for the team at Long Beach we were challenging for the lead when electrical problems dropped me off the pace. I drove much of the race with a collapsed front wing. (*LAT Photographic*)

ABOVE LEFT: Frank Williams was a great man to drive for, and he even got me out running with him at times. He loved his running, but he loved his racing even more, and his mind was perfectly suited to building the team that went on to dominate the sport for many years. (*LAT Photographic*)

ABOVE RIGHT: I didn't spend much time with my rivals, but James Hunt was an exception. He was such good company and a great bloke. I think he was also a better driver than many gave him credit for. (*LAT Photographic*)

After winning the Canadian Grand Prix I left the champagne shaking to others. We were sponsored by Saudi, and I felt I needed to respect their no alcohol beliefs … in public at least. (*LAT Photographic*)

Beverley was an important part of those early years of racing. We had a pretty fiery up-and-down relationship that eventually ended in the 1980s. (*LAT Photographic*)

My championship year and the FW07 was a great car. Patrick Head and his team of engineers built the best handling car in the field and it was enough for us to beat the much more powerful Ferraris and Renaults, whose challenge failed for a number of reasons. The biggest challenge was, however, from Nelson Piquet in a Brabham and here he is buried in the pack. (*LAT Photographic*)

On top of the 1980 World Championship, I came down to Calder Park in Melbourne where I had so many of my early races, and won the Australian Grand Prix. It was a great honour to join Dad on the winners list, and we're still the only father and son to have won that race. (*Autopics*)

ABOVE LEFT: Patrick Head, Frank Williams and I were a pretty good combination. Frank organised the money and ran the team, while Patrick engineered and designed the cars. Patrick was the perfect engineer for me, and the understanding between the two of us was one of the reasons we were successful. (*LAT Photographic*)

ABOVE RIGHT: Running a season with the number 1 on my car was something I had always dreamed about, and while I never won at Monaco and I didn't like the place, I would dearly have loved to have added it to my list of wins. (*LAT Photographic*)

Patrick and Frank's final attempt to keep me in Formula One at the end of 1981 was the six-wheeled car. I felt it had potential but it wasn't enough to keep me in England. I went straight from this test to Heathrow and flew home to Australia. For me, at that time, my career was over. (*LAT Photographic*)

No longer a driver but a farmer. I was breeding
Simmental cattle which I felt at the time was going
to make me a fortune. It didn't take long to work
out I wasn't a farmer.

Christian enjoyed the farm, though; the space allowed him to explore his own
love of machinery. Being around for him was one of the reasons I quit F1, but I
was still being drawn into motor racing.

This Porsche 935 was a bit of a weapon and I used it to dominate the Australian GT Championship in 1982. I was challenged by people like Peter Brock, but I won every round of the series. (*Autopics*)

In 1984 the World Sports Car Championship came to Melbourne and I drove a Porsche for the factory team. I made a silly error in qualifying and should have been on pole. After a couple of niggles in the race I ended up eighth with Vern Schuppan. (*Autopics*)

This is the race in which the world first truly noticed Ayrton Senna. Mercedes lined up an impressive list of world champions for a race at the new Nürburgring track in Germany; Senna got a late call-up and won the race, but only after my car failed while I was leading. Senna's car is still on display at the Mercedes-Benz museum – I would have liked that. (*LAT Photographic*)

ABOVE LEFT: Part of the reason I returned to Formula One was because Adelaide had won the right to run the first-ever Formula One World Championship race in Australia. The race and track were magnificent and set a new standard for grands prix, but my Beatrice was not so good and my two seasons with the team were very frustrating. If I wasn't getting paid so well, I'd have wished I never did it. (*LAT Photographic*)

ABOVE RIGHT: My year with TOM'S Toyota in Japan was also interesting. We won a couple of races, but only when we got the rear wing in its effective spot, rather than keeping the car pretty. (*LAT Photographic*)

I did win Bathurst, albeit the 12-hour race in a Mazda. I still find it frustrating that a lot of race fans in Australia don't love Formula One in the same way they love Bathurst. (*Autopics*)

Racing touring cars with Glenn Seton's team was enjoyable, and we were pretty successful too. We only got 52 laps done in this car in 1994, but the year after we nearly won the race. Second remains my best result at Bathurst in a touring car. (*Autopics*)

In 1996 I started Pack Leader Racing with support from Philip Morris. A lot of people think I did the dirty on Glenn Seton at the time, but both he and I know nothing is further from the truth. Owning the team wasn't a great experience, though, and eventually I sold the team to Ross and Jim Stone. (*Autopics*)

Meeting Amanda was one of the best things to happen to me. We have such a great relationship and we have a terrific family with the twins and her daughter. (*LAT Photographic*)

Amanda was brave enough to head onto the track with me at the Goodwood Festival of Speed. I'm not sure about the lack of helmet or glasses, though. (*LAT Photographic*)

These days I spend my time working with the Ten Network on its Formula One coverage and keeping my hand in the sport by working as a steward at some grands prix each year. My involvement with Lexus also keeps me busy, and I attend most of their drive days to 'entertain' the guests with stories and to take them on the track in the stunning LFA.

I am so honoured to have won the World Drivers' Championship but I also wish someone else could have joined me and Sir Jack Brabham for this photo. With Sir Jack's passing a couple of years back, we won't be able to have him join me with Australia's next world champion for a photo. (*LAT Photographic*)

were getting the same money as the drivers. That was a nice little earner for doing nothing – and I've never seen a team owner who didn't want more money.

For me it proved to be quite good because it paid for my tennis court at the farm and I ended up by winning a BMW, which I then put a few extra bob into, upgraded it to a black 325 convertible and sold it to a fairly wealthy lady in London for a tidy profit.

How it worked was that after practice if you were in the top six you went down and claimed your BMW M1 and they put your name on the windscreen and all the pro cars (as in the Formula One drivers) were done in white with the red and blue stripes that is now the badge for BMW's M spec cars. The privateers had their sponsors and their cars looked totally different. I think Niki Lauda had a privateer one, so he raced whether he made it into the top six or not, and that is how he won the first series.

The series was a great concept and a lot of fun – a great pressure relief on a high-pressure weekend. The cars were pretty good too, properly geared up for racing. But like anything with us drivers, it was also serious. At one race meeting in Avus we were all taping up the gaps in the panels and doors and around the pop-up headlights. We were all looking for that little bit extra on the long straights, and this would make the car more aerodynamic. If someone else was doing it, so were we.

It was a classic example of the purple-pole syndrome. If Mercedes today came out with a 90-foot purple pole at the front of its car, you'd bet your life that a few of the boys at the next race meeting would also have a 90-foot purple pole. They wouldn't know what the hell it did, but they'd have it and then work it out.

All us drivers had egos you couldn't jump over, so we all wanted to beat one another. And we felt we were the best in the world, and I think we pretty much proved that – it was very rare that we'd get beaten by one of the privateers.

Over time it became very clear to me that the cream would rise to the top. You'd go to circuits around the world, say in Can-Am or a race meeting on an airfield in Germany where we were all in Cortinas – the Formula One guys always ended up quicker than not only the locals, but also the guys experienced in that type of car.

We proved time and time again why we were all racing in Formula One – because we were the best.

One of the great things about the M1 was that it had guards and panels and was a little more forgiving if we touched each other. In a Formula One we'd avoid contact; we did touch wheels every so often, but it was a lot less forgiving and you knew every time there was a chance that could end your race. So we were very conscious of that and tried to avoid it, but in these things a little tap here and there was OK. Somewhere like Monaco in particular, in those things you were inevitably going to have some body contact . . . and we did.

If you saw a gap you went for it and if you had body contact you had body contact and you just hoped that it wouldn't rub a guard against the tyre. It was like when I went down the inside of Peter Brock at Siberia at Phillip Island when I was racing touring cars – I knew you could just lean on him and I'd be OK, so I did. We contacted pretty hard and I smashed all the windows on the left hand side of his car, but that was it. We continued racing. He didn't come up afterwards and he wasn't ranting and raving like

I'd just taken his first-born for a sacrifice. He realised it was a racing incident. Just like what Jamie Whincup did at Bathurst when he passed Scott McLaughlin in 2016. They took the race off him for that, which really annoyed me. I mean, do you want people to race or not?

You never consciously said 'I'm going to enjoy this because I can lean on somebody' or just belt the other bloke out of the way. The trick was *not* to do it, because there was always that chance you're going to damage yourself – put the bodywork in on the tyre or bend a steering arm – so you did avoid it.

This was an era where drivers were still getting killed in Formula One, so I think we all had respect for what we were doing. Look at those years, it's carnage. There were still people having crashes and getting injured, the carbon-fibre monocoques that revolutionised driver safety were still a year or two away.

I don't think any of us at that stage were driving through the tunnel at Monaco with the belief we couldn't get hurt. So even in a BMW M1, we treated the racing with respect.

15

The Championship Year

I TURNED UP for work for the start of the 1980 season confident but nervous. We were the team all the others had to catch, but that didn't mean it was going to be easy. The bookies had Gilles Villeneuve favourite for the championship in the Ferrari, but we felt we had the upper hand for a number of reasons.

Patrick Head wasn't going to let the others catch us though; he was as competitive as me. We had the Ford Cosworth engine, which was good and solid, but more than half the field was using it and it was clearly not as powerful as the Ferrari flat 12 or the Renault turbo, although they did have their own issues.

Ferrari, the reigning champ, had a new car, the 312T5, to race against our FW07B. There were stories going around that the engine was so bulky it made it hard to get the ground effects to work as well as those of us with physically smaller engines. Good.

We also had to pay attention to what was coming from Ligier – remember how fast they were at the start of 1979 – Renault, Brabham, McLaren and, of course, Lotus. There were lots of other changes up and down the field: Alain Prost was starting his grand prix career with McLaren and Carlos Reutemann had joined me at Williams. Carlos was bloody quick – he had won races at both Ferrari and Brabham and spent a year at Lotus before we lured him across.

Instead of going to Paul Ricard, we tested in mid-December in Argentina with the 1979 car updated to FW07B spec. Most of the main teams were there with us and we came away fastest, which meant to our eyes no-one had found a demon tweak yet. I flew back to the US with Mario Andretti, who was on his way back to Nazareth, Pennsylvania, while I went across to Los Angeles, California, and home. When the season started I was again based out of London, but I wasn't going to stay there until I absolutely had to.

'Shit, I hate to think what you're going to do in the new car,' Mario said – and it stuck in my mind. So Lotus was worried. He knew the FW07B was coming, and while it wasn't new it had some major improvements.

Testing in a place like Argentina for three or four days is a costly exercise – there is nothing cheap about sending a car, a driver, spares and mechanics 10,000 kilometres by air – but it proved valuable. We were able to dial the car into the circuit and do some very profitable work with Goodyear, who provided our tyres, and thus, when January and the race came along, we could just roll the car out of the trailer and assert our superiority over the rest of the field.

Or so the thinking went. We turned up in Argentina to start

the season in the middle of January with a brand new car and it never turned a wheel in anger. The Buenos Aires circuit had quite a long straight after you exit a beautiful right-hander, and the new car was porpoising down the straight, which meant it was just not pointing right. Patrick had moved the centre of gravity of the car back and it didn't work.

Luckily we left the car that I tested down there as a spare, rather than ship it back to England. So after the first practice session I just said, 'Hey, give me last year's car. I'll race that.' That was the best thing we ever did. My new teammate Reutemann was Argentinian, so there was a lot of attention on him that weekend, meaning I could avoid the spotlight and do what I wanted and needed to do.

The drivers were now becoming an even more vocal body – and we were all upset at the state of the track. Some were talking of boycotting the race, but that never entered my mind. I was a race driver; I was there to race, not play politics. I could control my own risk. My job was to race cars; it was Frank's job to deal with that stuff.

Sometimes, though, I got some enjoyment out of the politics, precisely because I simply didn't give a shit. I'd sit in the meetings and not say a word, then I'd throw a hand grenade into the argument and walk away.

Politics and sport don't mix. The Frenchman Jean-Marie Balestre had a few manufacturers from Europe on his side, and he was trying to wrest control of the sport from the Formula One Constructors Association – FOCA – which was largely being driven out of the UK by people like Bernie Ecclestone and my old mate Brian Kreisky.

I didn't know it at the time, but politics and other bullshit was going to leave a bitter taste in my mouth during 1980.

For me, I had one job, to win races. Sitting in meetings talking about bellybuttons was just not me. Fortunately there were enough like me who figured we'd come a long way, the crowd had paid their money and the track was the same for all of us, we just had to use our brains and get on with it.

So race we did. I qualified on pole and led away from the start. The track was breaking up as expected and with all the cars in racing mode they were tearing it up quite a lot. I got some paper in my radiator duct and had to pit to get it removed – the temperature was going off the dial and that wasn't going to end well. We didn't have telemetry or radio back then, so I had to make the decision for myself, and with a lot of pointing the crew knew exactly what was needed when I pitted.

In those days to make a pit stop for anything other than tyres meant you were pretty well rooted. I made a decision. We now had a system where the radiators could be repressed easily if they'd lost any water, and we did that and I got going again back in fourth. I managed to pass Laffite and then Villeneuve spun off because he just couldn't slow himself down for the conditions and I won the race from Nelson Piquet and Keke Rosberg – now there was a podium that told a story of the future.

It was a very rewarding race to win – I had made the decision to make the pit stop to clear the radiator, which I thought had buggered me, and we came back out and dominated. Pole, fastest lap and win . . . I liked the sound of that.

Mansour Ojjeh, who was running his family business, TAG, was sinking money into Williams at the time. TAG was an interesting business – they had an aviation arm, which distributed planes through the Middle East, as well as a few other technology-based businesses, and later they bought Heuer Watches and rebranded them as TAG Heuer. His younger brother Aziz was in Argentina and was staying with us until after the next round in Brazil. I flew into Brazil with him in his BAC One-Eleven and I was not in a good state. I was a little ill from the night before – read hungover – and I was lying down not thinking about anything, *not able to think about anything.* We had a really bumpy landing and I thought we were still at 20,000 feet and I shit myself. I thought I was going to die.

We had two weeks to kill. Charlie Crichton-Stuart and I went to a coffee plantation for a bit of a look and we sat there for three days drinking caipirinhas, the national drink, and going into the local villages.

I think maybe I was too relaxed, or that those days had an impact on me, but I wasn't myself when the race weekend started. I qualified 10th and then was equally as shit in the race, although I did finish third. After the race, the team said I had more fuel in the car than I should have had, so I wasn't using the accelerator enough. I wasn't being aggressive enough. They didn't have telemetry, but the buggers knew, and in their eyes I wasn't trying hard enough. Frank dubbed it the Mobil Economy Run!

I can't remember much about my mindset from that weekend, but I do know I was stung by that feeling. It wasn't going to happen again.

There was more of a shitfight in Brazil from the drivers. Jody Scheckter wanted to boycott the race well before we even got there. The Interlagos track was bumpy and the safety facilities were certainly below par. As it turned out, this was the last time I would ever race there. In terms of layout, it is one of the finest circuits there is, yet it is far from my favourite track. Getting there through city traffic is hell and, once you're there, the organisation leaves something to be desired, which is a polite way of saying it's chaotic.

But that's not all. It is also fiercely punishing physically, as Interlagos is one of the very few circuits around the world that runs counter-clockwise. This makes it very hard on the neck, because we are used to taking the g-forces the other way. There are a lot of fast corners, which puts the strain on the body, and after about fifteen minutes out on the track you become acutely conscious of it. It is the only circuit, for instance, at which I need a masseur; if he wasn't there to attack me for twenty minutes after each session, my neck would stiffen up completely and I'd be useless. The neck muscles, hugely built up to race clockwise, were simply not up to the strain.

South Africa's Kyalami, with its thatched-hut ranch and insufferably slow service, its icy pool in which only the bravest swim, its tennis courts where the Formula One family play, is high on everyone's list of favourite circuits, and it was up next.

I liked going to South Africa. It was a good place to relax – and you could order your meals in English. The circuit is interesting, challenging and fast, and at more than 1500 metres above sea level it was perfect for the turbo-engines. Renault was comfortably on pole – as they were at Interlagos, 800 metres above sea level, a month earlier.

The secret to the track was to get the car going as fast as you could down the long straight. I can remember the days when you had to get your car set up just right to take the approach corner, Leeukop, flat out after clearing The Esses. With the 1980 car that task was a lot easier, but it had plenty of other challenges too. Fast tracks carry danger, as Prost and Marc Surer found out in separate crashes in practice – both broke bones and missed races.

I qualified eighth and got a tremendous start and was actually leading the two Renault turbos down the straight as far as the bridge, and then they passed me. I was third and then Laffite passed me and that is where I stayed for 30 laps until the gearbox bearings gave way and that was that for me.

I was not in the best of moods, disappointed at not finishing. I wanted to get out of the track fast and told Frank as much. But he wanted me to go and shake hands, smile and sign autographs at the Leyland hospitality tent. Reluctantly I agreed; after all it was part of what I was paid to do.

Anyway, I went down to the tent and it was surrounded by barbed wire, cyclone fences and probably machine-gun nests as well. The guy on the gate said, 'You can't come in here.'

So I turned on my heels to go when someone inside noticed me and ushered me in. I wasn't in the frame of mind to be doing hospitality. It wasn't going to end well when a drunk car dealer came up and 'Hey, boy, you blew your car up, eh?' After a few more words and a stumble here and there, I just whacked him a couple of times and he hit the deck. Guards appeared from everywhere, and I left. When I woke the next day I was pretty worried about the fall-out, but when I picked up the paper my worry was over – 'Drunk Attacks Sportsman In Hospitality Tent.' It wasn't quite that way, but it saved us all embarrassment.

Renault's René Arnoux now had two wins in a row and led the championship, but I figured the two high-altitude tracks would be the Renault's best tracks. The next race was at Long Beach, just near my home, a track I really enjoyed. This weekend wasn't going to be one of them.

It remains for me a race marred by the serious accident which paralysed my old friend and teammate Clay Regazzoni. His brakes failed when doing 180 mph. For some reason, too, neither my car nor Carlos's seemed properly set up for Long Beach. Nelson Piquet in his Brabham was the man to watch; he was on pole and a second and a half faster than me. I had qualified fifth, Carlos seventh.

It was a race marked by numerous retirements and crashes. Some ten laps in, I was lying third, with Piquet in front and Depailler behind him. After a prolonged duel, I managed to overtake Patrick, but I seemed unable to do anything to catch up with Nelson, and two-thirds of the way through the race while lapping Bruno Giacomelli, he went into the side of my car and put me out of the race. It was after this race that I began to sense the threat posed to us by Piquet, who now led the championship alongside Arnoux. I also decided to have a few words with the new boy Jack O'Malley, as we used to call Bruno.

Not to worry though, because a month later the European season was about to start with the Belgian Grand Prix. This was my favourite time of the year. It was just more organised, and easier on everybody. There aren't those long flights; you get to the track on a Thursday and you have some chance of getting home by Sunday night; you get a rhythm going in your life and feel you have a base of sorts. I'm one of those people who always feels better if I know where I'm going to be and when.

After South Africa, we did a lot of testing for Goodyear. In fact, during the season, we tested at nearly every circuit, sometimes months before its grand prix. And, as we tested for Goodyear, we were able to sort our car out, too. All of it was a help.

Our testing duties were split though. Carlos did the Zolder test with the team and I went to Paul Ricard. When I got to Zolder for the race, the cars didn't have any front wings, because the Ligier didn't have front wings, and they were pretty good cars. Carlos thought that because they were winged cars, the front wings were offsetting the air going into the actual wing part of the car. He overthought things. He tested without the front wings and he was happy. But of course when he was testing, he was working on new tyres all the time, so when the tyres were worn a little it was a different story.

Zolder is on everyone's list of disliked circuits. Sandy, wet, inhospitable, it is many miles away from civilisation. At the time of the Belgian Grand Prix, the great battle between the warring authorities of FISA and FOCA was out in the open. Everyone's mood was sour, and few will forget the belligerent press conference Balestre held on race day: the sport would bend to his will, he implied, or he would force it to do so.

Though we were all watching the quarrel looming, my mind was only on the race and getting a result after two failures. During qualifying, however, I seemed to be unable to do much better than third or fourth in my race car, and finally, not far from the end, it simply broke down. I raced back to the pits to get into the spare car, only to find that Carlos was out in it. I admit to being pissed off at this, but Frank waited until Carlos had made the best use of his fresh tyres; then he put on another new set for me, put five gallons into the tank and off I went: to pole position! Satisfying, that!

But we had had serious problems with understeering throughout practice and I thought the race wasn't going to be kind to us. Didier Pironi had been just behind us in his Ligier all through qualifying and when it came to the race, he got a superb start and walked away with it. I couldn't get near him, I had to battle ever-increasing understeer to save second spot . . . which I did. As Carlos took third, the result was good for Williams, and I have no complaints about the six points I picked up for myself.

But I was pretty annoyed. Without the front wings, we had no way to control the understeer that appeared as the tyres were wearing out. I thought the front wings were really good for the balance; you can't just change the dynamics of a car that massively. If it was designed with wings, it needed wings and just because others weren't using them didn't mean you shouldn't. It's the bloody purple-pole syndrome. We did run some races later in the year without wings, but we understood it by then and had tested it properly.

Monaco was next, and I did not like it any more than before. It's not just the poseurs and their yachts, though they're bad enough; it's not just the aggro getting to and from the pits; it's the race itself, which is just a bloody procession.

I qualified third, made a good start and got into second place as I went up the hill, missing the shambles taking place behind me. I was surprised how slowly Pironi was going, and how he was holding me up. I was sitting there just waiting for him to make a mistake. Unfortunately for me, before he had a chance to make one, my gearbox blew up and I had to coast into the pits.

It was another disappointment, because I felt certain I could have won that race. Despite my dislike of Monaco, I would dearly have loved to have won there. Every point was going to count in the championship and here we were in three of the last four races watching the race's end from the pits.

I had 19 points up and trailed Nelson by three and René by two. The scoring system, of course, was 9-6-4-3-2-1 points for the first six in each race.

According to the history books, we didn't go to Spain for the next grand prix. We didn't race there because one particular Frenchman decided we wouldn't. We raced and I won – but there were no points on offer. The bitter taste lingers to this day.

There were warning signals flying from every flagpole at Jarama and the battle for the control of the sport was about to get real. Jean-Marie Balestre was not a nice man; he was a megalomaniac with delusions of grandeur, and as far as I was concerned the less I had to do with him, the better.

In one corner we had Balestre and FISA, the body that governed the sport. There were three teams in that camp, all vehicle manufacturers with Formula One teams – Ferrari, Renault and Alfa Romeo. That left 12 out of 15 teams affiliated with the Formula One Constructors Association (FOCA), headed by Bernie Ecclestone, who owned Brabham, in the other corner.

Balestre had announced a compulsory drivers briefing, but the lawyers for our FOCA teams said it wasn't in the rule book and we didn't need to go. So we didn't from Belgium onwards. For that we were all given a $2000 fine, which we refused to pay. On the day before practice was meant to begin, Balestre decided to suspend the racing licences for 15 of us, me included.

There was a bit of argy-bargy going on between all the parties, including the race organisers, who had the paying public and even bigger paying sponsors to appease. On the Friday morning Balestre declared the race would not be sanctioned – but would go ahead.

It was a heated day of practice, that's for sure. First, there were some teams who were going to go out and practise and some who weren't – in the first session only Renault, Ferrari and Alfa Romeo practised. Then when all the FISA officials were escorted from the track, we practised and they sat out – along with Osella, in its first F1 season, which was worried about other repercussions. The ones who refused to race were known as the 'loyalists' and the rest of us were branded as 'rebels'. Sounded like something out of *Star Wars*.

It was a stupid quarrel that came close to wrecking the sport and took more than a year to sort out.

Come race day, Osella had found a way to circumvent possible FISA sanctions and lined up, but the FISA loyalists were there with their cars watching. Not racing. We were there to race, and race we did.

For me, it was a lucky victory. I had three cars in front of me from the start, but all of them either broke down or crashed, and I ultimately won the race. To this day, I still can see no way in which the Spanish Grand Prix was not valid for the championship and, from a driver's point of view, I know that just as much effort, preparation and risk went into that race as any other.

To not get the nine points was a bitter, disheartening blow, confirming my low opinion of politics in the sport and my even lower opinion of Balestre.

As far as I was concerned, I went there on the Thursday, I went there and practised on the Friday, I qualified on the Saturday. I got on to the grid. I did the start. I won the race. I was presented with a trophy by King Carlos, and I went home with the Spanish Grand Prix trophy. But Balestre made it null and void, because of this bloody fight between FOCA and FIA that no-one understood.

And who knows why he chose Spain? They probably didn't have a seat for his wife or something.

Balestre was heavily backing the factory teams and perhaps it was because he knew that those of us with the Ford engines were winning the races and that his beloved Renaults were dropping off the pace. He used to call Lotus, Williams or anybody that didn't have a manufacturer behind them, garagists. They were just little garagists, operating out of a little garage somewhere. Whereas the other boys were big manufacturers. The garagists were essentially FOCA and aligned with Bernie Ecclestone, and to that mad Frenchman we needed to be defeated.

Bernie has got an ego, but is no fool. Balestre had a bigger ego, but he was an absolute fool. Up until this point in my career, he'd just been a bombastic tool opening his mouth at drivers' briefings and proving how little he knew about car racing. Now he was a major embarrassment for the sport and for the life of me I couldn't work out why the Europeans would align themselves with such a man.

Knowing that Renault had backed Balestre over Spain and that the French had combined with the Italians to put the season, and my title, into jeopardy, I went to France in a fighting mood. I not only wanted badly to win that race; I wanted my win to be a personal gesture of defiance. The Ligiers were far superior in qualifying, with Laffite and Pironi (always a dangerous rival) first and third on the grid; I was fourth.

I made a good start, raced against Arnoux and Pironi in the early stages and got past them. I settled down into second place and started to haul in Laffite. Eventually Laffite's front tyres began to go off and I managed to pass him and win. It was one of my most satisfying races ever – there was the emotional pleasure of beating the French on their own ground, but also, I think I drove one of my best ever races.

I had great delight in getting the Union Jack from one of the team as I was pulling up – and there it was flying high above the crowd that swamped me. Then I got to the podium and Balestre was there. I told the organisers I was not going on the podium as long as he was there. Because of the TV coverage they couldn't afford a long argument, so they kicked him off so I could get my trophy. I knew there would be consequences, but I didn't care. I didn't like him and I wanted to make a statement.

There was also a comical scene when they brought a horse up to the winner's podium at the end of the race – which I felt looked a bit like Balestre. There I was with this wreath around my neck and the usual celebrations going on and I thought, 'That's funny, bringing a horse to the podium.' Then they asked me if I would sit on it, and I said, 'Not on your life. I don't want to sit on a bloody horse.' What I didn't know was that I'd won the horse! Well, after my lap of honour, I was having a beer or two in the motorhome, winding down, when this man came back and said, 'Mr Jones, where would you like me to tie your horse up?' I thought the man was joking, so I said, 'Just tie it up to the bumper!'

Ten minutes later, I emerged from the motorhome and there was this horse tied up to the bumper as instructed! Eventually, I had to ship it from Marseilles to Holland, then from Holland to London and then eventually back to Australia; it did a few kilometres, that horse! But I reckon it won the lottery. If Jody Scheckter had won it, it would be pasturing in a Monaco penthouse, and, if a Frog had won it, it would have wound up on a plate! Instead, it made it to Australia as a thoroughbred's companion on the plane.

We all know that what's good for the goose . . . The British Grand Prix was next, and what we'd done to the French at Ricard they could do to us at Brands Hatch. When the two Ligiers qualified first and second, we thought it possible the French would indeed take their revenge.

Luckily for us, the Ligiers turned out to have a problem with their wheels. Pironi started well and was leading handsomely when his tyre started coming off the rim. That left Laffite in the lead, and I think he made a tactical error. He knew his tyre was going down – he could have stopped and changed it, but he opted to soldier on. The inevitable happened: coming into Hawthorn, the tyre came completely off the rim and he went off the track. Caution is part of the driver's stock of skills.

I spent most of the race with Piquet on my tail, and he kept me honest in a very good race. You come out of a corner, look in the mirror, and you think, 'Oh, I've gained a bit,' or 'I've lost a bit.' That's getting back to what I said about there being no replacement for laps under your belt: because when you see the other bloke has lost ground on where he was the lap before, you know that all you've got to do is what you did the lap before. Then you should be right.

After Laffite had dropped out, I kept the lead handsomely and won the grand prix I most wanted to win. England had become a second home for me; at home you like to prove you're a winner. I now had a six-point lead in the championship too over my fellow garagist, the rebel Nelson Piquet.

At this stage of the season things were settling down and we knew who our challengers were . . . not that I was thinking about anything other than just winning the next race. Nelson was going to be my biggest challenger: he was fast and consistent and was banking points. The Ligiers and Renaults were fast, but they weren't finishing consistently and that was hurting them. No-one else was a chance.

But there was always the looming spectre of Jean Mary, as I called Balestre. There was talk about Watkins Glen getting cancelled. Would I need that race? This is why I never did anything other than worry about each race as it came.

Germany and the Hockenheimring was a bit disappointing for me. It was worse for Patrick Depailler – he was killed there while testing in the lead-up to the race when he went off at the Ostkurve after the suspension failed in his Alfa Romeo. It was not long after this that they changed that corner to slow it down, which altered the nature of the track quite a lot. I felt danger was part of why we were there, so I never cried at a death on the track, I just got on with it. I mean, if you start to worry about that you shouldn't be there.

Drivers sometimes joke about death and people might think we are cold bastards. Patrick bought it last week. What does that mean? He bought it. We knew what it means. We seemed callous, but it was our way of dealing with his death. Or, potentially, our own.

Neither Patrick nor any other driver I've known who died haunts me. They are not ghosts. Nor are they forgotten. But when I went to Hockenheim after Patrick's death, I had a good look at the corner where he crashed. I analysed it. I knew I would be coming up against the same corner and I wanted to know where and how he lost it. And I decided if they didn't put some catch-fencing up there, I wasn't racing. The least we can do is learn from what went wrong for another driver.

It's only right that death in racing should be talked about, if only because more deaths could be avoided – by stronger cars, safer circuits, quicker medical attention, better marshalling. The cars do get safer and safer, but death is part of our job and you can't pretend it does not exist.

As a driver, you need to have confidence and even a misplaced sense of belief that it can't happen to you – but it can't be a blind confidence. As for fear – if it gets to that stage, it is time to pack up your gear and head back to the farm.

In 1980 Hockenheim was still a difficult track to get the set-up right; there was plenty of high-speed stuff to master and the tight and twisty stadium section, which was critical because of the passing opportunities. I quite enjoyed the track, and I liked it even more when I got pole position right at the very end of practice. In the race we just couldn't match the straight-line speed and acceleration of the Renaults and I spent 26 laps watching Jabouille run away from me in a straight line only for me to close in under brakes and through the chicanes.

Then his engine blew and the lead was mine. But what the gods give, they also take away, and I suffered a puncture with only ten laps to go. But this was one of many places where the discipline and spirit of the Williams crew showed to advantage: they did a lightning tyre change in the pits, I was able to come back onto the track in third place and I kept that to the end, and the four points that came with it. But the disappointment remained. Victory had been in the bag. Another proof of the old adage that you have not won until you see the chequered flag.

I finished one spot in front of Nelson, which extended my championship lead ever so slightly, and now Williams was well out in front in the constructors' title. People always think Frank would have been happy with that, and I am sure he was, but if we were doing well there we were also doing well in the drivers' championship, and that is from where prize money and start money is allocated.

I had won the two previous Austrian grands prix, so I was quite looking forward to heading back to Osterreichring. The truth is though that while I find the circuit very beautiful, it is also one of the most dangerous, and, while the circuit is very quick, it is also subject to unpredictable weather. So I didn't really like it all that much, despite my success.

As you might expect for a track up in the Styrian mountains, the Renaults were very quick and beat me to the front row, but again I was the best of the non-turbo cars. I made a very good start and led for the first two laps, but the Renault turbos just hauled me in and passed me on the straight as though I were parked. Eventually, Arnoux's tyres went off, but Jabouille still had an excellent lead.

And here I think we made a mistake. The pits didn't really keep me well-enough informed of the progress I was making against Jabouille. I was catching up – not spectacularly, but slowly – and

215

eventually, he beat me to the finish by less than a second. If I'd been told a bit earlier, I might have launched an attack and quite possibly won. As it was, another six points helped consolidate my position – Piquet could do no better than fifth, while the Ligiers were now virtually out of the championship.

The Dutch Grand Prix was a complete disaster for me. I was a bit twitchy because everyone was going round saying, 'Hello champ!' There was only 11 points in it with four races left, and that wasn't a big enough margin to have any confidence.

I was highly annoyed at everyone's presumption. Goodyear wanted me to sit on a pile of tyres with my thumbs up, getting their advertisements ready for the next year. I kept on telling them they were being ridiculous. 'If I don't finish the race and Piquet wins,' I said, 'that's going to make the title very, very tight.' And so it transpired. Perhaps because I was thinking of the possibility, because it was making me nervy. I could see all the Goodyear people tearing up their photos and their copy and replacing me with Nelson Piquet.

In this game, as long as anyone is in with a mathematical chance, nothing is really over. So many things can go wrong. I knew I wasn't champ, but the rest of the world didn't seem to want to recognise that fact. So when people came up and called me champ, I'd glare at them. They weren't thinking; they didn't realise they were putting extra pressure on me. If I didn't become champion, the same people would be saying, 'Oh, old AJ really blew that one, didn't he!'

A driver creates his own pressure. But he is the best judge of what is weighing on him and how to cope with it. That doesn't prevent many drivers from making something out of nothing and making additional pressure for themselves – and I was not immune to that. We come in different types. There are philosophical drivers who take things as they come; there are others who will hit the roof at the drop of a hat. Even the calmest driver will have a day when things upset him that normally wouldn't at all. The strain is in trying to be the same person every time you're on the track.

The sort of person I am on the track, however, is totally different from my other personality. On the farm for instance, any resemblance between myself and a racing driver was pure coincidence. I was relaxed and couldn't care about anything in the world. But when I got up and had to race that day, I was a driver again. I approached my whole day differently. I was a different being and, as I have said, not necessarily a nice one.

As if to prove me right and the rest wrong, I had a thoroughly nasty shunt in practice when my throttle stuck coming into the Hanzerug.

Come the race I was fourth on the grid and made a tremendous start, passing the Renault on the outside going into the first right-hander. At the end of the first lap I was two seconds clear in the lead. But then, coming back to the Hanzerug, I let the car drift a bit too wide and went off. When I came off I hit a rut, the car sank down and damaged the side skirts. These skirts were ceramic devices attached to the side pods of the car to maintain the vacuum. They had little springs that allowed them to move up and down to compensate for body roll. When you break one, you lose a lot of downforce and the car is very unpleasant to drive. They were one of Patrick's innovations. I pitted for some skirts, but my race and my points were gone. And, as I'd feared, Piquet won the race and was now only two points behind me with three races to go.

Imola, which came next, was definitely not one of my favourite circuits and that weekend it was high on my list of places to hate. The Brabham was going very well indeed and I only qualified fifth, but was ahead of Nelson on the grid, although I just couldn't match him for race pace. Gilles had a huge crash in the new turbo-charged Ferrari. Jody had crashed in practice and announced he was retiring, but Gilles, who I always said was never going to die in bed, kept charging on and raced the old 12-cylinder car. He had a tyre failure at Tosa and went head first into the Armco, tearing his car to pieces but somehow walking away. It was a bad season for Ferrari – they did not get one podium finish, after starting the season as favourites.

I had an ordinary start and dropped back to seventh, but Carlos led the field away until his clutch started giving him trouble. As people struck tyre issues and other problems, Nelson eventually walked into the lead and I had to fight my way to second nearly 30 seconds behind him.

So now, for all the 'champ' talk, we headed to North America with two races to round out the season trailing Nelson by one point. Bloody wished I'd studied harder at school sometimes, because now people were throwing maths around about the race to the title. Here is essentially how it was going to work.

We could count our best five finishes from the first seven rounds – should have been eight but for Spain – and that meant I had 28 (instead of the 37 I should have had) there to Nelson on 25, and we both had two retirements so we had no points to drop from the first half. Then we could count our best five finishes from the final seven races. Heading into Canada, I only had one retirement for the second half and Nelson had none, so we were both looking at dropping the points from one or two races to win the title.

So I had my retirement in Holland and the third place at Germany as my worst two races – so potentially I could drop four points. Nelson had a fourth and fifth to drop if he was going OK, so five points in total. Effectively, in my eyes, we were equal and that meant my task was simple – just win the bloody races.

So first of all, finish. Drive on instinct, go for the gaps when they appear and don't second-guess yourself. Don't take unnecessary risks, just do what comes naturally. I was calm and in control and I went to Montreal in a marvellous and serene mood, absolutely full of confidence. I was quickest on the first day, quickest on the second morning, and then – out of the blue, literally – Piquet found an extra second and a half! That surprised everybody, to put it mildly.

In those days, you could run a couple of chassis at a race meeting and swap between them as you needed. Nelson's car for that qualifying session was bent, no doubt. We think it had a trick with the combustion and they had to use a special fuel to stop it detonating. I wasn't too concerned because I knew he'd have to race in a car that was significantly slower.

So we lined up for the race alongside each other, the two title contenders on the front row. I always used to stop on the grid after the formation lap and do a couple of burnouts to leave a bit of rubber on the road, then when I came around to take the start, I'd make sure my rear tyres were on that rubber. I lined it up well and got a pretty good start – if you find the footage you can see I was spot on and Nelson wasn't. He got wheelspin when he changed into second, and I was away.

In Montreal, after the start, you have a series of corners and, if you want to go through those corners flat, as you should, you have to take exactly the right line. The start at Montreal will always be questioned by some people, but here's my version – and it's the truth. I out-dragged Piquet and, as far as I was concerned, I was in the lead and had the right to choose my line. If you get even half a wheel in front of someone else, you have a right to take your own line; it's up to the man behind to look out for you. If I'm behind someone – it could be the slowest driver on the circuit or the fastest – and I try to out-brake him and he cuts me off, that's his right and it's up to me to back off. (If you look at a restart of Montreal, you'll see that Piquet did exactly the same thing to Pironi, only Pironi had the brains to back off. He knew there were another 75 laps to go and that nobody wins a grand prix on the first lap.)

So in Montreal, turn 1, lap 1, I was in the lead and I couldn't see Nelson alongside me, so I took the line I needed to get through those corners as fast as possible. This wasn't a bluff; I could not see him. He didn't back off and we touched, which surprised me. It bounced him around a bit and kicked off a spectacular multi-car shunt. I had my rear engine cover, I think, come off, but apart from that, I was happy to continue. I opened up a lead only to be confronted by a red flag at the end of the lap. Bugger.

I'd never had what was essentially a start-line shunt at that point. If it's a gamble, bugger it, let the other man through: there's always time left to have a go at him. If you're in the last five laps, that's different; then you have to have a big, aggressive go at him. But early on, you have to say to yourself, 'Frank didn't fly the car and all those mechanics all the way to Canada for you to wipe the car out on the first corner.'

Aggression is necessary, but uncontrolled aggression won't help anyone win grands prix. Yet despite the fact that every driver knows this, there are still some drivers who seem prone to accidents. Look at Jean-Pierre Jarier in Interlagos the previous year: he had a five-hour lead and still went off. If all the cars had spun off where he did, that would have been different. But he was the only one that did – and someone else won that race.

If my lead is big enough, or if I have any doubts of any kind, I back off. I'll have put a lot of effort into building that lead, and I know if I need to, I can always build it up again. To win a race by two seconds is as good as winning it by forty. There were many races in 1980 where I backed off and did slow gear changes; I knew that whoever was lying second could get close to me, but the car had enough to rebuild the time I was losing. I concentrated instead on conserving the car, not over-revving it, not wearing out my brakes or tyres.

The smart driver plays each lap as it comes, and the really good ones win races in the slowest times, not the quickest. Unfortunately, I dearly loved having a go. Nothing pleased me more. Psychologically, I didn't like being on pole. Inside me, I think I preferred being on the second row so I could work someone over. It was a justification for driving that little bit harder.

Necessarily, you have occasional run-ins with other drivers. I never actually whacked one, but I had been mightily tempted to do so. I had that set-to with Bruno Giacomelli at Long Beach. He knew he was being lapped and he should have made it easier for me to pass. Bruno knew Piquet was leading the race, because Piquet had just gone past him: he could either screw me or make the whole thing neutral by moving over. I tried to outbrake him, and he just turned into me – which should not have happened since I was lapping him, he should have just let me pass. I had a go at him after that and brought it up at a drivers' meeting later.

Or there was the other side of the boot when I left my braking too late once and had to scream off up the escape road, which happened to be the entrance to the pits, and ruined a lap for Elio De Angelis. Afterwards, I apologised. It was my fault. When I said I was sorry, he questioned my motives. He said, 'Are you sure that's what happened – you just left your braking too late?' That was like a red rag to a bull. If I had the decency to apologise, he ought not to have questioned it.

So now we have to do the start again. For a driver, the sensation at the start is very different. He is concentrating, he is composing his mind. I had a process. I walked to my car and climbed in, knowing that I would not be getting out until my race was over. Once in the car, my effort was to try to relax, so that when the five-minute board is shown, I am completely at ease. The greater the tension, the greater the need for calm. At Montreal, fighting for the World Championship with the only man who could beat me sitting beside me, that was tension.

I used to play a game with myself. When the five-minute sign came up, I would say 'cinque minuti' and start counting down, or just counting, in all sorts of languages. It was a deliberate form of distraction from what is going on around me. I was no longer looking around at what was going on, I was getting my mind into that first corner.

The start of a race is neither joyful nor frightening. It is a commitment. I was there because I chose to be there. I do not sit in my car wondering what I'm doing there or wishing to get out;

nor do I think, 'Gee, this is great, I'm really enjoying this.' I simply go through whatever is necessary to get the best result. And that means going through a drill with myself.

For instance, I tried to leave the car in neutral for as long as I could, because if a driver puts it into first too soon and keeps blipping his accelerator, the clutch will burn out. By going through a drill, I am actually starting the race before the light turns green.

Mentally, I am thinking all the time, 'What might give me an advantage?' At the re-start of the race in Montreal in 1980, all I was focused on was getting my car to sit exactly on the tyre marks I'd left from my practice and my first starts. Piquet drove up and put his wheels between his tracks and I got the better start . . . again.

As the outsider might gather, the start puts a terrible strain on both car and driver, and it's my job to keep that strain to the minimum. I leave the car in neutral until the red light comes on; at that point I still have ten seconds to get into first gear. If you don't get excited or flustered, that's plenty of time. The five minutes of waiting for that first positive act – getting into gear – feels like a month. Like everyone else, I tend to think I've left getting into first too late. The truth is, it's a fine line between over-revving, which will wreck your clutch, and under-revving and stalling. By the time you've thought through all the variables, there's little time to have butterflies.

I used to spend that long five minutes, for instance, taking careful note of where the other cars were and guessing what each driver was likely to do. My aim was to outguess them. I think, behind me is so-and-so, he's going to try to scream up between myself and the wall; so I move the car fractionally closer to the wall to close up the gap.

I didn't check the drivers in front of me before the start. I simply concentrated on the lights. It's like keeping your eye on the golf ball: you're not supposed to be looking where you're aiming, but at what you're hitting. Of course, as soon as you line up your car, you take note of where you'd like to go. In every start, there's an ideal position to be in. And, as soon as the lights change, my eyes come right off them and I go as fast as I can into the position I have decided to take up. If I feel I've done a good start, but I'm aware that someone behind me has done an even better one, well that's his bad luck: I put my car where it's going to make him wait, because that is my right.

But a start is forever fluid – there are many factors outside of your control that change what you had planned. You need to be able to think quickly, rely on reflexes and make judgements on the value of a risk or an opportunity. You will not win a race on the start or the first lap, but you sure can lose one.

Knowing what you can and can't do is instinct. A good start simply means one in which you've got into the position you chose. If you are heading for a gap between the two cars ahead of you, you must actually be there already, so that they can see you out of the corners of their eyes and can no longer shut you off. The tyres are wide, the cars are quick: to pass someone or sneak through a gap is not a matter of speed, but of spoiling your opponent's manoeuvre. You have to position your car in such a way that he is the one who has to yield. When he backs off, you automatically get that little extra bit of speed that enables you to overtake him. You've taken away his line and established yours.

From the outside, a start may look like an almighty scramble. From the inside – at least in my day, when we were lined up two abreast – it was not so different from being on a motorway. The track is about three lanes wide and nothing obstructs your vision. What is more difficult is making the instant decisions that someone else's move may force on you. I've gone for lots of gaps that have closed up, and I've also been blocked and seen a gap open up before me. Suddenly there's this great big space in front of you and you can drive right through it! Afterwards, people say what a great start you made, but in fact it was just easy.

A driver has just enough peripheral vision to make this sort of decision. I worked on the theory that if I can't actually see them alongside me, then they were not there. If they were a quarter way into me, they didn't exist; if they're alongside me and I could see them, they were there. Even at the speeds we were going and with all the confusion of a start, you can always sense another car alongside your cockpit.

Just their presence, however, doesn't mean that I was going to give way. I could still try a bit of bluff and pretend I'm going to take my own line regardless. It quite often worked. The bloke thinks, 'Christ! He hasn't seen me,' and it's he who backs off. But the good drivers stick to their guns and if you see another car alongside you, you are the one who is going to come off second best if you touch.

After the shunt, Nelson along with a few others ran back to the pits to jump into their spare cars, which were now being warmed up as the debris was being cleared. The only problem for Nelson was that he now had to race his qualifying car and that was going to be interesting. In the race, they couldn't get away with using the 'special' fuel, but we didn't know if they'd changed the engine or not.

On the second start it was the same again, only this time there was no contact between Nelson and me, but he almost hit Didier Pironi in the same corner. I led the opening two laps from Didier and Nelson . . . but then that qualifying car came into its own. The next lap he was second, and then he was first, he passed me like he was driving a turbo-car . . . they hadn't changed the engine!

On the twenty-third lap, his engine blew. Then I knew for sure that, as long as I conserved the car, the championship was mine if I won, which I was pretty sure I could do when they put up a board telling me Pironi had been penalised for jumping the start. Me winning and Nelson not taking a point was the only scenario where the title would be settled in that race.

This was the only time in my Formula One career I can remember going into a fully conservative mode. I didn't need to race Didier, so when he challenged I let him through and all I had to do was keep Carlos behind me and finish within 60 seconds of Didier, which I did.

I was pretty sure Carlos wouldn't pass me, but as I learnt next season that was the kind of assumption I shouldn't make, but I did make sure I kept him far enough behind so as not to be any sort of threat.

Didier did finish first, but with his penalty he dropped back to third and I won both the race and, as the calculator told me, the championship.

I hadn't gone into the weekend thinking about anything other than winning the race; if I did that the other stuff could sort itself out and I didn't have to worry about calculators. When I saw Nelson as a steaming mess beside the road with his fragile qualifying car and I was told about Didier's penalty, I knew what I had to do. Just keep it on the island.

As a racer, it is not easy to drop back from 100 per cent and conserve. I wasn't an endurance racer and I didn't race compromised touring cars; I was in the most highly tuned racing car in the world. And when I was in it, we were at our best when we were going for it, not playing lap times. It wasn't easy.

I'd never been in that situation before. I'd never had to play the numbers to win a World Championship. It was a bit pointless saying, 'I'm a racer. I'm getting on with it.' I didn't need to win by a minute. I just needed to win.

In the modern era, they just push a few buttons and the car looks after it all. The engine's computer changes everything to conserve the engine and the gear changes are all made in safety mode. In 1980, that computer was my brain. When you've been taking the same lines, braking at the same spot, accelerating at the same spot for many laps in both practice and the race, and then you consciously ease off a little bit, you've got to be careful. You've got to get into a new groove, a new mark, a new reference point. I didn't back off all that much. I still kept doing reasonable lap times. I might have short-shifted a little and pulled the brake marker back in my head a metre or two. I just had to make sure everything was OK.

When I saw the chequered flag I was quite emotional. I would dearly have loved for my father to be there to experience that with me. Mum was living in Melbourne, but it wasn't the same without Dad. This was the culmination of something I had been working on since I was 13. I started crying in my helmet on the cool-down lap. I remember thinking, 'Jesus, pull yourself together. You cannot go back with tears.'

The feeling was and still is indescribable. There is an emotional release that only comes when the chequered flag waves. You know a few laps from home that you've got it. But you also know that motorsport is a cruel mistress and she can take it all away very quickly. The chequered flag mostly means that mistress is under control, and with no intervention from Balestre this weekend, no-one was taking this away.

Back in the pits the team was into it already. Remember, this team was really only three years old and we had conquered the world.

That weekend I did what now seems a silly thing. I had raced in Simpson overalls all year as I had pretty much done for a while – remember I shared a driveway with Bill Simpson. On the Saturday Yves Morizot, who ran Stand 21, which makes equipment for drivers, had brought over two pairs of green overalls, all badged up for me. Because they were green to match the car, I tried them on and used them in a session and I was quickest on the Saturday. I thought, 'Geez, these overalls are quick,' and I decided to race with them.

It was absolute stupidity, not thinking that poor Bill had supplied me with overalls for a long time, and then, I won the World Championship in someone else's gear. Here I am on the podium with photographs all over the world wearing Stand 21 overalls. You can imagine how that went over with Bill. No more free Simpson overalls.

I went back to the hotel, and I remember dancing in the shower and singing the Queen song *We Are the Champions* but with a little tweak to the lyrics: '*I* am the champion. *I* am the champion . . .' Then we all met down in the ballroom which Mansour had organised. His family owned most of Canadair that made the Challenger private jet, so this was a big weekend for him even without the championship win.

In that space of time, he had the walls covered in photographs, framed with non-reflective glass. How many people it would have taken and how much money it would have cost to do that in the space of a couple of hours, I don't know. But it was very impressive. The next morning I woke up with a very sore head and Mansour offered us one of his jets, 'Take the jet. Go wherever you want.' Charlie and I looked at it and then tried to work out where to go.

At that stage, I was seeing Dominique, a Penthouse pet of the year, who came to most races, but she was married to a New York copper, so I had to be a little bit careful. Beverley was back in our London home with Christian, but I wasn't going there with Miss Penthouse.

First step was to drop Dominique home, so New York. We had cucumber sandwiches and some champagne on the plane and flew to New York. I think we must have taxied to the wrong spot after we landed. This big New York copper came up and started abusing people in the plane.

It was a shemozzle on the plane, but Miss Penthouse got off and then Charlie and I looked at each other and said, 'Where do we go now?' In hindsight, we should have just gone down to Miami for a couple of days or something. Anyway, we couldn't make up our minds, so we flew to Elmira, where the next race was going to be at Watkins Glen. It's a nice part of the world and our motel overlooked one of the big lakes up there and we had a game of golf or two, but what a complete waste of a jet. It was just sitting in Elmira Airport while we stayed at the Ptomaine Palace, as we used to call it because you could get ptomaine poisoning.

I was determined to finish off the season as I had started it, absolutely competitively: if for no other reason than to prove that champions do still try! During the first days of practice, however, my engine was down on power and the best I could qualify was fifth. Frank and I had a discussion about it and when I told him I thought it was down on power, he just changed it. Come race day it was like night and day. I was quickest in the warm-up and thus pretty confident for the race.

I like the Glen. It wasn't the best place to get in and out of, but we solved that by getting a helicopter from the tennis court at the Palace up the circuit – no crowds and no traffic. It's a true driver's circuit and, when the old green light came on, I did a fantastic start, jumping into second place behind Giacomelli at the first corner. That bloody Alfa had so much power, it was his first pole and the first time he had led a grand prix, so this was going to be interesting.

The Americans have got this bad habit of spreading cement if anyone's had an oil leak. Someone in one of the support races obviously had a major oil leak down into turn 1, and there was about nine tonnes of cement everywhere. I was the first to slip off the track on it, but a few others followed me off too.

I thought I'd thrown it away, that I had damaged the skirts and my dreams of finishing the season with a win were gone. But when I got back onto the circuit and tried the car out on a couple of corners I found it was functioning all right. From there it became the most enjoyable race of the year for me. I came back on in 14th or thereabouts and, except for Giacomelli, who broke down, and Nelson, who cracked under pressure from Carlos and spun into the catch fencing, I literally passed one car after another to win the race.

I passed Carlos around the outside at the end of the main straight into this big, right-hand sweeper. He backed off a bit and I swung around the outside to take second. A lap or two later Bruno stopped and I had the lead and Carlos came home second for another Williams one-two.

It was a great finish to a great season for the team, and especially for me.

Mansour was back to help me celebrate and he lined up the jet to fly us to Kennedy Airport the next day for a Concorde trip home. Charlie was enjoying it, 'Champ, this is a bit of us.' He could call me Champ now. When we landed at Kennedy we actually taxied up beside the Concorde, jumped out of the private jet and straight onto it. 'Who are these people?'

I flew home and they had the big banner outside the house, which was made by my helmet designer John Lyall. I wasn't feeling too well at this stage but I had to pretend that I was OK and had to have a few beers again and just relax and soak it all in.

It was unreal, surreal even, and things just changed. There's no use pretending they didn't.

That's when I got the Citron because apparently to the French, I didn't make myself as available as I did the year before. There was a good reason for that: I simply couldn't. Obviously to most of those journos I would love to have just said I don't want to talk to you because you are dicks, but I couldn't and didn't. I made myself as available as I could given the increasing sponsor commitments and the like . . . and I still had to have the headspace to race well and win races. Talking to idiots was never going to help that.

While things changed for me, I don't think I changed. I was still going to be the same nasty race track prick as before, I was still the same bloke at home.

It is just that the world around me changed.

Nelson Piquet

Nelson and I really never saw eye-to-eye. I think he was rude, and I think he was unnecessarily undiplomatic. Calling Nigel Mansell's wife ugly publicly, I think, was unnecessary and unchivalrous. It's not like Nelson was that good looking, even if he thinks he was.

We didn't get on. I didn't like him. And to make things worse, he was my biggest rival in 1980. Invariably we'd always end up on the front row of the grid or within one or two cars of one another.

I think he showed his colours a bit when he jumped out of the car and tried to kick Eliseo Salazar in the balls at the chicane at Hockenheim. The fight continued when a van driver came to collect the pair, but it was Nelson who eventually drove off in the van to the pits, leaving the van driver and Salazar beside the track.

He didn't mind coming into our pits for a fight either.

Nelson and I raced hard, and when it didn't go his way and there was contact he always had something to say about me or whoever was driving the other car. But he didn't make mistakes himself apparently. Like at Montreal in 1980. I didn't care what he thought then and I don't care what he thinks today. I had the racing line, and it was his job to pass me safely. That crash was his fault and he has to live with it.

There was another one at Zolder, I screamed down the inside of him because the door was open. We rubbed wheels and he went off. He came back and walked through the pits and he said to Frank, 'I am going to break his arm.'

Frank just turned around and said, 'Well, I'm thinking you'll have one chance at him, mate. Make sure you're good at it.' That fucked him. He went, 'Um-um-um,' and just walked off.

The very next meeting was Monaco. He was leading and I was running second, and I could see him looking in the rear-view mirrors all the time. He had eyes like saucepans, and then he ran into the barrier. I thought, well, there's karma for you. That made me very happy.

I played mind games with him all the time, because I thought he was mentally weak. I once tried to check the ballast he was supposed to add to his car, and made sure he knew what I was doing. He went nuts.

He was quick, but his best skill was getting himself into the best cars. He was in the right place at the right time and he got three world championships. I thought he was a tool as a person, but he was a bloody good driver.

16

Australian Grand Prix

NOT LONG AFTER winning the World Championship I came home for the Australian Grand Prix at Calder Park.

As the season was progressing, my old boss Bob Jane was on the phone to get me to bring the Williams down for the Australian Grand Prix, which he was hosting at Calder Park, which he owned. My winning the championship had generated plenty of interest in Formula One in Australia and Bob was working on a plan to get Calder Park onto the World Championship schedule.

One would hope he had plans to change the track. Australia is a funny place with car racing: there is all the land in the world and then they – or we – build these dinky little tracks that are just not fun to drive. Calder Park was one of those. It was very Mickey Mouse and not complex – it claims to have 11 corners, but there are only three with three chicanes.

Just before I left London to come home, Bob said the media wanted a press conference and we could do it at his place if I wanted. So we did, and it was well branded for the Bob Jane Corporation. During the conference, he stood up and said, 'I've got a really successful Bob Jane T-Mart in my outlet, I'll give it to you for a dollar.' Then he proceeded to put a great big picture of myself with the laurel wreath around my neck on the wall at the centre in Melbourne, at that big busy roundabout at the top of Elizabeth Street, at the CBD's north-west edge.

So I got that for a buck, and let me tell you he got much more of a return out of it than I did. He ran his businesses as franchises, and now that Alan Jones had become a franchisee, Bob Jane had a great promotional tool, which he rolled out at every opportunity. I didn't see a penny out of 'my' Bob Jane T-Mart though, then he sold it, and I got even less. I felt completely screwed.

Anyway, the idea of racing in and even winning the Australian Grand Prix held a bit of romance for me, and if you've been paying attention you'll know there's not much that does. This was my home race, my father had won it and no other father-son combination had ever won the Australian Grand Prix. If I could win, it would mean a great deal to me.

I would imagine Bob had to pay a significant fee to Frank to get the championship-winning car. We brought that down with Wayne Eckersley and my other mechanic John Jackson – Skinny John – who used to put up with Wayne, which was amazing.

The only other Formula One car Bob could get was an Alfa for Giacomelli, but he had a brand new ground-effects Elfin F5000 car lined up for Didier Pironi. As it turned out the brand new car wasn't ready and he had to drive an older car alongside his team-mate, John Bowe.

The weekend was big. Channel Nine was covering it with Jackie Stewart leading the commentary team with Ken Sparkes, who I would eventually get to know really well when I started with Nine. He was a really nice bloke.

I got on pole a fraction ahead of Bruno, which is probably all you would ever get with a 36-second lap, and we were nearly two seconds clear of Alfie Costanzo, who was the fastest of the Formula 5000 cars. There were 15 Formula 5000 cars in the field, the slowest of which was six seconds behind me, and then a couple of Formula Pacific cars with little 1.6 litre engines that were 6.5 and 7.4 seconds off the qualifying pace. With a 95-lap race scheduled, there was going to be a lot of lapping cars. I donated my pole position money to a local charity, which I did because it felt right not because of the publicity it could get, but it went down well.

The temperature on race day climbed above 40 degrees Celsius – that's bloody hot anywhere, let alone in the cockpit – but the crowd was huge. I don't reckon they could have fitted another person in the place.

Off the start Bruno and I had a good battle, then going down the back straight we rubbed wheels and fell off the track together. He got back on before me and led the race, but I wasn't going to let that little Italian win the Australian Grand Prix in front of me. He didn't hold the lead for long and once I cleared him I sprinted away. No-one was going to beat me that day. Eventually I even lapped him too, so I won the race by more than a lap and had my own little way to honour my father.

It was also a final stamp on my championship year too.

We had a big party up at the farm to round out the year and get ready for a bit of downtime before the title defence. For years I enjoyed anonymity in Australia; this was no longer the case. There was a lot more attention now on Formula One, and while Bob's push for a World Championship was unsuccessful, there was a really good bid coming from Adelaide, about 700 kilometres west of Melbourne, that would succeed in getting a race for the 1985 season.

I had a few corporate things to do while in Melbourne, and I had to start managing my commercial interests and sponsors in general. I was part of the Marlboro World Championship team and that paid well, as did Akai, even if I didn't understand the slogan . . . 'Akai's Okay, OK!'

There was AGV helmets, the good old Italians. I was wearing a Bell helmet with an AGV sticker on it because I preferred the Bell, who then got dirty with me because they didn't want an AGV sticker on one of their helmets. They could have paid, so bugger them. But AGV was bloody hopeless, they took forever to pay. One time they said, 'The exchange rate's not right.' I said, 'For you or for me?'

Just pay me what you owe me. As I've said, I don't want any more and I don't want any less than what we agreed to. I just want the deal. The deal is the deal. If you weren't happy with it then don't do the deal in the first place.

Even with their slow payments, I wasn't short of dough though, that's for sure.

Opportunities were popping up everywhere. The old Aussie wasn't bad at coming out of the woodwork when you're a winner;

it was just the opposite when I was trying to climb the ranks. I had all these would-be entrepreneurs wanting me to go into business with them or endorse things.

I reckon sixty per cent of them were probably shonky. When you're in a semi-protected commercial environment, living in England, then you get home to all these people giving you these weird and wonderful ideas and solutions, you think, 'Oh, maybe I should have a go at that,' or 'Maybe this looks interesting,' such as Bob Jane with the T-Mart.

Getting a T-Mart for a dollar, I thought, 'That can't be bad.' The old adage, nothing for nothing. I've learned the hard way. I'm still learning.

At least I was OK when negotiating with Frank. I had signed a two-year deal with Williams covering 1980 and '81 and Frank thought that I already agreed a drive for 1981 for £600,000, but I didn't think I had. It became a psychological thing, I wanted to earn more than any other Formula One driver because of the competitiveness of it all, and I felt like I was the best.

There were plenty of people sniffing around, and while I didn't want to go anywhere else, I would have. Renault and Alfa were keen, but joining the loyalists would have been interesting. Renault even sent a lawyer to Montreal to do a deal with me. I made sure Frank knew about that. I knew I could make more than US$1.2 million at other teams, and that is what Jody Scheckter was getting, so I told Frank that was my price.

He said it was nearly the same on exchange rates anyway, but I dug in. Eventually we signed just after Montreal, Frank begrudgingly and me happily. I got what I wanted. Keeping the number 1 for his car was a good carrot too, because that went with the driver. Imagine a Renault with the number 1 – great marketing.

After I won at Watkins Glen, I went up to Frank and said, 'Well, there you go. The money hasn't slowed me down.' He just said, 'Piss off.'

So by the time I made it to Australia everything was sorted, and let me tell you now, that 1.2 mil is probably the same as 18 or 20 now. It was a lot of money. Unfortunately for me, plenty of people knew that too.

17

My First Final Year

THANKFULLY IN 1981 they moved the start of the season to March instead of January, which gave us a really long break after Watkins Glen in October the previous year. They did try to start the season in South Africa in February, but that bloody FISA-FOCA thing jumped up and killed the race as a part of the Championship.

There were big changes happening to the cars. The sliding skirts on the side of the cars that hugged the ground had been banned for the 1981 season in their old form and that meant the cars were going to be horrible to drive. In South Africa, we raced with them for the last time.

At least this time we went to the race knowing it was not going to count for the title, rather than having it stripped during the weekend like in Spain. The FOCA teams supported the race, which was won by my teammate Carlos, and ironically I was sidelined with a skirt problem after qualifying third behind Nelson and Carlos.

Without the teams from Renault, Ferrari and Alfa Romeo it was hard to tell where we all stood, and with the side skirts still in place there was still the possibility for some false readings, but it looked like Williams and Brabham had the cars to beat in 1981.

I returned to the fold for that race with my typical off-season weight gain. I'd try to get myself back to Europe three weeks or so before the first race so I could focus on stripping that weight off, as well as just getting back into the routine.

Patrick Head would always get stuck into me. 'You bastard, I've just spent hundreds of thousands of dollars trying to shave off a couple of pounds, and you've put on about four.' For the first couple of times you'd hop in the seat, which was custom-made and without adjustable belts, and there'd be grunts from both me and the mechanics as they tried to strap me in. After a little while of getting back to the not drinking, not eating so much, and exercising, it didn't take long to get back to my old fighting weight.

Paul Ricard was my first serious test without the skirts. And that was an eye-opener. Carlos had already tested a week before, but then we turned up with different tyres, which meant we really couldn't do a back-to-back test, which I thought was a bit silly.

The BBC came down and made a documentary called *Gentlemen Lift Your Skirts* (which makes good viewing on YouTube). We tried a few things on the car, but it was clear we would have to try something quite different that day. And so it was: Patrick took the springs out and he wanted to see what I thought. The theory was that we needed to maintain and control the gap between the side of the pods and the ground, and also that a constant angle of attack under acceleration and brakes would be good. Without springs we could do that.

Patrick was always into this concept – and the concept was proved when he had traction control, ABS and active suspension, which let him create his perfect world in a car that was driveable. That was when Nigel Mansell was dominating, and that is the car that Ayrton Senna thought he was getting when he went to Williams. But like this change to the skirts, they changed the rules without enough planning and altered the cars dramatically and quickly. But we weren't so badly off.

I wasn't against change; so long as we all had the same thing I didn't care, and the cornering speeds were pretty high. Although I was worried about ill-thought-out knee-jerk reactions born out of stupidity.

This was a case of one or two unqualified people in Paris jumping the gate and just banning skirts before they knew enough about what they were doing. After my first few laps in the car without skirts, I felt the car was a lot less safe than it was with them. It was slower, but if it was more dangerous had we taken a step forward? If the change was made to try and help the loyalists, then this was going to be interesting – they may have had better engine builders, but we in the garages had better aerodynamicists, so I felt we'd get our heads around this quicker than them.

And that led us to try no springs. I went around and the car was so rough and vibrating so much I couldn't see properly; the gearbox was bumping on the ground and the tyres were carrying all the suspension work. It was awful.

We were having a chat while I was still in the car and I was telling Frank and my mechanic how I couldn't see because of the vibrations, and I suggested maybe putting some suspension in the seat and then we'd know if there was some potential, which I felt there was. Frank said, 'That's actually a sensible suggestion,' and he paused before adding, 'You could sit on your wallet, Alan.'

I said, 'Why don't you give me something to put in it?' This was all on TV and that shut him up.

We ended up using springs: there is no point having a fast car that is undriveable. I felt we left that test with a good solution. There were other cars there that day and we were quicker, so I thought the FW07C was definitely OK.

At the end of the day, it wouldn't matter if the cars had ball bearings, as long as everybody else had ball bearings, because from there I'd back myself and I trusted Patrick to give me the right equipment. The only thing that a driver doesn't like is when someone's got something you haven't got. Mario Andretti had the drop on everybody with the first ground-effects cars in 1978. Now, had that been today, with social media everyone would be saying they were killing Formula One, like the talk about Mercedes recently.

Colin Chapman came out with an idea – ground effects that increased downforce – that blitzed everybody. Mercedes mastered hybrid power better than any other team and they blew everybody away too. Getting a jump on your competitors is the goal – that's always going to happen in Formula One. People say, 'Don't you think it's spoiling Formula One?' Did Michael Schumacher spoil Formula One when he was winning everything in a Ferrari? It happens, and it never lasts forever.

That's what it's all about. It's meant to be the top echelon of motorsport, and that means innovative solutions and ground-breaking ideas. No question about it though, if someone comes up with a new idea, the rest will catch them; it is just a matter of how long.

Our solution for 1981 left us with a really stiff car, they were really uncomfortable to drive . . . although less so when you were winning. There were all these little tricks for that season. One was having the car hydraulically lowered and lifted during the sessions and races, which Brabham pioneered early in the season. To see how well it worked just have a look at the Argentine Grand Prix – Piquet won easily and that was the first time the system was raced.

The cars needed to maintain a six-centimetre minimum ride height, but we could see the Brabhams lower at speeds. As a driver, I could see it. Despite a lot of talk, they were allowed to get away with it, so we all followed. But you had to be careful, because at the end of the session you had to have the minimum ride height when you were measured. We had a bloke stationed somewhere around the track with binoculars to check the ride height before we came in. If it wasn't right we'd have to spin the car into the gravel or Armco fencing to avoid the scrutineering.

Eventually we were all doing it. It was legal – much more so than Piquet's fragile qualifying engine the season before – but it was very borderline.

FOCA and FISA found some sort of common ground and signed what was known as the Concorde Agreement, which gave us four years of rule stability under FISA guidance, while FOCA retained control of the finances of the sport. The beauty of that deal was that it ushered in a period of unprecedented growth for the sport. If it was big before, it was now about to become massive – the biggest sporting show in the world bar none.

With all the testing done and my weight stripped off, the season started in Long Beach in the best way possible. We all turned up with newish cars with bigger wings and visible changes to the sidepods. We also had to adjust to Michelin tyres. Goodyear pulled out of the sport with immediate effect early in 1981 and we had to suddenly change to the new tyres.

We may have had the Concorde Agreement in place, but it didn't stop the politics. Colin Chapman at Lotus must have been listening in to my conversation with Frank at Paul Ricard – he turned up with a twin-chassis car. The car itself was incredibly stiffly sprung, but there was a separate chassis for the driver, in effect an internal suspension for the driver. It was clever, too clever for some, who protested. No-one really knew what rule it was breaking, but it was banned.

I had a great qualifying session with Riccardo Patrese in an Arrows which had clearly found something over the winter. We traded the top of the time sheet a number of times during quali-fying, and eventually he ended up with the pole and I was second, less than one hundredth of a second behind him. It was the sort of intense battle I loved, and I grazed the wall at one stage when the back stepped out coming out of the last corner, and Patrick got stuck into me over that, but I was giving it everything I had and that sort of thing happens on a street track.

At the start of the race, Gilles did a typical Gilles thing and made a wild dive for the lead from nowhere. He went off and we had to avoid him, and in that mess Carlos passed me for second and we stayed that way for the first half of the race, miles in front of everyone else. Didier Pironi was now driving for Ferrari and he was fourth, dropping away from me and holding everyone up. Perfect.

Patrese eventually retired and that left us with a Williams one-two, and with that I started to charge at Carlos. I had looked after my car in the early part and I had plenty up my sleeve, half a second a lap in fact. The three-second gap was soon nothing, and Carlos ran wide while trying to pass Marc Surer and I jumped through into the lead and sprinted away for a nine-second win, even after I eased off.

Brazil in the rain for the next race was a little more interesting, but not necessarily for the racing. Frank had drafted a new agreement for Carlos for the season, which had all these clauses in it and what I thought was a pretty improbable scenario; if we were more than twenty seconds in front of whoever was third, and we were less than three or four seconds apart, I was to win. It wasn't just that I was the old boy at the school – which I was – but he didn't want to transport two cars to the other side of the world, have them comfortably winning a grand prix, and have them take each other off while they fought for the lead.

So in other words, if the race was dead in terms of anyone challenging us, I was to win. Frank drew up the agreement and Carlos, with his eyes wide open, signed it. If he didn't like it, he should have said something. I am a firm believer in living by the agreements you make, whatever they are and whether or not they become less palatable over time. Carlos, as it turned out, did not see things that way.

We were back at Jacarepaguá, since it was felt Interlagos was unsafe and that the slums of Sao Paulo that surrounded it were not in keeping with the image that was required of the sport. So Rio it was, on a much less interesting track. It was pissing with rain on race day and I started third behind Nelson and Carlos.

We quickly cleared Nelson and I spent most of the race right on Carlos' backside.

We were nearly a minute in front of Patrese with a handful of laps to go when the team hung out a board, 'Jones-Reut'. I'd also won the first grand prix, so by letting me win, that would have consolidated my championship lead. Then there was the matter of what our contracts said. We did another lap, we did another lap, we did another lap, and I thought, 'I know what he's going to do. He's going to wait until the last corner, make the big magnanimous buddy hand, like, OK you go through, and then tell all the journalists that he could have won, but team orders dictated that I win.'

Anyway, on the last lap it became clear he wasn't going to honour the terms of his agreement. I thought, 'This prick's not going to do it.' Sure enough, he didn't. He kept going. I was furious, I could have challenged him many times. If it wasn't for the agreement I would have. I was faster and felt I could easily have won, and Frank knows too well that without the agreement I would have slipped it down the inside, or I would have had a go somewhere. That could have ended in tears, so I didn't have a go, because it was wet, which makes it a lot easier to lock your wheels up. And we had the agreement.

I thought, 'No, I know what the team orders are, I know he signed the deal, so I'll just consolidate another nine points.' That would have given me 18 in the championship for the first two races. He would have had second in both, that would have given him 12. Everything's hunky-dory.

The agreement was there to stop us taking risks with each other. Carlos didn't abide by the rules of the agreement that he signed. That's the thing that upset me.

Now, purely circumstantial, it was still pissing with rain, and I pulled up in the designated zone and climbed out of the car and no-one was there, in true Brazilian fashion. There was no-one in sight. I thought, 'Screw this, I'm not hanging around in the rain, I'm going back to the garage.' Now, of course, that was interpreted as me having the screaming shits. It wasn't, it was because I didn't want to stand around in the rain with no bugger there.

I didn't talk to Carlos after the race. I just said to Frank, 'All bets are off.' Frank only paid him for finishing second that day as a sort of fine, but if Carlos expected me to give him any help in the Championship, that just went out the window. I'm a bad loser anyway. Carlos was good enough to drive elsewhere, it was not like Williams was his only option.

Of course, even to this day the whole aftermath of the race is reported as a dummy spit by me and that gave the next race, Carlos' home grand prix in Argentina, a great build-up. Although it wasn't good for me.

I needed armed guards for the most of the weekend and I had a police escort from the airport to the hotel. Taxi-drivers were pulling up and giving me the finger. The first time I practised the marshals were into me as well. I thought, 'This would be bloody nice, if I have a shunt or something, they'll just let me burn.'

The front row of the grid was dominated by Nelson with his new 'illegal' suspension and Alain Prost, who was now at Renault, then it was the two of us with me in third and Carlos fourth. Good luck, I thought. He was off my Christmas card list. In my eyes we just weren't teammates. It was every man for himself. Hopefully we'd make it past the first corner.

Brabham had come up with a clever solution to the side-skirt problem and dominated the race – so good even Hector Rebaque was able to run second until his car broke. There was nothing we could do about them. I had an uninspiring race and finished fourth and Carlos got onto the podium to take the Championship lead.

For some reason I was a little down on my qualifying speed at Imola for the next race, which was now called the San Marino Grand Prix. San Marino is a little principality maybe 100 kilometres from the Imola track, entirely encased by Italy. The rules were that only countries could host a grand prix, and countries could host only one, except the USA, which was a market Formula One was keen to crack. The Italian Grand Prix was back at Monza, so San Marino was the answer for Imola, which wanted to keep hosting its grand prix. So the San Marino Grand Prix was not run in San Marino.

Starting the race eighth in the rain, I was quickly into it. By the end of the first lap I was challenging Carlos for third, while the two Ferraris used their turbo power to sprint away. Carlos didn't like me challenging him and we hit – one of the race reports at the time said he had 'driven into' me, so you can read into that what you like. My front wing was damaged and I had to pit.

I finished two laps down and out of the points while the two people I thought were my biggest challengers for the title were on the podium and pulling away in the points. Carlos led on 25 points from Nelson on 22 and me on 18. It should have been both of them on 22 and me on 21, and who knows what else if Carlos hadn't hit me.

Zolder was up next and it was a bit of a shitfight, and it needed to be. The pit lane there is narrow and there were so many people allowed in the pits you could sometimes not even find your own pit when you came in. There were no speed limits in pit lane then, and it was dangerous. During practice, one of the mechanics from Osella stumbled on the pit wall and fell in front of Carlos, who hit him. The mechanic died in hospital and we drivers decided we needed to take a stand, so we organised a protest on the grid, which really just created confusion.

The start was all over the place. I was starting sixth and Carlos was on pole, Nelson was late making the grid and while he was taking his place Riccardo Patrese's Arrows stopped. A Formula One car is great at many things; sitting stationary with the engine running is not one of those things. As he was waving his arms to stop the start sequences, one of his mechanics jumped the fence to start his car. The race started while the mechanic was still on the track behind Riccardo and right in front of me. I couldn't believe what was happening. I managed to clear both the mechanic and the car, but as ever with a start you jump at gaps you see appearing. Siegfried Stohr in the second Arrows saw a gap and went for it only to plough straight into the back of the stranded car, cleaning up the mechanic at the same time.

When the field came around for the end of the first lap we could see the carnage, then on the second lap they were still clearing it up. Nelson in the lead didn't slow one little bit, and then the rest of us decided to stop. This was bloody dangerous, so we in effect did our own red flag while Nelson kept racing until he came around the next time to find us all stopped. The mechanic, Dave Luckett, survived with just a few broken bones, but it could have been so much worse – and it didn't need to happen at all.

When the race restarted I was really strong and I worked my way into the lead battle with Pironi and Piquet. Pironi's Ferrari was so fast in a straight line he could keep a gap, but both Nelson and I were faster than him over the whole lap. We just had to fight him. I put a move on Nelson on the 10th lap and we had contact, which sent him off the track and into the catch-fencing and out of the race. He came in after the race for a fight, but if that is what he wanted he picked the wrong bloke. I simply didn't give a fuck if he was upset.

Once he was out of the way, Didier was no problem for me, and I was leading by the end of lap 12. I was in a great rhythm and started to pull a gap before settling down the pace a little. Seven laps later, after running through the fast right at the same speed in the same gear and with the same line, the side skirt on the car got stuck and I lost all downforce. I had no grip and went off the track and into a wall, ever so gently but with just enough force to cause damage. The radiator burst and scalded my thigh, but I was more pissed at losing the race, which I felt I really needed to win at that stage of the season. To make it worse, I had given Carlos, who won the race, nine points that should have been mine.

This race in Belgium combined with the Monaco Grand Prix, up next, turned out to be critical events in my title defence. Both races should have and could have been wins, 18 points in total; instead, all I got was six points from a second place at Monaco.

Firstly, I really needed to get on top of my qualifying pace. Seventh was just not good enough when the car had speed, but I was still trying to work out the single lap on Michelin tyres. It was purely me, Carlos was out-qualifying me and I didn't like that at all. In the races though, I had speed and race craft to help me out.

I always felt I was a better racer than qualifier, but I was making my life hard here.

And seventh on the grid at Monaco was much worse than it sounds; it was a tough place to pass people. But we did. I picked off a couple, including Gilles in the cumbersome but quick Ferrari, and then took second when Carlos retired with gearbox dramas. I closed in on Nelson and put the pressure on, and then he cracked and spun when he couldn't lap the slower cars easily enough. No contact from me, Nelson, but same result for you.

Then I was walking away with the race despite the discomfort of my burns from Zolder. This was probably the worst place to have an injury like that, you're turning left, right, left, right and putting pressure on it constantly. I nearly had to have a skin graft on the burns, but they put all this oily gauzy stuff on it and wrapped it up and I just got into the car and made myself as tight as I possibly could to stop the movement and it was working well in the race.

I had a 20-second lead over Gilles when fuel vaporisation problems started to affect my lap times. It was inconsistent and hard to drive, but we held on for many laps. It only got worse and eventually Gilles passed me like I was standing still on the pit straight. I watched the highlights later and Murray Walker was shouting, 'What a fantastic overtaking manoeuvre!' He passed me down the bloody straight, for Christ's sake. It's not like he went past me sideways down the inside into Mirabeau.

Then I thought I was running low on fuel and a top-up would help, so I pitted and got back on the track still in second, which is where I finished. That was my best-ever finish in the most prestigious race on the calendar, and typically under Jones' Law this

253

was the only podium on the calendar where only the winner was present.

So straight back to the garage, this time without the shitfight in the media. Not only did I not win, but I didn't have a chance to go up onto the podium and have a look at Princess Grace, who was alive and kicking in those days. That was Monaco. As much as I didn't like Monaco, I really wanted to win there.

We went to Jarama in Spain for the last time three weeks after Monaco. Quite funny really – it was felt Jarama was too narrow with the speed of a modern Formula One car, but Monaco was OK. There was a sense of Spain being the sacrificial lamb. After the disaster of the 1980 race being removed from the calendar, the crowd was tiny, but at least the politics were kept to a minimum.

I finally had some qualifying form back and put it on the front row beside Jacques Laffite. In the race I got away best and was leading by more than ten seconds over Gilles Villeneuve when I fell off the track. It only took a fraction of a second of not driving at 100 per cent for it to happen. I lost a heap of time and had to pit for some minor repairs. I stayed on the lead lap but I missed out on being in a great battle for the lead of the race.

Gilles was in the turbo Ferrari, which looked like a dog to drive but it had so much power it was hard to pass. His lap times weren't that great, but he was leading and one by one the challengers lined up. In the end, the first five cars finished within 1.24 seconds of him. I finished seventh, so no points again . . . three races in a row which all could have been wins.

Carlos finished fourth and pulled out a 13-point lead over me. The pressure was mounting now, and this was going to be interesting. There is no way I was going to let him take my title that easily.

The Renaults were again great in France, and that is about all I'd like to say about that race. Only a few laps into the race I was in the pits with several issues, the worst was overheating. I lost four laps and was the last car home in a rain-interrupted race.

If I thought my season was tough so far, there was more to come, and my enjoyment of the sport was fast waning. At Silverstone I got caught in a Villeneuve incident when I couldn't avoid his spinning Ferrari, so that was another retirement for me. John Watson won the race in the first carbon-fibre car, which McLaren had released earlier in the year.

My qualifying form was now OK, but the turbos were just dominating that part of a weekend. They'd turn the wick up and get another 50 horsepower and take pole, second, third and whatever else was available. If we could get onto the first or second row that was a great achievement. In qualifying the rest of us were fighting over the scraps knowing they'd come back to us in race trim.

When we got to Germany I wasn't in the best of moods; when I left it was worse. Carlos and I managed to qualify on the second row behind the Renaults. I got a good start and ran third for the opening laps, Nelson hit Arnoux on the opening lap and the Renault had to pit to replace a punctured tyre. So that made it Prost in his Renault from Carlos, me and Nelson.

Carlos was relatively easy to pass, Prost not so. I was all over him in any corner – Hockenheim doesn't have many – and then he'd blast away in the straights – of which Hockenheim has plenty. Lap after lap I ducked and weaved in the stadium section, only to watch him pull away when we got out of it. I tried a couple of moves at the end of the back straight. I had to go so late on the brakes the car would twitch and buck as I went in, but I just couldn't get through cleanly.

Around 20 laps into the race we were coming up to lap Arnoux in the second Renault, and I figured he'd let Alain through easily and then hoped he would get out of my way. As it turned out, we caught him at the stadium section, and while Prost was being cautious I dived between the two of them at Sachs Curve.

It was real balls-in-the-mouth stuff, but with my mood that weekend I was going into that gap. I pulled it off and then walked away from Prost, who dropped a spot to Piquet when it started to rain. With around 10 laps to go my car started to misfire and I started to drop heaps of time. When I was passed by Piquet and Prost I headed to the pits with steam coming out of my ears. I finished a lap down and with another win handed to someone else. This could have been my fifth win in a row, I was leading all of them except for Silverstone, when some mechanical gremlin cruelled my day.

There was always this myth about no-one could ever do back-to-back championships. No-one had done it since Jack Brabham in 1959-60. No-one really knew why. Frank and Patrick said I drove better in 1981 than I did in '80, but it was all these stupid little things that were hurting me. I was now in fourth in the Championship and 19 points behind Carlos.

As luck would have it, the car held together in Austria, where we just didn't have enough speed to challenge for the win. Jones' Law. I was in a great battle for third place for many laps with Didier, Nelson, Jackie the Foot and eventually Carlos. It was a familiar story, Didier's turbo Ferrari would pull away on the straights and we'd close in on the corners. Nelson and Jacques were swapping spots in front of me as each tried to pass the Ferrari. As they did that I kept inching closer.

Jacques Laffite was the first to clear Didier and he went on to win the race. The rest of us cleared the Ferrari too, but the extra lap or two allowed a huge gap to appear and that was it. Both the Renaults out in front had issues, Prost's suspension failed and Arnoux killed his tyres, but they had enough of a gap for Nelson and me not to catch up and I finished fourth. It was nice to finally finish and get some points, my first since Monaco.

Zandvoort was next and even from my early days I had a good record there. I qualified in the second row and jumped Nelson off the start to follow those bloody Renaults again. Arnoux was easy pickings, but Prost was hard. I followed him for lap after lap looking for gaps, trying to make gaps where they weren't. I was all over him, but it was hard work for both me and the tyres, and eventually the tyres went off.

I tried to settle for second, but Nelson, who hadn't been in any battles, still had good tyres and by the end of the race he rounded me up and took second. Third for me.

I was starting to get very frustrated with racing. I was driving my heart out and getting no real reward. It was either mechanical dramas, other people's problems or just having to work things too hard to battle shitboxes with great engines.

Monza was more of the same, only this time it was second place. John Watson had a huge shunt in the McLaren, which a season or two earlier would have killed him. The car was destroyed and left debris everywhere, but being a carbon fibre monocoque he walked away with bruises. That was impressive.

It looked like no-one really wanted to put a mark of authority on the 1981 Championship. Carlos and Nelson had been out in front for most of the season but weren't putting up enough wins and points to take control. In Italy, Carlos joined me on the podium. It was only his second podium since his win in Belgium eight races ago. Nelson was collecting points, but not in an emphatic way . . . and that left the door open ever so slightly for Alain Prost, Jacques Laffite and myself, who were within two wins and striking distance of the title.

Despite this, my enthusiasm wasn't lifting any and it was pissing down with rain in the Canadian Grand Prix and I banged wheels with Carlos into turn 1 – remember, no favours from this boy – and led the early laps. The car was a pig to drive in those conditions and I spun out of the lead and then retired. If I was having little fun before, now I was having none at all.

I was out there risking my life every lap of every race, giving my all and getting nothing back. I thought, 'Fuck, all these mechanical failures I've had, I haven't got any chance of winning the championship, I'm not going to stick my neck out. Screw it, I'm going home.' I made the decision to quit from Formula One. It was that easy and that sudden. In hindsight, the urge to walk away had been growing, I just couldn't see it.

We had been looking at getting residency in Switzerland when I made the decision, and Bernard Cahier, who was a very well-known photojournalist who had been around forever, was helping me out with that and to find a house on Lake Geneva. We went there with him for a look one weekend, and he was good mates with Peter Ustinov, who also lived there, and we ended up all having lunch together. We had this fish they said was only found in Lake Geneva. Well, that's what they said.

The house Bernard had found for us had its own little acre or so beside it with its own vineyard where the guy would come in and make wine and you could keep a certain number of the bottles and he took the rest. It was all terrific.

I was paying for an advocat – Swiss lawyer – to go back to Bern and get the OK from the mayor of the Canton de Vaud, which was where the house was located. They had the VD designation on their number plates, which always amused me. We were still looking at adopting another child, so when I said, 'Fuck it. I'm going back to Australia,' that knocked both Switzerland and the other child on the head.

In hindsight I should have stayed and at least got my residency, which I would never have lost, and that's always a handy thing to have. But, anyway, it was typical of one of the impetuous and stupid moves that I make all too frequently. This was perhaps the one snap decision of mine that Bev didn't mind – she was happy to pack our bags and move back to Australia.

The next week I went home to do Bathurst, in a Holden with the upside-down suspension for Warren Cullen. He had some special suspension which he thought was going to help him win the race, but it wasn't that good. I remember Kevin Bartlett and people like that coming up and saying, 'What are you driving that piece of shit for? There's better cars to drive.' I got $50,000 to do Bathurst. That was more than the bloke that won it. You couldn't turn around to the likes of him and say, 'Yeah, is that right? I'm just doing it because I love it, mate.' I got my airfare paid back to Australia, 50 grand, and then back to Vegas. Thank you.

Honestly, I couldn't have given a rat's arse about Bathurst, still couldn't really. I had my eye on the brown paper bag, and that was what it was all about, which is in essence all touring car racing ever was to me.

Then we had my final grand prix. It was meant to be at Watkins Glen, but the people who ran the race there went belly-up during the year, so we lined up in the car park at Caesars Palace hotel in Las Vegas. This was a funny little track. It ran counter-clockwise, so that was hard on the drivers, but the surface was really smooth and the track with all its little straights and hairpin-like bends had plenty of places to overtake.

I was out of title contention, but Carlos led into the final round. I didn't need to remind him I was not there to help him; I think the whole world knew that at the time.

Frank took four cars to this race, one each for qualifying and one each for the race. That was to give Carlos his best chance to win the championship, but Frank didn't want to be seen to be giving favouritism to either of us, so we both had two cars. I'd bent a valve in the engine of my qualifying car, so I took over my race car to qualify, and it felt fantastic. I qualified second, not that far behind Carlos, who had pole.

I thought I'd play with him. 'Have you seen where pole is? It's just a disgrace, there's shit everywhere, I don't know how you're going to get off the line.' It worked. Carlos said to Frank during a debrief or something that this was a big problem for him. I said, 'Well, you know the man who gets on pole can claim whichever side of the track he wants to start,' and I just left it at that.

Sure enough, he's gone up to the organisers, 'I want to start on that side.' I got on pole thanks to my mouth.

It was only about 50 metres down to the first corner. You could have done the worst start known to man, and you still probably would have led into the first corner if you started on the inside line, which I now had. In the morning warm-up, I ran down the inside all the time, shit flying everywhere, but I was cleaning it all up. Frank knew exactly what I was up to.

Of course, I out-dragged him into the first corner, as did Villeneuve, Prost and Giacomelli. He was fucked from there on in and he went backwards. I lapped him. They had a jumbo full of Argentinian journalists that flew in to see him win the world championship. Piquet, the man he was battling for the Championship, was rooted, feeling ill. He was spewing and carrying on. All Carlos had to do was finish in front of a sick Piquet and he would have been World Champion – because I was going to win, and that ruled everyone else out.

In the end, I did win. Easily. I lapped Carlos and probably laughed when I did so. Prost and Giacomelli finished on the podium with me and that was a very satisfying way to end my Formula One career. I hadn't just won, I dominated and let the whole world see that I may not have had the Championship, but I was still the best.

Nelson finished fifth, which moved him one point in front of Carlos who missed the points altogether, and won the Championship.

After the race, in all the interviews, I was asked time and time again about Carlos missing the title. My favourite quote was: 'I don't see how I could help him. I would not care for holding up people, as I'm a member of the British Commonwealth, Australia specifically, and I would consider that unsporting.'

But he didn't deserve to win. There was a doco made about that season, and it had a very funny bit in it. 'And down at the pits, we've got blah, and in the meantime, here's Carlos!' And there was footage of Carlos laying by the pool. 'Now we're down at the Renault pits, and you can see Alain Prost going through his telemetry with his team, and here's Carlos!' Down by the pool again. It took the piss out of him like you wouldn't believe.

I finished my career finally satisfied with a race that year. It would have been a shame for it to end any other way. We had a major party in my room, and Frank was still trying to talk me out of it. I just wanted to go home, I was essentially one flight away from Australia and I had no desire to go anywhere else. 'Alan,' Frank said, 'come back and drive the six-wheeler.' That was the new car he was getting ready for 1982. I debated with him as best you could after a few Foster's, and he ended up winning. Fuck!

I went back to England, and it was freezing cold. I stayed in a motel near Donington. I had a Jaguar, which in those days didn't have central locking, you still had to put a key in it. I had to boil the kettle to pour hot water over the lock so I could unlock the car, that's how cold it was. We went out to the circuit, got in the transporter and all the metal was cold to touch. When the sun eventually came out and the circuit dried up, we did some laps. It didn't really feel all that much different. It wasn't blindingly quick, and certainly wasn't good enough to impress me.

I said, 'Right, we finished?' With an affirmative response, I jumped in my car and went down to Heathrow, boarded a Qantas jet, went up through the clouds, overcast and dull, and into bright sunshine. I had an ice cold Foster's, and I thought, 'I'm on my way home.' Although for me I was always sort of home already on a Qantas flight. I hated the weather in England, and that alone played a big part in my decision to quit.

Whether the six-wheeler had potential or not we'll never know – they banned it before it even raced, so that put Williams back a little for 1982. I was sure I'd made the right decision and I felt I had done so honourably – as soon as I knew I told Frank. Frank still says I didn't give him enough notice, but at least I did it near the end of the season and not part way, like Reutemann did to him in 1982.

My decision was quick. I was over the weather and living in England. I'd tried commuting from the US, where I liked the weather, and that didn't work. I could maybe have done something from down south in Europe, but again I would have been flying a lot and I was missing Christian as it was.

I was over it. Over the weather. Over the travel, over going to countries where they didn't speak any English and you could not talk to anyone. We had no mobile phones or computers back then, so you couldn't easily talk to home. The TV was crap and invariably I couldn't understand it. I didn't socialise because that wasn't good for my racing. So aside from the occasional enthusiast of the female kind, I was pretty much alone.

It all bubbled up inside me on one weekend and I decided that was it.

Frank Williams & Patrick Head

If I hadn't had such a great working and personal relationship with Frank Williams and Patrick Head I'm not sure I would have had the F1 career I had.

Even when I was with Shadow I got on reasonably well with Frank because he's a very personable bloke, but I didn't really meet Patrick until I went to the factory to have a look at the car. I had about half an hour with Patrick, and found him very down to earth, very matter of fact, and that was enough to convince me about what I should do.

You could see he was aggressive, competitive and single-minded about what he wanted and where he wanted to be. That feeling was only confirmed the more I got to know him. There was a standing joke at the workshop, Frank would be up in his office and you'd hear Patrick stamping up the stairs. A part wouldn't have arrived or something else had gone wrong and he'd come storming up the stairs to vent at Frank.

There was this great mutual respect between them. It just all worked out. I joined the team, we're all similar age, and it gelled. It was a really good place to be.

I had missed out on Ferrari – but I think Ferrari would have been quite different and ultimately wouldn't have suited me as much. Yes, I would have had the equipment to do the job, but something would have gone missing for me in the memos telling me where to be and what to do. I still would have driven at Ferrari though, because as a driver you hunt for the best car you can find – friendship disappears fast when you are at the back of the grid.

I reckon I could have even driven for people like Colin Chapman and Ken Tyrrell if needed. Colin seemed not to take his drivers into his confidence and he was rude and aggressive, which is not behaviour I like . . . but he was very clever. Ken was a very dominant figure in his teams, I'm not sure he listened to his drivers enough and simply wanted them to do it his way. They would have been hard work for me, but if it meant winning I would have found a way to cope. I mean, I survived both Graham Hill and John Surtees and we weren't winning. But I was at Williams – and I was happy about that.

Patrick and I shared a dry sense of humour, and he too did not like to lose. At Long Beach once, I went wide in qualifying and I scraped the wall. He let me know in no uncertain terms, 'Why the fuck did you do that?'

'Well, Patrick, I thought I'd just put it in the wall just for a bit of fun.' We used to have our words, but we all had the same goals. That meant everything that was ever said or done was for a reason.

I got to the stage with Patrick where he understood exactly what I needed by what I was saying. I could do a warm-up lap on the morning of the race and think I needed a bit more grip at the front, or the back; he'd make a change and nine times out of ten it'd be right.

He always used to say to me, 'Don't tell me what to do,' which suited me because I had no idea what I wanted to do anyway, 'just tell me what it's doing that you don't want it to do and what it's not doing that you do want it to do.' That I could do, and then I trusted him to get it right and bang, it'd be brand new.

You look back now at the people that have come through in Formula One under Patrick, people like Adrian Newey, Rob

Smedley, Neil Oatley and Ross Brawn, who is now the Director of Motorsport for Formula One. He's had some brilliant engineers that have later gone on to become leading designers in their own right. He's had some really good guys come through. Patrick is a brilliant engineer. His strength is his ability to be able to simplify things and use parts for more than one job.

Formula One is enormous now, but even in my day it was big business. It was and still is equal parts sport and business, and as such is at the mercy of all – and requiring different talents for each. The variables make it so complex. There is the personality of the driver to mollycoddle; there are sixteen mechanics each with different skills and different problems; there are the factory staff who build and repair the cars, each of them a technician and a specialist. In the 1970s there were few enough for you to know them all, yet too many to spend all your time getting to know their individual psyches. There is sponsor-chasing, there is the logistics of carrying cars and people all around the world; there is negotiation with the tyre people, and suppliers of engines, gear-boxes, spark plugs, any one of an inventory of thousands – all that has to be kept in your head, alongside the main business of getting out on the track and winning.

And Frank is exceedingly good at it. Anyone who can run a Formula One team successfully can run any other business there is.

Frank was the commercial bloke, the one with the vision. I think the fact that he's still going to grands prix in a wheelchair after all this time shows a bit about his determination and drive. I couldn't do it, there's no way I could go to that many grands prix as an able-bodied person.

I liked Frank even before I worked for him, even if he didn't really know me. He was jovial and polite, and I put a high value on politeness.

Civility is very important. Being civil doesn't detract from your inner combativeness or your interior strength. You don't have to be arrogant or rude to be a good fighter. The popular notion of the driver as arrogant, rude, macho and boorish, derives from the Teutonic, aggressive Lauda and Jochen Rindt – the 1970 world champion, awarded posthumously after he died in practice, his throat cut by his seat belt. They set a style: if you weren't rude and arrogant then you hadn't the balls to be a top racing driver. Not true of course – James Hunt wasn't like that.

I was somewhere in between, and I knew what was required of me on the track and what I had to do to achieve that. But even in my most focused times, I never dropped my values. A waiter is not a pig for spilling the soup. The world is full of my equals. I'd like to think I was the best in my sport and I would do anything to keep myself on top. But the rest of the world remains my equal.

Frank's politeness doesn't get in the way of his competitive-ness. As we got closer to a race, he got more wound up inside – but I never saw him be impolite. The truth is that, like myself, he's a very controlled man. And also extremely determined, competi-tive and intelligent. He's by far the best man I've driven for. But then I've had some lesser ones, haven't I?

Frank is a racer, an absolute racer, no doubt about it. He lives and bloody breathes it. He used to share a house just near Heathrow and they used to get up to all sorts of things. At that stage Frank used to operate out of a phone box, that was his office.

He'd leave the number and he'd wait outside the phone box and answer the phone. No one would be any the wiser.

When he was trying to lock down the Saudi deal, and even after that make it work, he'd go down to Saudi Arabia and he would sit in one of the sheikh's waiting rooms for eight or nine hours. Of course, those bastards knew that you were there. Half the time, I think, they just did it for a bit of sport, but he wouldn't leave, he'd stay there until he saw them, very determined.

He never drank or smoked, so I did have some doubts about him. He used to run about eight miles a day with his mate Dave Brodie, who raced touring cars. Frank always got this magazine with different running shoes and cross-trainers and he and Dave would look at it the same way I'd look at watches. But I've never known two people to have so many colds. They reckoned if you're really super-super-fit you're more inclined to pick up colds and things.

He would leave Didcot and call into my place in Kew. He'd get changed into his tracksuit and have a 'fix' as I'd call it, going for his little run. Then he'd come back, go into London, have his hair cut, which he did once a week, same barber, always wore a navy blue pullover, and then when he had his hair cut he'd go back to Didcot, which was a little more than an hour away. I think he was just a bit OCD.

His wife, Ginny, died in 2013. She was a lovely woman and together they were pretty powerful. He was as tough as she was nice. When they started getting a few bob, they'd buy a house, and she'd decorate it and do it all up and sell it and make a few bob. The boys used to call her the Duchess of Didcot, because she had a very posh accent. So does Frank, but it wasn't like Ginny's.

Bev, Christian and I used to go to their place and play tennis on Sunday and stay for lunch. There are very few people I worked for that I socialised with like that; I really enjoyed going up there. Nine times out of ten Patrick would be up there as well and we'd all end up having a game of tennis. It was really pleasurable, and it just meant that when we went to the races it was almost like a continuation of being at Frank's place playing tennis.

Driving for Frank and Patrick was absolutely the best team I have ever driven for. It was happy and comfortable. Frank was able to get the very best out of me, not through threats, not through promises of rewards; he just knew how to get me giving my best. I think that's a bit of a bloody thing in itself, an art.

My time there has also ensured that Australia has a soft spot for Williams, and Frank feels the same about Australia. He always had a lot of Aussies working for him too. My chief mechanic was a guy called Wayne Eckersley, who unfortunately passed away a couple of years ago. Then there was Sam Michael, who has come home and joined Triple Eight Race Engineering in Brisbane. Wayne was good value and fitted into Williams very well, but he was hard work. He was a bloody good mechanic. He would not leave that circuit until he was absolutely satisfied everything was 101 per cent – that always gave me faith in the car.

So not only did I get on well with Frank, but he chose good people to work with us. And he trusted me as a driver. There was one time when I had no speed and I said to Frank I felt the engine was down on power. Rather than doing a Graham Hill or John Surtees and questioning anything other than the engine, he just changed it. Didn't question it, he just said, 'Well, if you think it's down on power we'll change it.' Then I was quickest in the warm-up, went off in the first corner and climbed from 14th to win.

He gave me confidence in the team and I wanted to do the best I possibly could to reward him for doing it. He was very clever. And a good bloke, a really good bloke.

I am not surprised in the slightest about the empire and legacy that he has built. He always poured a lot of money back into the team, while others were pocketing the cash. Eddie Jordan might have a big yacht that he travels around the world in courtesy of his little stint in Formula One, but the Jordan team no longer exists. Whereas Frank was always putting it back into the team to improve it, buying machinery, improving the factory.

His daughter Claire now essentially runs the team and she will take up more and more of the backroom duties over time as well. She is very much like Frank and they've got enough good people around them to be successful again. People like Rob Smedley are very smart.

Williams has now outgrown Didcot and the team is up in Grove, at an amazing centre. Now they've got a museum and a lot of the old cars there, and a convention centre. There is a bar named after me, which shows Frank's sense of humour.

Alain Prost

Prost I liked. Once again, a tough little bugger and he has this nickname of The Professor. He was good at working the system, you see. He was one of those guys that when he came into Formula One you knew that he was going to be a show. Even when he was in the McLaren, before he went to Renault, I knew he was going to grow as a threat.

He was more of a thinker than many – hence the nickname – certainly more than someone like me or Ayrton. Senna was more entertaining to watch, he used to get the car and strangle it a bit more than Alain. I think Alain would spend a lot more time setting the car up to do what he wanted it to do, whereas Senna would just jump in it and do it.

They were very different people and very different drivers, and that is what made them so interesting to watch.

Ayrton Senna

I raced against Senna in Formula One in my Beatrice days, which meant I really didn't race him as such. I had breakfast with him a couple of times during 1986 – and he was such a nice guy. He's the only race driver that's ever sent me a Christmas card. Now, whether that was just a bit of process for him or whether he was just generally nice and said, 'Let's send Alan a Christmas card,' I don't know. I also don't know how many others he sent them to, but it was something I will always remember.

He was always very respectful. I remember I bumped into him at Adelaide one year and he was with his girlfriend and he said, 'This is Alan Jones, he's an ex-world champion,' which meant you need to treat him right. He liked the sport and its history, and he understood what you had done and what it took. He was very quiet and I liked him a hell of a lot.

He got a bad run from the English press because he wasn't English and he was keeping Poms out of the seat they expected for their people.

But here was another guy that would do anything to win a race, and he was very focused. It was all about winning. He grew horns when he hopped in the car, except it wasn't the devil's horns, because he was a devout Christian.

The thing that used to astound me with Senna is that time after time after time he would wait with literally two laps left and just jump in and go whoosh, and whack it on pole, and by a lot. That takes an unbelievable amount of confidence in your ability, because anything can happen. Someone could blow up an engine, oil could be dropped, the session could be red-flagged . . . He just seemed to get away with it all the time.

My work on TV had me watching him a lot, analysing what he was doing, which was normally something more than everyone else. There was one particular instance I remember in the wet at Donington, and I thought his brakes had failed, but they hadn't. I don't know how, but he passed a pile of cars like they were parked. He just went that deep under brakes it was amazing, staggering car control.

Every now and again a genius comes along, someone that's blessed with an innate natural ability, and he was certainly one of those.

His death when driving for Williams was a great tragedy, a freak outcome from a seemingly light crash. He went through that left-hander and I suspect the tyres hadn't built up their proper pressures, because they had been under a safety car, driving at a much lower speed. Then there is a bump there and I think he's hit that and he's gone into the fence.

It was absolute nonsense to think a modern Formula One team would start hacksawing a bloody steering rod in the pits, as some alleged. The carry-on from the Italians was embarrassing. A lot of people think it was the steering rod that went through his helmet, but it was a piece of carbon fibre. He lost so much blood that he died, otherwise he wasn't all that badly knocked about at all. I know that crash affected Sid Watkins too; he was very fond of Ayrton.

Carlos Reutemann

Carlos Reutemann lost me when he dishonoured his agreement with Frank. The reality is, I did not care who my teammate was and I never asked for any agreement. It is unlikely I would ever have agreed to any terms in my contract where I had to give wins to people – but he did and he should have stuck to his agreement. He had every opportunity to take it to his solicitor, he had every opportunity to go and sleep on it, he had every opportunity to say to Frank, no, I don't like it, but he signed it and as far as I was concerned that was that. I could have passed him in Brazil before he was asked to let me past, but I knew he would be asked to, so I didn't have a go. I waited for him to do what he should have done.

They showed him the Jones-Reut sign for a few laps but he ignored it. I kept expecting him to do it, I would have honoured an agreement if I had signed it and I expected the same from him. He didn't and that was it for me. In hindsight, I wish I'd had a go at him and just passed him.

I told Frank from that point on to forget about me helping him, and perhaps the mind games I played with him at the final race that year helped him to cough up the title to Nelson. It must have broken his little heart too, and then Keke Rosberg, who in effect replaced me in the team, went on to win the title in 1982 when Carlos walked away.

It was kind of appropriate he became a politician, where his dishonesty could work for him.

Gilles Villeneuve

We used to call him Jiles Vile-Enough. I used to come up with names for lots of people, or just say them in different ways. Patrick Tambay was Patrick Tampax and because he was French he never knew what was going on. Gilles was Jiles.

He was not a bad little bloke, a complete lunatic though. I once said, he was never going to die in bed, and he didn't. Even when he used to fly his helicopter from Monaco up to Fiorano he'd get there with about one pint of fuel left in it. He was a risk-taker.

I think that's why the Italians and Ferrari loved him, because he personified what they'd like to be, brave and fearless, and he never left anything on the table. If you passed Gilles you had to earn it. He'd never leave the door open, and even if you were right beside him you'd be rubbing wheels and he'd still try to slam the door on you. I remember we raced at Montreal and Frank said, 'Wait until your fuel load gets down a bit before you start really hopping into it.'

Gilles did a better start than me and I followed him for what seemed like a long time right up his gearbox and he just left the door open a little bit too much into the hairpin and I dived down the inside, and he came over on me and we rubbed wheels, which in hindsight was a bit silly because it could've ended his race and mine right there. As it turned out, it didn't.

As soon as I got in front of him, I thought I'd get away because he was holding me up, but I didn't. The little bugger stuck right up my arse until the end of the race. He was a very tenacious little fighter, and you had to earn everything.

At Zolder in 1982 his new teammate Pironi was giving him a bit

275

of a touch-up and ignored team orders at the previous race – hello Carlos. Gilles was keen to prove a point and was going to out-qualify him no matter what. He came over the brow of the hill to go down through a big left-hander at Zolder. I think he may have double-guessed Jochen Mass and he clipped the back of his car and it flew into the air and started to disintegrate as it tumbled down the road and he was killed.

He let Pironi get to him – he was furious and I think he made a poor decision. He had qualifying tyres on, it was near the end of the session and he should have been smarter. Jochen did nothing wrong, he stuck to his line and Gilles just got it wrong when he should have slowed and cursed him for ruining his lap.

The anchor points of the seat came out, ripped through the bloody floor, and he was thrown across the track and into the catch fencing. Not that seeing any big crash is good, but this was shocking. You can ask whether the anchor points should have come out, but he should never have made that mistake.

If you have a look at the amount of shunts that he had he may have been lucky to make it that far. He had a complete disregard for anyone and everyone on the track. There's quite a few things he did I thought were ridiculous. Too much bravado and all the shit that the Italians loved – Forza Gilles.

He was fast, but reckless.

18

Retirement . . . Part 1

I wasn't enjoying my racing anymore. It had nothing to do with what Jean-Marie Balestre was doing to the sport, which a lot of people at the time thought was a factor. It was becoming a job. I wanted to live in Australia. I probably wanted to increase my chances of being at Christian's 21st. There were a number of factors.

I was really just flat and looking forward to life in Australia. Today I'm not sure why that was such a big pull for me, but it was. Perhaps I'd climbed my Everest and maybe the next climb didn't seem as much fun.

But you have to look at the other side of the coin. I was living out of a suitcase and getting on too many planes. People reading this today might think, 'Oh, poor bugger,' but let me tell you – getting on and off planes all the time is not fun.

And if you wanted to ring home, you'd pick up the phone in your room, and the person that answered the phone couldn't speak English. Then you had to go down to the reception, give them a piece of paper with the phone number on it, and either race back to your room or wait next to cubicle number three to speak to whoever you wanted to speak to in England, the US or Australia.

Today you could go back to your room, watch any number of TV channels in pretty much any language you desire, or you could ring up somebody from your mobile. It is a different kettle of fish.

When you're stuck in a foreign country and you don't speak the language and all you've got to do is listen to a foreign language on TV and you can't make a phone call, it gets a bit boring.

From the start of my time at Williams, if not before, I was really ten-tenths all the time, and as I said if I didn't qualify in the top three rows I used to bash myself up. So I was hard on myself and that is draining – ask any athlete. When I did come back to Australia, I was only a few months into my retirement when Didier Pironi ran up the back of somebody at Hockenheim in his Ferrari. Lo and behold, Ferrari rang me to see if I could come over and fill in.

Very stupidly, in typical fashion, I've deliberately buggerised them around, which I thought would be a bit of fun, because I thought they'd done the same to me in 1977 when they signed Villeneuve and cancelled my contract. I got a mate to answer the calls and spin them out a bit. 'He's just down the butcher's, he'll be back shortly.' Because they couldn't get me quickly they signed Mario Andretti, and he stuck the thing on pole at Monza and then made it onto the podium.

Funny how the world turns: in '77 they would take me if they couldn't get Andretti and now it was the other way around. If I hadn't have been so stupid I could have milked that dry. I could have said the only nation in the world I'd come out of retirement for was Italy, and the only team I'd come out of retirement for was Ferrari. I tell you, I would never have paid for anything in Italy ever again. Free spaghetti sauce forever.

The minute Bev found out about the offer, she flung herself on the ground and went into one of those fits only women can do. I thought, 'Oh Jesus. Is this worth the shit?'

She didn't want me to do it. Probably more so because she thought she might have to go back over there and go through all the crap again. Maybe if I had said she could stay in Australia and do whatever she wanted she would have been OK, but she was pretty clear about it.

I just didn't know whether a temporary drive for Ferrari was really worth the aggravation.

I'd been doing some racing in Australia and I was quite enjoying the low-stress nature of what I was doing. Without the pressure of racing in the biggest show in the world, and with the stakes lowered, I just started driving cars for the fun of it. I've always been competitive and I always wanted to win, but the pressure was different because, to be blunt, it didn't really matter that much to me.

Although I am not sure you would describe racing a Camaro touring car at Amaroo Park as fun – there was probably not a greater mismatch between car and circuit anywhere else in the known world. But that is what I did in March 1982. I decided I needed to get a little serious about touring cars, so I got George

Shepheard, who was well known for his work with the Holden Dealer Team and for building rally cars, to do me up a Falcon, and he charged like a wounded bull. I think I paid something like three hundred grand for it, which was big money.

I just hated the car. Bob Morris drove it at Oran Park in a 100-lap race and won, and I decided I preferred the Mazda RX-7 I had run with Barry Jones a couple of weeks before at Amaroo Park, where we had won an endurance race together. I kept running Bob in the Falcon and I ran the Mazda – with number 27 on the door – for a DNF in the Sandown 500 and then paired up with Barry for Bathurst, where we broke a gearbox. I was cross-entered with the Falcon there and practised but did not race.

Earlier in the year an opportunity came up with Alan Hamilton, who I had been friends with since we were kids. Alan was the Porsche importer for Australia. He was having a look at running a Porsche 944 in the Australian Sports Saloon and GT Championship and he rang to see if I was interested. Of course I was, but even more so when he decided to do it with a 750-horsepower Porsche 935 – that was more me – and he ran Colin Bond in the 944, which is how I got to know Colin.

We went out to Calder and did a test day. It was a lot of fun. You could turn the boost up, and being a rear-engined car you could almost lift the front wheels of the bloody thing under acceleration. After that test we agreed to do the series and I thoroughly enjoyed it. It was terrific.

Along with Colin, there was Peter Brock – who was a big deal in Australia back then – in a Chev Monza for Bob Jane. That car was a beast and wasn't short of horsepower. I thought the biggest threat, however, should have been from Rusty French, who also had a Porsche 935. Brock beat me at Sandown in a non-Championship race, but I won all the rounds of the Championship to take the title comfortably. I wasn't averse to the concept of cruise and collect.

But with such a powerful and tough car to drive, I could never relax. I nearly had a big one at Symmons Plains down in Tasmania. I got a wheel on the outside, she flicked sideways on me and threw me off the track. That got my attention back and I said to myself, 'I think you'd better start concentrating a bit.'

The week after that we raced at a place called Baskerville, in Hobart, which was a bit different – spectators could watch from the comfort of their cars. It was so tight in one of those race cars, in fact it would have been tight in anything, so I really had to be on my game.

In the middle of the year we raced at Lakeside – and that was the catalyst for making my mind up to move to Queensland. Not because I liked Lakeside mind you, because I didn't. But it was a cold, miserable, overcast, windy day when I left the farm, and then I landed in Brisbane to a stunning day and I was in a T-shirt and a pair of shorts. That was much more me.

I went to the Gold Coast for a look and bought a penthouse in Main Beach. I started going home less and spending more time up north, then I thought I'd ration myself with three months straight. I didn't want to fall into the false holiday atmosphere that was prevalent there – lounge by the pool, drink champagne and basically just remove yourself from the world. And then one day check the bank balance and think, 'Shit, I'd better do something.'

Funny you know, when I stopped racing, I was really looking forward to Australia's weather – and then promptly moved to the farm in Victoria. In winter you sat next to the heater freezing your arse off. It took me only that one winter to realise I wasn't a farmer. The countryside was beautiful, but winter was freezing and in summer you slept with one eye open waiting for the bloody bushfires to scream through.

That was in a place called Glenburn, halfway between Yarra Glen and Yea. I remember the manager coming in one day and saying, 'Alan, we've got a fox in paddock three.' I remember saying, 'Who gives a fuck? If he wants to take a couple of sheep, he can have them, I'm not getting out of bed.'

He was disgusted. 'What sort of a farmer are you?'

I said, 'I'll tell you what sort of a fucking farmer I am, I'm not.' I'd always come back in the European winter when it was summer in Australia and the weather was great – aside from the bushfire risk. You'd be making hay and going down to the local pub and having a well-earned beer afterwards. I thought, 'This is not a bad life.'

Of course, the first winter I spent there, I thought, 'Jesus, come back, England, all is forgiven.'

Then I did a deal with Kubota for some tractors that had climate control and a radio. I was out slashing a 100-acre paddock, and I was about a quarter of the way through it when I started to second-guess myself. 'Jesus, what am I doing here? I'm cutting straw.' The sum total when it's all finished was about $2000 worth of hay. I could be down in Melbourne wheeling and dealing in cars and making more than that in a day.

Then a plane flew over and I thought, 'I wonder where that's going.' Yet a year earlier, I vowed and declared I didn't want to see an airport ever again. After the experience of the winter and my life as a 'non' farmer, I had started to think about Europe again and serious racing. Maybe deep down I hoped the Gold Coast was going to settle that down.

At the end of three months, I'd decided, I was going to go back to Melbourne and the farm to sell everything and move to the Gold Coast permanently. It took a while to get it all done, but eventually I had shed myself of the cold.

Then I was happy. I was enjoying my C&C, but not the tracks. Most of them were, and still are, shitholes. There's only one permanent track in Australia that is any good, which is Phillip Island. Lakeside, Winton and Calder Park just weren't interesting and with all the space in Australia, you wonder why they kept building these Mickey Mouse circuits.

You go to America and you have places like Road America and Watkins Glen, beautiful, big, long circuits with challenging sweeping corners. They're all proper European style circuits, great to drive on. In Australia though, not only do we make them small and tight, we build them near emerging suburbia, so we know they won't last. When the houses are built near the track the new residents start complaining about the noise and get the track blown up. It's a joke.

Or we build a place like Mallala on the edge of a desert north of Adelaide with wind and sand like you could never believe. It was really funny, we went there many years later testing with the Stone brothers when Paul Romano was driving for me. I went down to the local convenience store to get some sandwiches or something, and the woman behind the counter said, 'Alan Jones, what are you doing here?'

Well given the fact that it's a Mallala race track and I'm a race driver and you've recognised me, one guess. Instead, I said, 'I'm here for the holidays. I bring the wife and kids over once a year and we stay in a caravan out in the circuit, we love it.'

'Really, you do?'

Not that I was too bothered by the quality of the tracks: I was winning and I quite enjoyed that. Alan gave me a great Porsche to race and it was really well prepared. I was challenged a few times, particularly by Brock, and I hopefully repaid Alan and crew for all that effort with the results.

I raced a little Ralt RT4 at Winton in late October for a second place, and that was it for my racing in 1982. I started the year thinking I was a farmer, and I ended it in a Gold Coast penthouse knowing I wasn't a farmer and that I still had a motor-racing itch to scratch. If I hadn't have been so silly, I might have been preparing for a year as a Ferrari driver, since Didier Pironi wasn't coming back after he smashed up his legs at the German Grand Prix and Gilles Villeneuve was killed in Belgium during the final qualifying session, while Mario was a stop-gap at his age and Patrick Tambay was never going to make it. They eventually signed René Arnoux and he gave the title a real push in 1983.

I do wonder what life would be like if I'd won a Championship for Ferrari. I wonder if I could have done that. But I don't wonder for too long though.

In March 1983 I was thrown off a horse on the farm – which I was still trying to offload – and I broke my femur. I was in hospital having it pinned when Jackie Oliver rang. He said he had a multi-billionaire ready to put money into the Arrows team and would I come and drive for them. Which was complete bullshit, he didn't have any bloody billionaire; what he wanted was to be able to say that he's just hired the ex-world champion, so he could snag a sponsor – hopefully a billionaire.

I was too stupid not to see through that, so I went back and drove the Arrows at Long Beach and then I did a race at Brands Hatch, the last ever Race of Champions. Remember, this was going to be a full-time drive with lots of money behind it. As soon as he has said 'billionaire' he got my attention and from there it took a few weeks to get my head straight.

We went and did a half a day's practice at a little track east of LA to familiarise myself with the car. Because my left hip was still far from perfect, I remember getting a sledgehammer and bashing the inside left-hand side of the monocoque so I wouldn't be rubbing my hip there. Then we raced at Long Beach.

I was replacing Chico Serra in the car. He had qualified 23rd in Brazil while I did 12th at Long Beach, so I figured I was proving some of my worth. In the race I was running inside the top 10 comfortably when I had to stop. The constant rubbing on the pins in my femur was causing too much pain to keep going, so it was a return with promise.

Bloody René Arnoux was on the podium in the Ferrari and his teammate Patrick Tambay had been on pole. So if I had done Ferrari, not only would I have not broken my leg because I would have been in Italy, I would have been driving a bloody fast car.

That was 27 March and two weeks later we ran at Brands Hatch. It wasn't a full Formula One field but there were plenty of good drivers in good cars there. Keke Rosberg, who had won the 1982 World Championship, took pole from Arnoux, and then it was me, which felt pretty good. Arrows had a car there for Chico as well, and he was down in 11th and five seconds slower than me . . . Remember, the first target is to beat the bloke in the same car.

The race went OK for me and I ended up with third, which felt good with a crap engine. I thought the Arrows A6 had potential, but I wasn't seeing this billionaire or his money. So I put the hard word on Jackie.

I got a lot of stalling and 'ifs' and 'buts', so that was it for me. If I was going to do Formula One they were going to need to be as serious as me. I hadn't changed my standards since the days of Mr Nestle Van.

Before I could get on a plane home, Ron Dennis had word of what was happening and said, 'Niki's not well, do you want to come down to Monaco? I can't guarantee you'll drive, but I'll pay you 20 grand just for coming and I'll pay you 50 if you do drive.'

I should have done that, I mean 20 grand for doing nothing wasn't bad pay. I had twigged something was going on between Beverley and our horse trainer and that was on my mind when I turned him down. McLaren was all over the place in '83 – at some places they were struggling to make the grid and at Long Beach, for instance, they finished first and second. As it turned out Niki did drive but he didn't even qualify.

So I have two regrets from that time: I should have gone back and driven for Ferrari and I should have gone to Monaco as an emergency driver for McLaren.

When I walked away at the end of 1981, I didn't miss it at all. Then while sitting on a tractor I started to have second thoughts. When I got the call from Jackie, his timing was just right – I was easy pickings.

While I was floating around England I got the chance to race a Porsche 956 for the Porsche Kremer Racing team – or the Brothers Kremer as I used to call them – at Silverstone. They turned up with the long-tailed car, which was a mistake. I think they thought with the high speeds of Silverstone that the Le Mans spec with its low downforce body would be better than the shorter car with the bigger wings.

That might have been true in the dry, but this weekend was wet. I led the race for a bit, but then started to get a few niggles in the car and came home in fifth with Vern Schuppan. I did quite enjoy driving the car though; some cars you hop in and you don't even have to turn a wheel and you're immediately comfortable. This was one of those cars. Of course it can be different when you start to drive, but this was a Porsche and that didn't happen. It was a great car. We were lapping faster than a Formula One car.

I did Le Mans with the Brothers Kremer the next year, 1984, and while it was an experience it wasn't really me. Yes, it was fast, but I cynically used to say my favourite place to be skilful was in a straight line. Whether you're doing 600 Ks or 400 Ks, as long as nothing flies off, it's not a big deal. All you've got to do is keep the steering wheel straight.

The thing at Le Mans, though, is that sharing the track with Frederick Fuckin' Fucknasty in his cravat, driving his Sprite coming over from London to do his annual Le Mans, is dangerous. He's going down there at about 160 and you're doing 420. You're just thinking, 'Please look, don't move.' In the drivers' briefing, they're told not to move over or to make room for you, that you will find a way around them, but they either forget that when they're out there under the pressure of driving a Sprite, or they just panic.

That's bad enough in the dry, but when you get them at three in the morning in the rain, and all you see are some tail lights coming at you fast and you've got to second-guess them, that's when it gets a bit dicey. In those days, Mulsanne Straight didn't have the chicanes, just the kink. It was quick and straight for quite a distance.

I was sharing this car with Vern and Jean-Pierre Jarier, who both had many races at Le Sarthe under their belts. Vern even had a win – the first Aussie to do it in nearly 60 years – in 1983. I'd raced in the same team with him at Macau and I knew him in England, our paths had crossed many times. I was reasonably friendly with him, but then he is not a difficult man to be friendly with anyway, he's a gentleman. A bloody good driver too.

Aussies were at a geographical disadvantage and he had done the hard roads in Europe a year or two before me. We both went there with a dream at a similar time. We got no support and we had to scratch around for both the money needed and the opportunities. He won Macau a couple of times and also had a British Formula Atlantic title, and he did race Formula One, but he found his real forte in sportscar racing.

We didn't have the outright speed of the Lancias at Le Mans, but we were still rated as one of the favourites for the race and we qualified third – the best of the non-Lancias.

Less than an hour into the race, Vern had taken the lead. Twenty-two hours later we were still in contention when the engine gave way and we had a long spell in the pits. There was no way to repair the engine, but with 10 minutes left Vern went back out to complete a slow lap and take the chequered flag. We'd lost

23 laps and could have easily won the race from where we were; instead we were sixth.

I didn't really enjoy the race though. Yes, I could tick it off my bucket list, but I figured I was never going back. I worked out I was a sprint driver, not an endurance one. I put in 110 per cent when I was in the car, and that left nothing for when I was out of it. To me, when the helmet came off it was beer time. I struggled with hopping out of the car knowing that I had to get back into it an hour or two later. I was also not that good with sharing the car with anybody; doing driver swaps just didn't do it for me. I'd even struggle today at a grand prix when they have to get out of the car after the formation lap for the national anthem and all that carry-on.

My time with the Brothers Kremer was good. I liked the car and I really liked them and their approach to the sport. We thought the same way, we gelled. But that was it for me with them.

Later that year the World Sports Car Championship went to Australia for the first and only time, to race at Sandown – opposite the cemetery where Dad is buried. I was approached by Porsche in Germany to drive a works car in that race, again with Vern. I wasn't as fit as I should have been for this sort of thing – I was up on the Gold Coast running car businesses. I said yes anyway.

I should have been on pole for that race, but I missed because of my own stupid mistake. They had the start-finish line in a different position to where they did the time for the laps. I've screamed past what I thought was the finish line, and then eased off with about another 150 metres to go to where they actually timed the lap. I ended up third quickest, which shows how quick I was. I was pretty shitty. I did take the lead off the start, but we had trouble during the race and dropped a few laps to finish in eighth.

For me, the race was more convenient than special. But I think it put a little wood under the fire – I knew I still had the urge. The question was always if I could apply myself. I felt I was now at that stage.

I had another run with Warren Cullen at Bathurst and I think the suspension was in the right way this time. We qualified just outside the top 10 and then had a trouble-free run into fourth behind the two biggest teams in the class – the Marlboro Holden Dealer Team (read Peter Brock) which got first and second and then Peter Stuyvesant International Racing (Allan Moffat). So that was a pretty good result, as was the brown paper bag.

I was selling Alfas on the Gold Coast and for 1985 an opportunity came up to race a V6 Alfa in the Australian Touring Car Championship with Colin Bond. This was good for me, firstly because Colin is a great bloke and we got on so well, and secondly because it could blow the cobwebs out properly. You're not in a Formula One car, but it's better than just sitting in your lounge room, and I was doing it with number 27 on the door again.

We weren't going to win the title, but we had a good shot at winning our class. Bondy had one GTV already and then he imported a second one for me from Luigi Racing, which always tickled my fancy a bit. It was a left-hooker while Colin drove the right-hand drive one – I figured mine came from Italy so it should have been better, but who knows.

The first two race meetings were at Winton and Sandown, two very different tracks. We started the season with a pair of fourths to many more powerful cars than us. The Alfa was a great car to drive for a touring car – you could throw it around and try all sorts of things. I had a great dice with Neville Crichton in a works BMW 635 at Wanneroo coming out of Kolb, which was the second last corner on the track and a big hairpin. He'd get about nine car lengths on me, but by the time he got down to turn 2 I was right up his arse again.

It was a real David and Goliath thing, which I really enjoyed as much as when I was running the V6 in Formula 5000 all those years ago. What it lacked in power it made up for under brakes and with handling. But quickly for me that season became a training run for a proper return to Formula One and I only did six of the nine rounds. I was leading my class when I bailed out and could have finished as high as third overall, which would have been amazing in that car and that field.

But no matter how much fun it was, it wasn't Formula One. It wasn't racing with big dollars and big stakes and uncompromised vehicles, and maybe I was ready for that again.

19

Beatrice F1 – American Muscle

LATE IN 1984 my old mate Charlie Crichton-Stuart called from England. Carl Haas was putting together a deal to do a Formula One team, and Carl was testing the water with him to see if I would be interested. I was – especially as in 1985 Australia was getting a World Championship Grand Prix in Adelaide, and I would love to be on the grid for that.

Charlie wasn't getting anywhere on the phone, so he jumped on a plane and came and spent some time with me. He started talking dollars, which had me sitting upright . . . 'Look, I'll level with you, AJ,' which is probably Charlie being Charlie, 'I've been told I can start at X, and I can go to Y. Why don't I just go to that now, and I'll spend four or five days down here and we'll go fishing.' In hindsight he probably had a Z as well, but I was happy anyway.

The Alfa stuff to me was just a training run in preparation for this.

Beatrice Foods, which was backing the Formula One team, also sponsored the Newman-Haas team in the CART IndyCar World Series. Mario Andretti had broken his collarbone and scored a hairline fracture in his hip from a crash in the final stages of the Michigan 500, and they wanted me to fill in for him at Road America in Elkhart Lake. I said yes to this because it wasn't an oval track. Apparently Mario was a bit defiant about his injuries and when they took him off to hospital and told him the news he said, 'This can't be right, I'm Mario Andretti.' They said, 'We've got news for you. You are, and you are in hospital.'

Because I hadn't raced an IndyCar before and because they ran their own licensing system, I had to do a rookie test. Apparently, in America, if you win a World Championship and have run 100 grands prix or whatever, you may not be good enough to drive an IndyCar. So I did my rookie test at Firebird International Raceway. I had to do half a dozen laps without putting it in the fence, and then I had to do one or two pit stops where I came in, did a pit stop, and took off, and that was it. As you might have guessed, the whole test gave me the shits.

Anyway I went to Road America, near Elkhart Lake in Wisconsin, which is a fantastic circuit. I'd raced Can-Am there so I was familiar with it. I don't think I qualified all that well, but the race was good. I had two things going for me: first you had to turn left and right, and in those days the Americans weren't all that clever at that, and secondly there was a drizzle of rain and they were even worse at that. Al Unser Jr had a big accident down the back straight, and a few others speared off too.

I ended the race in third, which was great for my one and only IndyCar appearance. The team was called Newman-Haas Racing. The Newman was Paul Newman, and didn't he love Foster's. After the race we were down in the motorhome and he was drinking one of those big cans of Foster's. We sat down and had a few beers, which, as you know, was what I liked doing after a race, and eventually I said I had to go. 'No, it's all right,' he said, 'I've organised the company jet to take you back to JFK.'

When I flew into America, they gave me a brand new Cadillac to drive from there to Elkhart Lake, and I had the whole thing planned until Paul baffled me with Foster's. I was on a late British Airways flight from JFK to London: all I had to do was drive that Cadillac two hours to O'Hare in Chicago and then get on a plane to JFK and then home. The company jet he was referring to was one of Beatrice's jets sitting near their Chicago headquarters. So relax, AJ, take the easy way home.

If only.

When I finally jumped on the jet we sat on the runway for two hours; they wouldn't let us take off for some reason. When we were finally allowed off it I had to jump on a cattle train with wings to fly to LaGuardia, which was as close as I could get to JFK, not that it mattered since I had missed my flight anyway. I got in there at some unearthly time of the night and stayed in a motel where your feet stuck to the carpet. I don't know what time I got to bed, but I had to get up early because then they booked me on the Concorde to London.

I got on a helicopter at LaGuardia to go to JFK but the thing stopped on top of the Pan Am building to pick up some others and I thought I was going to miss my second flight in two days.

Anyway, I finally got it. That was a bit of an aside to that weekend, and it left me pretty frustrated, but I did get a third place and some prize money.

Back in England, they started to put together the team. A deal had been done with Ford to use its new turbo engine when it was ready. The chassis was being built by a new entity known as FORCE (Formula One Race Car Engineering), which was created for this purpose, and ran as Lolas even though Lola had nothing to do with it. Key staff were coming on board too. Teddy Mayer, or the Weiner as James Hunt and I used to call him, was a former owner of McLaren and a big deal in the States, and he bought into the operation, which he would run. We got Neil Oatley on board and Ross Brawn as well, and anyone familiar with Formula One today will know those names.

All the ingredients were being beautifully sourced. It was now just a challenge to see if it could all be put together properly. Our first race was at Monza in September 1985, with Hart engines instead of the promised Ford V6, since that wasn't ready yet.

You could probably have argued that the Hart wasn't either. A couple of back runners were using it too, but it was nowhere. It was a 1.5 litre inline four which was theoretically the same configuration as the BMW, and its only real claim to fame was Senna's second place at Monaco in 1984. I used to call it the hand-grenade engine, because it would always blow up. It was a boy trying to do a man's job. It was basically a Formula Two engine that had been stretched – it was over-stressed. Mind you, when it was running it was better than the Ford when it finally arrived.

At Monza I qualified 24th out of 26 and managed six laps before the Hart engine died with some sort of distributor issue. I wasn't allowed to run in Belgium because of some stupid rule – the race weekend had started earlier in the year but the track fell to bits and the race was rescheduled. They said only the teams that were entered in that first meeting could run, so we had to twiddle our thumbs and wait for Brands Hatch, where this time I got 13 laps done before the engine suffered from terminal overheating.

South Africa was an awkward weekend. Renault and Ligier were encouraged by the French government not to race there as a protest at apartheid, and other teams tried to get the race cancelled, but it was going ahead regardless. So we fronted up there to race. All around the world the politics around South Africa was getting interesting.

Beatrice was a huge company that not many people knew much about. I think they were trying to raise awareness that it did more than just ice cream, which is how it began operations a century earlier. In my time there it had brands like Danone yoghurt, Krispy Kreme doughnuts, Tropicana orange juice and even businesses like Avis hire cars, and it was privately held. They also had manufacturing and operations in South Africa – which you could do when you weren't on the stock market – so when we went there it was a big deal for them.

During the Friday I was summoned to see Bernie Ecclestone in his penthouse. Not sure what I had done this time, I fronted up. As I went in the door Bernie said, 'How do you feel?' Standard greeting, although he had a look in his eye, I gave him a standard reply, 'Pretty good, thanks.'

'What do you think your chances are of winning the race tomorrow?' he asked.

Again, I felt no need to be subtle: 'Bernie, I think you know the answer to that question. If I start now, probably pretty good.'

'Well, I've got a bit of an idea. If you pull up sick and can't run again this weekend, we'll give you first-place prize money. Go home and visit Australia.'

The background was that US civil rights activist Jesse Jackson had said that if a Beatrice car raced in South Africa he was going to get all of the black workers – thousands of them – at Beatrice around the US to go on strike. Beatrice couldn't be seen to be backing down to an individual like him, but if they didn't back down there was a chance of the strike.

So Bernie came up with an idea. 'If the driver falls crook and can't drive, then the Beatrice car doesn't race. It's a force majeure. Jesse Jackson can't get on his soapbox and say, "I forced that company to withdraw," and he also couldn't call a strike because the car didn't race.'

The idea was that I would wait until Saturday morning when everyone went to the circuit. I would quietly check out, and jump on a plane to Harare to get home (because Qantas wouldn't fly to South Africa).

This could not afford to leak at all. I'm pretty sure only Teddy and Carl knew from inside the team. I could not tell the mechanics or anybody.

And so, on the Saturday morning I was gone. I just didn't turn up. They had the car out ready to go, when they were told, 'AJ's been struck down by a virus and we are not racing.'

I made a miraculous recovery for the Australian Grand Prix, which was just as well. Bernie allowed me to drive the first lap of the track in a Formula One car before the 10am practice on Friday, which was a pretty special thing to do on what was also my birthday. This pissed off Ken Tyrrell who thought we were being given an unfair advantage. I wish sometimes he paid a little more attention, one lap wasn't going to help us at all . . . nothing was that weekend. That said, I did the lap, to the cheers of the fans – this was a big moment for Australian motor racing.

We had a troubled run all weekend with engine and turbo problems, but I managed to qualify in 19th. I stalled at the start and was last after the first lap, but I turned the boost up to at least put on a show. No matter what boost I was using it was going to break, so why not have some fun. I was up to sixth on lap 20 when the electrics shut down.

The Australian race, however, was a huge success and set a whole pile of new standards for the running of a grand prix. Firstly it was a great track for a street circuit and that made it good for the drivers, it just seemed to flow even though there was a series of 90 degree turns. On top of that, it was the final race of the season it always had a great atmosphere among the teams, some of whom had already shut down. I'd like to think I played a small part in getting enough inspiration in Australia to get the race up, but I had nothing to do with how well they did it. I was a pretty proud Australian that weekend. Bernie Ecclestone announced at a press conference that the standard of organisation was bad news for Formula One. Registering the dismay on everyone's faces, he added the kicker: now everyone else would have to match such a high standard. Typical Bernie.

Carl warned me not to expect to spend Christmas in Australia, since he was hoping to start testing the Ford engine. I spent my Christmas in Australia with no sign of the first engines, and that let me know what 1986 was going to be like.

Patrick Tambay was my new teammate for the season and I am sure he was wondering where his career was headed. In 1984 he was with Ferrari and in 1985 he was a factory driver for Renault, now he was here living the great American dream with Haas.

To start the season we both had retirements in Brazil, and in Spain for the second round Patrick managed to get a car home for the team's first finish. Eighth place and six laps down. I had a first-lap crash with Jonathan Palmer, so who knows what was possible that day; maybe I could have been five laps down.

Then I got the Ford engine. The much talked-about and well-hyped engine that was essentially a V6 Cosworth engine with Ford electronics. I knew there would be a settling-in phase, especially given we didn't have enough engines to fit Patrick out yet. So I got to run it and I was more than two seconds a lap slower than Patrick. On the bright side it may have been more reliable, since I got 28 laps before overheating while Patrick got just five with the Hart.

At Monaco, which was next, I was sixth fastest in Thursday practice – Friday's a lay day for Formula One there – and they're all going around saying, 'Oh, yeah, now it's showing its true colours.' I kept silent, but I thought they were kidding themselves. Sure enough I dropped back to 18th in qualifying and then crashed out on the second lap, but at least we qualified.

I was classified as a finisher in Belgium, but I didn't see the chequered flag after running out of fuel on the last lap. In Canada, Patrick was injured in a warm-up crash when the suspension failed. We were continuing our trend of nailing it with one car while the other struggled. I qualified in 13th and drove into 10th only three laps down.

Patrick had to miss the next two races and I got Eddie Cheever as a teammate for one of them, but we failed to finish in both of them, and the next as well. Adrian Newey had now joined the team as well, but there was no great turnaround. The cars were slow and unreliable, so even when we did finish we were laps down.

Into the Hungarian Grand Prix we started to see something positive. Both of us qualified inside the top 10 and Patrick finished seventh, two laps down, high up the order because of the attrition rate. I wish I could tell you more about these races, but I have really tried to forget them.

It was the same again with my memory of Austria, where we got our first points with me fourth and Patrick fifth, again two laps down on the leader, in what commentator Murray Walker called a race of attrition. We didn't get points through speed, but strangely through reliability.

I got another point at Monza in Italy, but I was really worried about where we were headed. I think it was in Hungary that a rule change was announced for 1989 that turbo-charged engines would be banned, and that meant only two more seasons with the Ford TEC engine from Cosworth. They shut up shop on development. Qualifying 18th and scrounging around for a point is not my idea of fun.

This season was now well and truly in brown-paper-bag territory, I'm afraid. We were going nowhere. I love the way from the outside people wanted to give me advice, and I'd listen and nod and then walk away with the money and buy a farm, or a plane, because nothing I could do would change anything. I bought Carl's Mitsubishi MU2 plane, which we used to call

The Widowmaker. It was a turbo prop, but it didn't have any aileron, just spoilers, and very narrow little wings. It was bloody quick.

The guy that was flying it for me was named Jeremy, who later became Frank Williams' permanent pilot (Frank at this stage had become a quadriplegic after his car crash in France early in 1986). Having the plane and Jeremy made life a little bit easier, we had a bit of a standing joke that we'd like to be back at my favourite Chinese restaurant in Chiswick before it closed on a Sunday. Jeremy used to get sandwiches and beer in the plane, we'd park it at the closest airport to the circuit, which we could do because this thing had a very short take-off and landing capability. I didn't hang around long after a race.

In Portugal I was fed up with the team, the car, everything. It was huffing and puffing and banging and farting – and going about 20ks slower down the straight than anybody else.

I said to Jeremy, 'Get it ready, mate. Get the sandwiches, get the grog, because we're going to be leaving early.' He said, 'How do you know?' I said, 'Because I'm going to throw it in the sandpit,' which I did. I made sure it was in the sandpit right behind the pits, so all I had to do was jump over the fence and go to the motorhome and get changed, and we're in the plane and on our way home and an hour or so later I made the Chinese restaurant again. I'm not particularly proud of that, and it's the only time I ever did anything like that, but that's the way it was.

Even in testing I gave it my all, so this was the writing on the wall for me. If I was that uninspired we were in trouble.

The reasons I came back to Formula One were quite clear to me. First it was the attraction of Adelaide and the Australian

Grand Prix. Also, this team looked to have it all. I was told the Ford motor company had this great new engine and we had the works deal for it. We had Goodyear tyres and we had plenty of money.

So I come back to my cooking analogy. We had all the right ingredients, but when the chef put it into the oven it was either undercooked or overcooked and it tasted awful. The engine was at the root of all the problems. The Hart was so unreliable it was a waste of space. The Ford wouldn't pull the skin off a rice pudding.

The Americans from Ford just couldn't get their head around the electronics. They'd play around with it and you could either drive it out of the pits beautifully and it wouldn't go on the track, or it would blup-blup-blup out of the pits and it would be OK on the tracks. It was just hopeless.

I had two races to get through and then it would be all over for me in Adelaide. This team was just a joke. I got paid extremely well and that compensated for any disappointment I might have had, but worse for me was the loss of my motivation.

In my whole time in Formula One the only place I had really been happy was Williams. Shadow was OK, they were nice people to work with, but it was a struggle on the money side of it. I had enjoyed working with Carl in the Can-Am Series and I had hoped this was going to be the same, but it just wasn't.

I got only 16 laps done in Australia and Patrick got 70. Beatrice pulled out of the team and shortly after the end of the season Carl shut up shop and sold the assets of the team. That was the last race for Team Haas (USA) in Formula One, and for Patrick and me too.

At the age of 40, I had run in 117 grands prix and had 12 wins (or 13 if you count that one in Spain). There were pole positions, fastest laps, a World Championship and mates both alive and dead. Yes, there could have been more wins and more titles, but mostly I raced without regrets in my career; my decisions on the whole were right for me at the time.

The way it ended this time there was going to be no itch to scratch, just a wound to heal. Formula One, for me, was over.

Carl Haas

Carl is the second-best bloke I ever drove for. Like Frank Williams, he realised that you were the driver and he took notice of what you wanted, within reason. He was very easy to get along with, and gave you the best equipment – or at least tried to – and the best mechanics. As a driver, that's all you can ask for.

He's a funny bugger too. He used to come up and bless the car when it was on the grid. He had the cigar sticking out of his mouth, not lit, and he'd touch all the suspension bits, blessing them. I'll tell you, you can take the piss out of it, but they rarely broke in the Can-Am days. I remember going to the Long Beach Grand Prix and I actually went out of my way to get him to come up and touch the car for me. Who knows, maybe there was something in America that he has, some divine right he had only there. It didn't seem to work on the Beatrice, but that was rarely in the US.

I first met him when I was driving for Shadow and after I won in Austria I started doing Can-Am for them. Patrick Tampax – Tambay – was driving the Carl Haas Lola T332 or whatever it was. At Riverside in my second outing in the Shadow, I put it on the front row beside Patrick. I think I led for a while, the bodywork scraping and everything, and most people knew that it shouldn't have been there in the lead.

I knew Patrick from doing a few other bits and pieces in Europe, so I went up to the motorhome, I was having some sandwiches with him and I said, 'Patrick, another C&C, eh?' They all looked up. I said, 'Cruise and collect,' and I said it loud enough for a reason.

When Patrick left Carl to do McLaren in 1978, Carl offered me the drive. I hadn't signed a deal with Frank at the time and really only had Shadow as a firm offer, so I signed up and did a year of C&C with him. When I eventually signed with Frank I told him about the deal, and he was OK so long as I could manage it.

At the first race meeting in the car, the president of First National City, the chief sponsor, was there, and he was doing the barbecuing. Typical American, you could hear him from the other side of the river. He said, 'Where are you from, boy?' I said, 'London.'

'Oh, London, Ontario.'

'No, London, England.'

'Oh, my, God, how do you manage that?'

'Well, it's a bit of a hassle. It means I've got to fly over here and do a Can-Am race and I've got to fly back and do a grand prix.'

'Why don't you take Concorde?'

I had to explain to him I couldn't afford that yet and he got on to Carl. 'Hey, Carl, we got to get this boy on Concorde.' Carl said, 'Well, you pay for it, and we'll do it no dramas.'

Of course, being a barbecue with 100 people around, 'Yeah, whack this boy on Concorde.'

From that time on, I used to fly Concorde backwards and forwards. The Concorde lounge at Heathrow used to open up about an hour-and-a-half before departure. It was like the opening of a Myer sale, I'd be at the doors ready to go. They had three phones and you could phone anywhere in the world and they had all these little canapés full of caviar, which I love. I'd be on the starting blocks and as soon as the doors opened, whoosh, I was in. The flight itself was only three-and-a-half hours and then I'd get a connection to wherever, and then on Monday morning I'd fly back and get a connection home. It really did help a lot.

The Can-Am thing was quite small. We had Jim Hall, who was a very well-known engineer and designer in the States, Carl and Bernie, his wife, and the three mechanics. They had a nice transporter and the car was always immaculate and had very good engines, obviously, and we got the job done.

Like Frank, Carl was able to come to grips with the fact that his racing career was over. But he had knowledge, he knew what to do and he understood the driver and his role. We got the job done and I enjoyed my time with him then. I wasn't so happy with the Beatrice thing, but it didn't change my relationship with him.

Bernie Ecclestone

Bernie is a terrific bloke. He has a wonderful sense of humour, which is probably not apparent to the public. I like spending time with him.

He is a man of his word too, which I admire. If Bernie shakes your hand, that's it, it's binding, and he expects it to be the other way around as well. Which is good for me since that is the way I like the world to run.

There's some great stories about Bernie, and as far as I can tell they are all true. I went to a function in Melbourne with Amanda and she said to him, pity the grand prix is on such and such a date, it clashes with something I've got to do in Queensland. Bernie said, 'I'll go change it for you. We'll change the date.' I think Amanda believed him for a little while, even though I was kicking her in the ankles. He was very convincing.

Not that changing a GP date was beyond him. For the first Hungarian Grand Prix, 1986, the country was still under Communist rule. When they had a date locked in some clowns over there saw an opportunity. They went out and booked all the hotel rooms of any note in Budapest, and then thought they'd charge a premium for each room and make a tidy little profit.

Bernie apparently found out about all of this, got his men to go to the hotels and say, 'We had a conference here last year, we were very happy with it, very happy. If possible we'd like to book the whole hotel out to such and such a date.' Which was a different week, and when he had all the hotels tied up he then changed the date of the Hungarian Grand Prix and left his communist mates with about a $150,000 bill for the rooms. He was very sharp in business, I'm not sure anyone could outdo him.

There's another famous story. We were in Brazil, down by the pool and it was one of the rare times I was poolside since we often had a couple of weeks to kill before the race. A lot of the drivers were seeing how far they could swim underwater. Bernie just quietly piped up and said, 'You're all bloody idiots, I could do three laps underwater easily.' Which was more than any of them.

I said, 'You're kidding, no way in the world.' He said, 'All right, I'll bet you $100 each.' As soon as he got the $100 from each of us in his hand, he said, 'Herbie, go and get the snorkel and flippers.' He was underwater, so we had to pay up. That's the way he thinks, he is so clear and so quick. He's a lateral thinker, that's for sure. He won the bet and said thank you.

He was terrific for the sport too – he turned it into the biggest regular sporting event on the planet. The Olympic Games come around every four years, World Cup soccer the same. Grands prix come every couple of weeks and have just as many people watching. An extraordinary achievement.

He's also the one that kept demanding that the promoters upgrade the facilities. Before that we used to operate out of a side-awning of the team truck. That wasn't good enough for him. He's been responsible for making Formula One what it is, and it will be interesting to see where it heads without him at the helm.

20

Racing After F1

I WANTED TO keep earning money after Formula One – I quite like the stuff. I lined up some TV work with the Nine Network doing special comments for its Formula One coverage, and I went racing in Japan.

Not long after I landed back in Australia I got a phone call from John Wickham. I knew John from my days fooling around with March and then from around the paddock with other Formula One teams in which he was involved. In 1987 he had taken up a position with TOM'S GB in the UK, which was like a division of Toyota that built the serious race cars.

Strangely, it was this arm of Toyota that was to run sportscars in the All Japan Sports Prototype Championship, and he wanted me to race for them. The thing that turned me on a bit there was that it's only a seven-hour flight from the Gold Coast or Brisbane and there's only a one-hour time difference, so there's no jet lag. There was plenty of yen involved too.

So I went up and did a deal with them to race the Toyota 87C, and for a couple of races in the TOM'S Toyota Supra in touring cars. The thing that I both love and hate about the Japanese is that they are always looking for something new and a way to innovate. But not all new ideas are good ideas . . .

I turned up for my first race with the team at Fuji and I was partnering Geoff Lees. I don't like sharing, but I do like yen. I looked at the car for the first time and the rear wing was down and forward, and I asked Geoff why the wing was there. 'Isn't it the same regs as Europe?' He said, 'Oh, AJ, don't go there. If you can get them to shift that wing, you're a better man than me.'

I went out and did some laps in the car and came in to chat with the engineer. 'Why is the wing there?'

'Designer,' was the one word response.

'Yeah, but why is it there?'

'Designer.'

'Hmm, okay.' I said, 'Can we try it up and back?'

Then, after much sucking through teeth and carrying on, which they're given to do, I said, 'I'll tell you what. I'll pay for the bracket.' Of course, that was it, as soon as you might be seen to lose face they would burst into action. 'Put the wing at the furthest point back that we're allowed and the highest point up that we're allowed. If it's no quicker, or I don't like it, you'll never hear me utter a word about the rear wing again.'

Anyway, TOM'S made an aluminium wing stay and we were instantly quicker by some margin, and about nine times more comfortable to drive. The wing stayed in that position, for the domestic championship.

I finished third with Geoff at that first round, but we knew we had some work to do if we were going to beat the Porsches, even if they weren't Brothers Kremer cars. We were a minute behind second after 500 kilometres, so that wasn't too bad for a first race in a new car. A few weeks later we blitzed the field at Fuji and won a 1000-kilometre race by five laps from a Porsche spearheaded by Vern Schuppan. I still had Geoff with me for that race, but we also had Masanori Sekiya with us, which was good because it meant less work for me.

We also went to Le Mans for me to do what I said I would never do again – funny how money can make me do silly things. I started the car and before the first pitstop it ran out of fuel on the track and that was it . . . shower, change and out of there. We were more than 12 seconds off the top qualifying pace there, and qualified 14th, so we knew we had some work to do if we were going to match the best in the world when it came to hitting 420km/h. We didn't.

Back in Japan we had trouble at the next Fuji race, which strangely was a 500-mile affair, and didn't do enough laps to be classified. I missed the next race and the final race of the domestic series, but ran the World Sports Prototype Championship round at Fuji in October. I was given the heads-up before I arrived: 'We have a special lightweight car for this.' I gave them all the right words of encouragement because they knew as well as I did that we were racing against Jaguars and Porsches that made us look silly at Le Mans, but then we also knew Fuji was a different story.

So I front up to Fuji and look at my lightweight racer and guess where the rear wing was? Down and forward. I said, 'Why?' 'Lightweight car.' I know this sounds incredible to believe. I used to come back and tell stories and people would say, 'Oh, Alan, that's impossible. These are the people that make Sony and everything.' But it was true.

I said, 'Now hang on, it's a lightweight car, but the aerodynamics . . .' I mean, I couldn't believe it. I'm not all that clever in any of this, but I just know that if the regulations allow you to take advantage of something, you do it. 'Can you put the brackets on, please, and put it back where we had it before.' 'Hmm.' Sucking through teeth, looking at each other. 'The bracket's back in Tokyo.' I said, 'Right. Well you'd better get somebody to go and get it, because I'm not driving, unless it's on.' I'm sure most of the guys in that team hated me, but I wasn't going to make a fool of myself for them.

TOM'S duly went and got the brackets, and we led that race for a while after qualifying second, in front of all the works Porsches and Jaguars. Just before half distance we had electrical issues from something in the wiring loom. Carrying on the conversation from the start of the weekend, I told them they would need another gaijin for the next season, because I wasn't going to do it. I put up with Surtees and his shit because it was Formula One, and I even walked away from that. This didn't really matter that much to me and I didn't need the aggravation.

But you don't give them the arse, they give you the arse. Loss of face. They said, 'You want more money.' I said, 'No, I don't. I'd have to give half to a psychiatrist anyway.' 'You want a psychiatrist?' I said, 'No. See, this is what I mean? This is why I want to leave.'

Anyway, guess what? Next morning I turn up, there's a sport psychiatrist there. I went, 'Geez, this is ridiculous.' I did the race, and at the end of that stint, I just said, 'No. I'm out of here.' I couldn't stand it. You'd go to a debrief. There'd be 130 of them in a garage, all smoking. It was freezing cold outside, so they'd all have parkas on. Then you'd get the report from one of the 130 and it would take 10 minutes to say how he's going to get down on his left knee and use his index finger and thumb to undo the valve cap. Like, who gives a fuck? You just wasted 10 minutes on explaining how he's going to do the valve cap. Please, just say, 'Matsu, you're going to do the valve cap.' That's it.

In the end it was driving me nuts, I had to say, 'I'll be wherever, hopefully a warm motorhome, if you want my input or you want to just come and get me.' That sort of ended my career with TOM'S.

What a nightmare. There were so many little things that I thought were holding them back. The lightweight car had a gull-wing door. I lifted up the gull-wing door to stand on the sill to hop in, as you do, and my foot's gone straight through the sill. Light fucking weight? It was tissue paper. It's gone straight through.

'Oh, very big problem.'

We used to take the piss out of them, literally. You'd go to Fuji and you'd go to Suzuka and everything would be different. Go to Fuji, you'd have to stand on your right foot, with your left foot bent up with both hands over your eyes for five seconds before you got in the car, because that was what you did at Fuji. Then you had to do a urine test to check everything was OK, and then you had to grip something to prove to them that you've got power in your hands. That was just basically showing, I suppose, you could hang on to the steering wheel.

Then you go to Suzuka, and it'd be the left foot. We used to say, 'Ah, Fuji, left foot circuit.' For our urine test, we used to go into the toilet and all the gaijins, Geoff Lees and all the boys, we'd swap our piss and see if they worked it out.

Vern had a T-shirt made. They have these things on the back of their cars, particularly the touring cars. 'We are friends joining hands over the bridge of freedom,' or stuff along those lines. So Vern had this white T-shirt made with a red circle and all these teeth, saying 'We are friends . . . We are across the water to be on the boat with you.' We read it and would say, 'Fuck, what is that?' They were rapt though, they wanted to buy them.

You talk to anyone that raced there or for the Japanese you get the same stories. They're excellent at building things, but no good for instant decisions: they'll go to a board room with a hundred people and take four days to make a decision. The old gaijins will make a snap decision, say, 'Right, that's it, boys. Let's get on with it. Let's do it.'

It didn't suit me and the way I liked to operate.

That said, the Supra was actually quite a nice car and because it was a touring car there were enough restrictions to not have the same issues as the sports prototype. I co-drove with Eje Elgh at Sugo and Geoff was running in another car with Kauro Hoshino. Sugo is a lovely circuit, on the northern island of Japan, nice big sweeping corners that suited me. We started on the front row and won the race from a BMW.

The internal politics were interesting. There was TRD and TOM'S, and while both cars were entered under the TOM'S banner, Eje and I actually raced the TRD-prepared car. When we beat the TOM'S car, which didn't even finish, you'd reckon a Nissan had won by the level of drama. Anyway, we won and that was it.

We ran the next round of the Japanese touring cars at Suzuka, the Super Final as they called it. We finished sixth there and just couldn't repeat the speed we had at Sugo. There was one final outing for me in that car, which was at Macau, and that was a very different story to the tracks in Japan. The Supra had such a long wheelbase I thought I was going to have to do a three-point turn at Melco.

Because the race was just a week after the final round of the World Touring Car Championship in Japan, all the big guns from Schnitzer BMW and the like were there, and that is a track that was great for those little M3s. The old Supra wasn't the best car for that track, but I had fun until the turbo let go.

With Toyota done, I still wanted to keep my bum in a car. I still wanted to be waiting for the light or the flag to drop and racing. Then being able to come home on Monday. Whatever I did also had to work with the TV commentary I was doing with Nine, which meant my only real option was touring car racing in Australia.

Now touring cars are pretty much the exact opposite of Formula One or sports prototypes. Those have been built specifically to do a job while the touring car has been altered to do a similar job. One is a thoroughbred race horse and the other is a draft horse. You can still ride them, but it's just a little different.

The sensations are different and to me not as enjoyable, but when you are racing you almost forget the compromises in the machinery because it is all about the bloke next to you. You're waiting for the lights to change, whizzing off the grid and you're racing. You've got people around you and you're racing them and when you win it's very satisfying, no matter what car you're in.

Or even what sort of vehicle, in fact. I won a celebrity lawn-mower race in the Czech Republic when we went there with the A1s. It was a big slalom course on a tarmac and I won a bloody big ride-on lawn mower, which I donated to charity. Anyway, I still enjoyed riding it and I was over the moon because I'd won.

I didn't have much lined up for 1988, but I had resigned myself to the fact that I was going to have to race touring cars if I wanted to keep racing. It was the only thing in Australia where there was any money, and I was done with the international thing.

I drove a Ford Sierra with Colin Bond in the Asia-Pacific Touring Car Championship late in the year where we finished second overall, even though we didn't run at Fuji along with most of the rest of the Australian teams. The other three rounds were Bathurst, Wellington and Pukekohe.

When we talk about compromised race cars being modified for a task, the Sierra was a perfect example. It was under-tyred and over-powered, which is fine in itself, because everyone else in a Sierra was in the same boat and that was the car to have. Strangely it proved OK on some tight tracks, I got pole at Amaroo in 1990 with one, so while you could keep the tyres going it was fine everywhere.

The tracks we did race on that year were an interesting mix . . . Bathurst is long and fast and the bit over the top is quite challenging – you needed power and Colin's Sierra had plenty of that. Wellington was a street race, so it had all those close walls and the like, and the weather was just something else. I remember being bloody cold in Wellington, and having my overalls on while lying down inside a sleeping bag in a caravan just to warm up.

This was at the circuit and I was just freezing and thinking how can anyone live here?

The last race for us was at Pukekohe, a challenging and fast track. There was a bump in the first corner, which was interesting in one of those things. I don't mind bumps actually, it gives tracks a bit of character and leaves a bit more to the driver. There was also a good bump at turn 1 at Lakeside, a terrible bump right through it that you had to be wary of when you went through there in a touring car. I won a round there with Dick Johnson right up my backside, and that bump would unsettle that car every time and if you were going flat out you only just had enough time to settle it for the right-hander straight after it. When you are being pushed, you had to be especially careful.

We also did Sandown for the 500 which was a traditional lead-in to Bathurst, but this wasn't part of any Championship. I was meant to drive there with Colin, but we split a bore in the engine during the warm-up and we retired that car before the start. To get laps in, I was then moved into the team's other car, but it didn't last long enough for me to get a steer.

At Bathurst we had good speed, but then Tom Walkinshaw protested all the Australian-built Sierras, ours included, and we had to pull the car and engine to bits for the protest. After pulling apart the good engine, we were forced to run the spare and that was noticeably down on power, Bondy reckoned at the time it was 50 horsepower less than the engine we wanted to race. The others cars were similarly hampered, so Tom got his way in a very distasteful manner. Tony Longhurst went on to win the race and we finished in third. We were disqualified a month later and then reinstated a month further down the track.

We backed up that podium with a fourth at Wellington and then we had a retirement at Pukekohe after qualifying in third. The points system in use was what they called a Double Can-Am, which meant you got points for where you finished in your class as well as the race, and that meant we ended up losing the Championship to a class car.

The next year I joined the Benson & Hedges Racing team for the endurance races and then turned that into a full-time drive for 1990. At Sandown and Bathurst I was to drive the team's second car with Denny Hulme, but at Bathurst Tony Longhurst joined us after his car expired early in the race. In those days with cross-entering, you could actually race in two cars during the same race. Brock got two of his wins there that way.

The team was really Tony's even though Frank Gardner was there and running it. I'll tell you this for nothing, and I know Frank is dead now, but there are few people in this world that are as fantastic self-promoters as Frank was. He was great for the one-liners and the jokes and all that sort of stuff, and he was quite a cunning businessman. He always made sure he was at the right place at the right time. He knew where his bread was buttered. If you had, for instance, a Tony Longhurst alongside you with a wallet the size of his father's, or Paul Morris with Terry beside him, you knew who was going to get looked after the best. Frank knew that is where his future lay more than Alan Jones who was just there collecting money.

It was a well-structured team and it had, I believe, pretty good sponsorship from Benson & Hedges. Frank was very good at getting on with the right people, a bit like Graham Hill. He had a great relationship with Ron Meatchem at BMW, which saw Ron in our pits on a regular basis even though we were running Fords, but Frank had a plan there.

Tony was good fun. I quite enjoyed his company and enjoyed driving in the team with him. As a teammate, he was bloody quick: I knew if I was outpacing him I was doing well. He was probably a little mad too.

In my Formula One days I didn't have much to do with my teammates, I was there to do a job and that was it. Touring car racing was a little different for me; it mattered, but not to the same degree. I'd go out to dinner with Tony; I don't remember doing that with Carlos or Clay except when I had to.

I started out my Australian Touring Car Championship career with a pole at the most unlikely of venues for that car, Amaroo Park Raceway, which was little more than a go-kart track. My old Azusa kart would have been better suited to that track. I didn't really enjoy it – it was all stop, start, and a goat track with a little hill, built among rocks out the back of Dural in the north of Sydney. It is a luxury housing estate now.

I got eighth overall in my first outing and was steady for the next few rounds. I got my first podium in the series at Winton, another track that wasn't much fun. Our cars had plenty of power, perhaps more than anyone else, so we generally qualified well before struggling to keep the rear tyres alive during the races.

I missed Lakeside and then had two retirements in the final three rounds, which reminded me of the Beatrice days. Although I didn't go into a race wondering which lap it would break, there was a chance we'd do the distance, but we did go in knowing the tyres would go off.

I think in many ways the endurance races of 1990 were a write-off because it was already decided we were racing BMWs in 1991, which I was quite looking forward to. Both the team cars failed to finish at Bathurst, which is what happens when you stop stocking the shelves with the latest bits. I did get my first run in the Top 10 Shootout, which is a single qualifying lap for each of the drivers who qualified in the Top 10. I didn't mind the Shootout. I liked the build-up and the fact that you couldn't make a mistake. If you gamble a bit and lock a wheel or put a wheel on the dirt and lose one or two-tenths you might be buggered, but if it comes off you could be on pole. You've got to try for the perfect lap, of which there's no such thing . . . so you are really just trying to get as close to that as possible.

I was pretty sure my car was the one getting the lesser equipment. It wasn't as fast as Tony's but that was OK, he was putting up the money and I knew where we were headed and I felt that was going to be a much more enjoyable place for me. I would enjoy my money a lot more if I was enjoying the racing too, not that I was getting that much really, but it was OK.

The compromises bothered me though. With the Sierra, you could melt your rear tyres in a lap or two if you weren't gentle enough with the throttle, so a lot of the time you were not racing at all, rather you were just hanging in to finish, after racing for just a few laps at the start. The BMW M3 promised a very different experience; while we were not going to have the power of the Sierras, we were going to have a car that handled really well, had great brakes and wasn't going to melt rubber every time you powered out of a corner. I was very much looking forward to 1991.

I was quite comfortable in the team despite the presence of Frank, and that was good for me at that stage of my career and life. In some ways that was more important than the equipment I was getting. I wanted to be comfortable in my surrounds and friendly with the people I was with. I took that very much into account.

The BMWs were ex-Schnitzer and were left with us after the Wellington street race in New Zealand. They were upgraded to the latest spec with slightly bigger engines and revised aero. It was a lot more forgiving and a bit like the GTV Alfa. You could go to somewhere like Lakeside that really required handling and just wait for their tyres to start going off a little bit on the Sierras. Then the little BM would start chewing at them.

But things were changing in Group A: the Sierra was no longer the car to have, the weapon of choice was now the Nissan GT-R – or Godzilla as it was dubbed by local journalist Mike Jacobson. This car was built to the very edge of the rules: turbo, four-wheel-drive . . . everything you wanted or needed to dominate . . . and they did. I didn't have a clue how it even worked, but I appreciated the fact that the Nissan had a major advantage over everybody else. That's the car you wanted to be in, particularly in the wet, but I think we had the next best thing.

As the season went on, it was clear they were going to win and for the rest it was a different battle. We won the non-Nissan battle. The format for the season didn't suit us as much as one longer race, so we had I think three races a weekend where points were collected and they were added up to determine a winner.

Gentleman Jim Richards won four of the first five rounds from his teammate Mark Skaife, who won the other one. 'Gentleman Jim' – what a load of shit that is. He's far from a bloody gentleman, let me tell you. He's certainly not a gentleman on the track. Tony was the first guy to beat them all season in round 6 at the Amaroo Park goat track, and then he won again at Lakeside. He was the only round winner for the year that wasn't Richards or Skaife. He also finished as the first of the non-Nissans three times.

I did that in the final round, with a satisfying second at Oran Park. Skaife won that day and Richards had a DNF, which he knew he could afford and still win the title with a silly drop-your-worst-round point system. Skaife actually got more points than Richards over the season but finished second when the points were adjusted. Tony was third in the series and I was fourth, although when I dropped my worst score I was on the same points as Glenn Seton.

The Sandown 500 had a slimmed-down field and I finished second there with Peter Fitzgerald, again to a Nissan GT-R, but not Skaife or Richards, just to prove how good the car was. The main team didn't even front up, so Mark Gibbs and Rohan Onslow were there to win by six laps. 'Who?' I hear you ask. And that is my point: it was a great race car.

At Bathurst it was decided to pair Tony and me – and our car broke. The car was terrific across the top and down through the chase, but on the big long straights we were just eaten alive, and we needed everything to go our way to have a chance. We were running as high as third in the early stages and we were on target for a really good result when I got a puncture going up Mountain Straight. I had to limp around almost an entire lap with the tyre shredding itself, which caused a bit of damage to the body-work and the suspension. We lost ground, fought our way back to fourth – then the car shut down on me and that was it with

25 laps to run. The team's other car came home fourth and maybe we could have finished second, but that's motor racing.

We did the New Zealand races again and Tony was leading at half distance in the car I was sharing with him at the Wellington 500 when he got clipped by John Sax, who he was lapping. The car hit two walls and the second hit was so hard Tony cracked his helmet on the concrete wall. It was a pretty scary incident, and Tony was theoretically OK, but many think he was never the same driver after that.

The next season, 1992, I switched camps after the championship and drove for Glenn Seton Racing in the endurance races, which was more about looking into the 1993 season given Group A was getting the boot and a new formula for V8 Holdens and Fords was coming in. Aside from the fact that Paul Morris was now nosing into the BMW team with pocket loads of cash, I felt Seton was better prepared for the new era and that all made sense.

The 1992 championship itself was not that much fun. CAMS had lumped both our cars and the Nissans with extra weight to slow us down, and it killed us. The Nissans dominated the series again, but the Sierras and Commodores were closer. Lakeside was again our best weekend with Tony first and me third, and aside from another podium for me at Oran Park, that was pretty much it for season highlights.

During Easter they ran the second ever Bathurst 12-Hour race for production cars. BMW entered an M5 for Tony, Neville Crichton and me and we came home second behind a Mazda RX-7. The M5 was such an easy car to drive there, I think I turned the radio on at one stage. It felt even better because I was no longer enjoying the other part of my racing.

Joining Glenn's team was such a good move for me. Both his dad, Bo, and he were terrific to work with. The whole team was really nice and even Ken Potter and Kerrie Godfrey from Philip Morris, who was sponsoring the team with the Peter Jackson brand, were great. They all put on a really professional show.

Mike Raymond, who was a little more than just a commentator at Seven, helped me get that drive. I think he suggested to them that I would be a good bloke to come and join them. I was talking to him on a plane on the way back from Perth and I think I'd probably had enough of Frank at that stage and let it be known. Getting right back to the start of this book, it's called working the paddock, only this time I was working the plane. Then we teed up a meeting and I ended up with Glenn.

All the bloody fans were horrified that I was switching cars, especially mid-season. But I was attuned to Europe, where it didn't matter at all. Many of the race fans were really not that bright when it came to this sort of thing. I didn't care what they thought – as I have made clear, I went racing for myself. Fortune was planned; fame was a side effect.

Glenn's team was a good set-up. For Glenn's sake, there is no doubt it would have been easier to have it run by someone other than himself, but it wasn't and it made no difference to me. I was given a good car and a great place to go racing from. He is genuinely a nice man, Glenn. How he got on with me I don't know.

For my first race with the new team we ran the 1993 Spec Falcon rather than the Sierra, which we could also have run, but Glenn was keen to get as many laps in the car as possible before the next season began. We were allowed to run these cars – which a few years later were rebranded as V8 Supercars – in the endurance races. So we raced the Falcon at Sandown and Bathurst. Looking to the future was what attracted me there in the first place, so I thought this was good.

We had retirements in both races, but the potential was clear. At Bathurst Glenn was the fastest qualifier in a 93 car and there were a few running them. We made it just past half distance of the full-length race, but this is the 92 Bathurst where the big storm hit and most of the field, including the eventual winners, Jim Richards and Mark Skaife, ended up crashed into a wall or buried in a sand trap. The crowd was incensed that a crashed Nissan could win, and they gave it to Jim, who lashed back with the famous 'you're all a pack of arseholes' line.

The 1993 season was structured in an interesting way. After qualifying there was a thing called the Peter Jackson Dash, where we pulled our starting positions out of a hat and then raced to decide the first three rows of the grid. Then we had the 2-litre cars race, then the 5-litre cars and then a big race for all of us, and the way the points worked was so complex I didn't bother trying to work it out. I just went racing.

Amaroo Park was the season-opener, and Tony was still allowed to run his M3s during the season so I thought they had the box seat. I was wrong. The new cars dominated, and by that I mean both Falcons and Commodores. Glenn had a good weekend and mine was OK. At Symmons Plains my car was really good and I won both my heat and the final and had enough points to be the overall winner for the weekend.

I won't say it was like winning my first grand prix, because it wasn't, but it was very satisfying to finally win in a touring car in Australia. Again, the Holdens were up the front of the field and the first six spots for the weekend were evenly spread. Glenn won the next round at Phillip Island and I didn't even make the Dash, but the Falcons were pretty good here and I raced into second place in the final race and had third overall, so this was the first time Glenn and I were on the podium together.

After Phillip Island I went back to Bathurst for the 12-Hour race, this time in a works Mazda RX-7 with Garry Waldon. Allan Horsley at Mazda had put together the team as he did the previous year. He also worked on the homologation for the car and made sure it was a potential winner. He did an excellent job running them. The bloody race started at four or five in the morning and by the end of the twelve hours I had my first Bathurst win. Unfortunately it isn't the one the race fans in Australia covet, but it was a win. Charlie O'Brien was in the team's other car with Gregg Hansford, and they finished second with a couple of laps less than us.

Back into touring cars and Lakeside was all mine, and I won the Dash (I drew pole out of the envelope and made my famous comment, 'I'd rather be lucky than good,' which hung around with me for a while) and the Final to get the win for the round. I could have won the heat as well, but I got out of shape over the bump leading into the second turn and that let Dick Johnson through. Then Glenn started his winning streak, I got a couple of podiums during that run of Glenn's but the Holdens were still there and Tony was back in the game after he reduced the weight of the M3.

So with Glenn winning the third, fifth, sixth and seventh round of the series and me winning at Symmons Plains and Lakeside in the second and fourth rounds, we won six rounds in a row. Now comes the politics. I had not really paid much attention, but there were little lobby groups and whingers all over the place.

The Holden teams had started complaining about our Falcons, saying we had some sort of advantage. They were better at this game than Glenn and Dick Johnson, who was leading the other competitive Falcon team. So what happened was if you spent enough time complaining instead of working on your car, you could get the rule-makers to help you out. They killed our car mid-season. We lost some of the front undertray and the Holdens were given some other little tricks to boost them.

The effect for us was immediate, we lost speed and we lost front downforce, which meant we started to work the front tyres too hard. The Holden teams eventually got on top of their changes and the pendulum swung the other way. Glenn put on just enough points to win the title and I was second, but no-one was listening to us about what they'd done to our cars. After Glenn's win at Mallala, no Falcon saw the podium again in the championship. That tells a story in itself.

Glenn did win the Sandown 500 after switching out of the car he was sharing with me, which broke early in the race, but that is not an aero track and we struggled overall for speed. Bathurst was different altogether, the first two rows of the grid were Holdens and we started from the third row alongside Dick. The only other Falcon in the top 10 was Paul Radisich in Dick's second car – otherwise it was all Holden and that is the way the race was run too.

Our car died on top of the mountain in the closing stages when we were running fifth, which was as good as we could have expected after what they did to us. Glenn was a great driver, but he wasn't a politician and he had been totally outmanoeuvred.

For the next season, 1994, both brands of car had new aero packages, and we were still a little off the pace but it was nowhere near as bad. We had these little vanes on the front splitter, and that had the Holden teams complaining again, but they had the better packages and dominated early.

I had a puncture at Amaroo to open the season and Sandown was OK but no-one in a Ford could touch the Holdens there. I was mid-field in Tasmania when I developed a misfire in the heat and that left me down the order for the main race.

The next race was the non-championship support race for the IndyCar Grand Prix on the Gold Coast. I was having a really good weekend, finishing second in the main race on the Saturday, and was then leading the Sunday sprint race until the closing laps. I clipped a wall with two laps left I think, and drove over the top of one of those stupid tyre bundles, where it got stuck and that was it. Darrel Eastlake was commentating that race, and as the cameras showed me walking back to the pits he said, 'That will be a terrible place to be when he gets back, let me tell you, he gets cranky.' He was right, but only because it was my fault.

We did OK in the wet at Phillip Island – I won the Dash after starting last, so I felt good for the race. The rain made it all a gamble. The first race was good, but then I slipped off the track in the second. This was kind of how this season was going for me, we struggled and then when we had a track that suited us, something went wrong.

I got caught up in a tangle between a few other drivers in the first race at Lakeside and then slipped off on some oil in the second. I led at Winton, Australia's Monaco, before I spun and handed the race and the round win to Glenn, but I was happy because we had found our speed. Eastern Creek wiped the smile from my face, as I just had no speed. Mallala we were no match for the Holdens, and that took us to Barbagallo Raceway in Perth.

I had a run-in with a bloke on the gate at Barbagallo, and maybe that revved me up enough to have a good weekend. I was running late on Saturday and this bloke wouldn't let me in the gate, I couldn't find my pass and that was it for him. Now I'm not shitcanning the volunteers at the track – most of them do a wonderful job, but you do get the odd weekend warrior who says to himself, 'Right, this is my moment of power . . . I don't give a damn who you are.' Or, even worse, 'I know who you are, and I know you've got to go racing, but you can't come in because you haven't got a pass.'

Who knows, maybe this bloke was a Holden fan. Anyway, the argument grew and because I'm an idiot, one thing led to another and I biffed him. I had to go before the stewards and I copped a whack for that, but I did end up winning the meeting, so maybe it was good for me to get fired up.

That would be my last round-win ever.

In the final of the season, I had a retirement in the first race and then charged into third in the final. That was a great race, I really enjoyed that. It was enough for me to finish fifth in the championship, which I thought was a pretty amazing result. Glenn and I were the only two Fords in there.

I was pretty philosophical about my racing at that time. It was always nice to win, but I wasn't going to go home and slash my wrists if something went wrong. I really just wanted to get paid and enjoy myself and take the good with the bad. In that sense Big Daz was wrong, but he was also right. I didn't like it when I made a mistake, and maybe Beatrice softened me up to retirements, but they didn't hurt the same.

Which was just as well because Sandown and Bathurst were both retirements for me. Sandown was with Glenn, and I think they were hedging their bets at Bathurst and split us over the two cars, and I drove with David Parsons. Both cars failed.

The next year, 1995, started OK when I won the Eastern Creek Triple Challenge in January with an old EB Falcon, but then a rough year started when the championship began with no points at Sandown in the updated EF Falcon. Out of the 10 rounds, I had two races with no points and only two third places to my name – the rest were somewhere in-between. Glenn had a good run in the other car and nearly won the championship, but there were issues starting to grow inside the team.

Glenn and his father Bo were arguing and it was affecting the team, and particularly my car. As things were bubbling away, the guys at Philip Morris were getting pissed off. At Sandown I ran to a retirement with Parsons, and then for Bathurst I was paired with Allan Grice.

My relationship with the Philip Morris people was really good, and the guys there offered me a bonus if I finished on the podium. Glenn had that race in his control and then the engine died with nine laps to go, and that gave us the famous footage of him and the talk he gave to the TV while sitting in the car, I really felt for him that day. We saw a lot about the character of Glenn Seton that day – the failure was ripping his heart but he still sat there in the car doing a TV interview. Bo was in tears in the pits.

I was a little bit pissed off at the team because I was actually leading at one stage and my brakes were starting to go. I was changing down early and probably, if anything, slightly over-revving it, going into the corners, using the engine as a brake. I didn't realise that, of all people, Larry Perkins was catching me at a great rate of knots. They weren't giving me that information. Before I knew what was going on in that final stint, he was right up my arse, out-braked me and went on to win. If they had told me what was going on I would have pushed a bit harder. I was a bit disappointed in that. I think they'd just forgotten they had a second car out there while Glenn was leading.

So I was in the car at the end and I was a second or two behind Larry when Glenn's car stopped. I couldn't catch him, even though I'd have dearly loved to remind him of the Formula Three race way back when by taking that race off him, I couldn't. Second was a great result, and I got my bonus.

After that weekend things began to change fast. The relationship issues between Glenn and Bo were having a big impact on the team and Philip Morris was looking at exiting the team. They approached me to see if I would be interested in running a team. I made it very clear that yes, I would be, but I didn't want to be seen to be pulling the rug from under Glenn. I would only do it if they were definitely not going to sponsor Glenn. They guaranteed me that was the case and we formed Pack Leader Racing.

I think Glenn knew what the deal was, so we didn't really have any issues. Since I was in charge of getting as much money as possible for the team, I went to talk with the CEO of Ford Australia, who offered me sweet FA, probably because of the way the media were portraying the set-up of the new team as shafting Glenn.

Everyone in Australia thinks I'm a Ford man – I'm not. It's just purely coincidental that every single team, with the exception of the BMWs, was either a Ford Sierra or a Ford Falcon. I always wanted to race a Holden, because I thought they were a better race car. They had a smaller frontal area and they always seemed to handle a bit better than the Falcon. So I was pretty pissed off with Ford for what I saw as a token amount. I was so pissed off that I went onto the grid at Bathurst wearing a Holden cap just to show them what I thought.

Regardless of Ford's effort, Philip Morris supplied enough money to set up a workshop and get all the equipment, transporter, engines, dyno . . . the whole deal. I then contacted Ross Stone, who always prepared a good car, and got him and his brother Jimmy on board to look after it all. I knew Jimmy because he was working as a fabricator at Norwell when I was with the BMWs. Notice I use that word, fabricator, because he was not an engineer.

I knew I wasn't mechanically minded enough to run the cars and I didn't want to worry about the small things, I just wanted to race. The Stone brothers looked to be the perfect solution. I offered them a percentage of the team if they were to come across as an incentive in addition to wages. Which they agreed to and we were off and running. We also got Campbell Little to build our engines and he was, and still is, a really good operator.

Jimmy came across and was trying to be an engineer, which he's not. The proof of the pudding is that not long after they established Stone Brothers Racing, Jimmy ceased to be the engineer. They got engineers in, I mean proper engineers. I was always having trouble with the rear grip and Jimmy was no help at all.

We ended up with sponsorship issues when the government blocked cigarette sponsorship on cars – bloody Jones' Law, here was a good sponsor and the relationship was already terminal. That is when we switched to Pack Leader with a colour scheme that evoked the Peter Jackson brand.

The government cracked it with us – but they did say we could take the sponsorship money but not market products. Eventually we weren't allowed to take their money, even if we were driving a plain white car with no stickers, which I just find extraordinary. What do they think, that some kid doing a project was going to find out on Google that a car is sponsored by Marlboro and then immediately go out and buy a packet of fags?

Anyway, the relationship lasted a couple of years until they closed that door on us. At that point I was in a bit of trouble. We had the team and all the equipment. I had a factory up and running and I had my office at the front and the Stone brothers were operating the workshop at the back. Because I was having trouble getting sponsorship for 1998, I sold them the team. They didn't have all the money they needed at the time, so they agreed to pay extra rent to make up the difference of the purchase of the team. I thought I was pretty generous, but I'm sure they think differently.

So I was running the business side and they were supposed to be running the motorsport side. I was involved with them as far as the major decisions in regards to the financial situation and what we spent money on, but in terms of what engine went on what dyno and when we went testing, it was up to the Stones. I didn't really want to get involved in the day-to-day things. If people came around to the factory, I would take them through as a tour.

Paul Romano joined the team as a second driver and he brought some cash, and in the endurance races we had Allan

Grice and Andrew Miedecke, who was very thick with the Stone brothers. The first half of the season was tough, Jimmy just wasn't able to help me get the car sorted and it took until the middle of the season to get any results and any sort of flow. I finished second in two of the final four rounds and felt we were getting somewhere.

Paul and Andrew got 10th at Sandown, where I got a retirement with Allan. At Bathurst we were fast. I qualified third with a really good run in the Top 10 Shootout, where I was nearly a second quicker than I was in qualifying. That was very satisfying when most dropped time. On the 15th lap of that race I passed Peter Brock in the wet to take the lead and I was pulling away from him and opening a gap at more than a second a lap when the car caught fire going through turn 2 going up the mountain.

In the wet the car was fantastic. Going across the top there's little rivers that run across the track and you've really got to be prepared for them. You need to make sure your steering angle is straight when you hit them. I loved the challenge of that sort of thing, and to race like that and open a gap was very rewarding. I enjoyed the small amount of time I had in the car that day. And there was only another 140 laps to go, so it was anyone's race at that stage. If I didn't own the team I would have been most of the way home by the time the race finished, but I hung around to see our second car finish in 11th.

To round out the year we ran the two races in New Zealand and I had Paul Radisich in the other car. At Pukekohe we both retired in the final, and in Wellington I missed the final two races of the weekend. I was in the box calling the final race with Darrell Eastlake, which I enjoyed through gritted teeth.

Can I say the 1997 championship was just 10 rounds of frustration? While in 1996 we were a consistent top 10 car, this season we were not. The thing handled like a bloody blancmange most of the time. It wouldn't put its power down. I would dearly have loved to have gotten a decent engineer into that team. I was pulling in one direction and the Stone brothers were headed in another.

I battled my way through the season for just one race win at Oran Park. There were too many retirements, especially in the first race of the weekend, which makes it hard.

When the car was good I really enjoyed myself. Barbagallo Raceway in Perth and Oran Park in the last round were two of those. Perth was great, I fought my way through the pack, picking them off after our tyres hung in well – I'd like to think it was my clever driving, but I was never that patient – and we were able to make ground late in the dry races there.

At Oran Park I wanted the round win after winning the second race, and the car was really good. I got a good start in the final race only to have Greg Murphy pass me like I was standing still. After a couple of laps I was on his tail and constantly looking for a way past. I put the pressure on pretty hard but he held steady. Lap after lap I stuck my nose down the inside at the end of the main straight and then coming onto the straight, which were two great overtaking spots. With only five laps to go I pulled right inside Murphy at the last turn, he squeezed me, as was his right, and I went onto the kerb and ended up clipping him. I took the lead but then went off at the next corner. I damaged the front suspension and that was it.

So with the sprint races done, we could think about how to salvage the season with good runs at Sandown and Bathurst.

Sandown with Jason Bright was pretty good, the first Falcon home, in third. Mark Larkham – Larko – in the other car had speed too and he qualified second while I was fourth. In terms of this season, we couldn't have gone to Bathurst with any more confidence, which was actually my second run in a Bathurst 1000 in 1997 after running a Renault in the Super Tourer a couple of weeks prior.

For that race I kind of reunited with Williams to run a Renault with Graham Moore. Graham put the deal together and while I was over in England I went and had a sit in it and got it all under control. Very nice team and the Renault was a front-wheel drive Laguna – I hated it. We ran two cars, one for me and Graham and the other for Alain Menu who was the British Touring Car Champion that year, and Jason Plato, both good blokes.

I came through The Cutting about 40 laps into the race and there was some oil there and being front-wheel drive, the bloody tyres have hit that and they've just spun. I've gone straight into the wall and that was it.

It was good to be back with Williams, even if it wasn't the real team – people like Frank Williams and Patrick Head had nothing to do with it. But it was a European team and they had all the right computers. Everything had a place and there was a place for everything. It was a well-oiled machine, which made me think a little more about my team.

For the V8 Supercar race, Conrad Casino put some money into the team for us to use Scott Pruett, who'd been out for the Indy at the Gold Coast. They had some sort of relationship with him and they wanted him to do Bathurst, so they put up some money and I banked it for the Stone brothers to spend. Being American, he struggled with the right-hand drive and changing gears with his left, and it didn't help when we started the weekend with a really poor car. We got the car OK and I made the Shootout, but it wasn't an easy car to drive, which wasn't good with 1000 kilometres in front of us.

We were there or thereabouts for most of the day, running in the top three or four for the first half of the race and settling into second for the run home. Then things started to go wrong and a series of pitstops cost us eight laps and we finished 11th. Larko brought his car home in third.

I was up and down like a yo-yo with everything that happened in 1997, and when Ross and Jimmy came to me with a deal I didn't have to think too long. I sold it to them with probably too much haste and joined with my old mate Tony Longhurst for 1998, while the Stone brothers went on to win Bathurst, since they made the changes they should have made when working with me.

Racing for Tony was a way of using his spare parts, which wasn't the best, given I had brought sponsorship from Komatsu with me. If the gearbox had a few too many kays, put it in AJ's car. I missed the first two rounds and then did the remainder of the series, which was actually a bit of a waste of time. I don't remember being competitive anywhere, so we'll just move on. Finishing 16th in the Australian Touring Car Championship was not a career highlight for me.

I was going through the motions. It was pointless getting bothered by it. Just grin and bear it, or as my wife would say, smile and wave.

I've never worried about my reputation, so that didn't bug me. All I really cared about at that time was my immediate family and that's about it. It's like when I went back to Formula One – people were saying, 'You left on such a high note, you're the only driver to have ever won his last Formula One race. Then you came back and spoiled it.'

Yeah, so what? So what if I had a shit season in in 1998. Who really cares? I guarantee I don't go to bed thinking, 'Oh, 1998, Christ, oh Jesus. I wish I hadn't done that.'

There were times when people probably perceived me as arrogant during my touring car years. I remember when AVESCO was formed and they started all these things we had to go to, and you'd get a fine if you didn't go. I scored a $1000 fine for one non-attendance at something, and I worked out I could just pay for the whole season and do none of them. So I did.

In touring racing in Australia at the time there were just too many idiots. People like Peter Wollerman. I just didn't see why I had to be answerable to someone like him. I had a slight case of diarrhoea at Winton – you could say Winton gave me the shits but this time that would be unfair. I went into Benalla to get some tablets and I missed the drivers briefing because of that and he fined me. I threw the old force majeure at him, I was either going to shit my pants or I was going to go to Benalla to get the appropriate tablets. He didn't care, he still fined me. A year or two later when we were having an argument over something else, he said, 'Why didn't you tell me that?' I had! He's still around.

It wasn't like this in Europe. Mostly you'd get great people who were involved for the love of the sport – but then you'd get the dickheads.

Anyway, I didn't even get off the grid at Sandown 500 and

the car sat there for the entire race at the side of the track. I was able to jump the fence to the pits and get out of the shit weather. We got 58 laps done at Bathurst after qualifying 11th. We weren't really going all that well after a couple of extra pitstops when I was coming down to Forrest Elbow when I got stuck in the middle of a five-car crash. That was that.

I walked away from that season and from full-time racing. I still enjoyed racing and I enjoyed driving fast, but as ever I didn't enjoy it when it was a shitfight. I did three sets of endurance races with Anthony Tratt and that included a couple of extra races in the championship to get ready. We had no speed in 1999 and finished the Queensland 500 but then retired at Bathurst in the closing laps of the race. We finished neither race in 2000 and then finished both in 2001 – but we weren't racing, we were making up the numbers.

My final opportunity in V8 Supercars came up with Dick Johnson Racing and the chance to drive a Falcon with Greg Ritter while Paul Radisich and Steve Johnson ran the lead car. It was good to be back in a serious team. This was 2002, at the end of the era where the team was a powerhouse of the sport. Greg's aspirations sometimes got a little bit in front of his ability, but we finished eighth at Queensland and seventh at Bathurst. Greg actually fell off the track near the end when he was trying to pass my old mate Larry Perkins, then he fell off again and lost a chunk of time, before deciding he wasn't going to win and he just needed to get home before he put it in a wall.

I never announced or even declared a retirement proper from racing. I would never close the door to a good opportunity if it came up, but I was now in my late 50s and knew I was stretching it. I just walked away from it, no fanfare, no farewell tour, just me being me and doing it my way.

So in a very quiet and private way, that was it for my motor racing career as a driver.

Weekend warriors

One of the good things about Formula One is that you are removed from some of the day-to-day stuff, like scrutineering.

When I was racing the Porsche with Alan Hamilton, we raced at Adelaide International Raceway and they scrutineered the car and deemed it to be something like a millimetre longer on one side than the other, and therefore illegal. I just shook my head and thought, 'Fuck me, here we go, welcome to Australia.'

Another time the splitter on my car was too sharp. The splitter is the aluminium part that comes out from underneath to create down force. You can take it out and put it in and that affects grip. It means you can play around with the car's balance in corners. It was too sharp.

I said, 'Listen, if I hit you at a hundred and twenty miles an hour with a blunt one would that be better?' Straight over his head, he had no idea. It was too sharp. Nowhere in the book does it say the degree of sharpness that your splitter must be. Once again it was old mate, with white overalls on saying, 'By Christ, I've got some power this weekend.'

I just shook my head. I think I might have even dropped the clutch and gone towards him, my foot must have slipped. And anyway, there's nothing in the book to say you can't do that, so long as I don't hit him.

At the time it felt like some of them just wanted to put me back in my box, and to say to their mates down at the pub, 'I did this to Alan Jones, he's such a wanker. Yep, put him in his place.'

I had a few run-ins with that type of person. I don't suffer fools, and I've met plenty of them.

Vanilla

I'd hate being a Formula One driver today. There's too many corporate games, too much bullshit.

I'll give you an example. When I went to Shanghai for the very first Chinese Grand Prix in 2004 I did some laps. After I came back, I was speaking to a few of the drivers and I said, 'It's too samey. It's got one hairpin, after hairpin, after hairpin, after hairpin.' They agreed, it was a bit ordinary.

Then you see them on TV. 'Oh wonderful facility, great circuit.' So I'd ask them why they said that. 'Mate, I drive for X manufacturer and if I told the truth they're going to get the shits because they're trying to sell cars into China.' I didn't have to worry about any of that crap. You just told it the way it was. I think there's not enough of that at the moment.

Even when they get interviewed there's always a girl next to them recording what they say. It's got to that stage.

Then if you do show a bit of personality, everyone gets stuck into you. It is all very controlled and wouldn't suit me.

You don't see a lot of personality in any motorsport these days. Nelson Piquet jumped out of the car at Hockenheim and tried to kick Eliseo Salazar in the balls, which given his Brazilian background is not entirely surprising. Twenty years ago you had Tony Longhurst jumping out of his car to punch his teammate through the car window in Australian touring cars. It just doesn't happen anymore.

See, Bernie Ecclestone loved all that. The best thing that could have happened to Formula One in 2016 would have been a major blue on the podium between Lewis Hamilton and Nico

Rosberg. I mean a big punch-up. Bernie would have been over the moon.

There's just not enough controversy or personality to give it life outside the cars and the racing. It is all there, they're just frightened to open their mouths. There's some great personalities under those facades and that is the tragedy of it all.

21

Not a Racing Driver, Not a Journalist

ONCE I CLOSED the door after getting out of a Formula One cockpit for the last time, plenty of other doors opened. One of those was to move straight into TV commentary in 1987 to work with the Nine Network on its motorsport, especially its Formula One coverage.

I got to work with some characters there. That's where I got to know Barry Sheene. And Big Daz, Darrell Eastlake. Daz was terrific to work with, a really nice bloke. He was bigger than big; he loved what he was doing and that came across in his commentary.

Baz had you in fits of laughter all the time, he was such a character. For example, our studio set had all this sporting memorabilia in the background behind us. One day he draped a black bra over a tennis racquet and it was there for the duration of the show. That was typical of the pranks he used to get up to.

I didn't see myself as a journalist, I would never admit to that even if I was one. I was there for special comments and analysis. I really enjoyed it, which is why I still do it today. It combines really well with my work as an FIA steward at various grands prix, which keeps me in touch with people face-to-face a few times a year. You never want to be forgotten. I still enjoy going back to England for the Goodwood Festival of Speed, especially the two-kilometre Hillclimb race up Lord March's driveway.

There was always travel involved, but the travel was never anything like being a Formula One driver. A quick flight to Melbourne or Sydney is easy and generally involves at most one night away from home – and it's in the same time zone.

It was Channel Nine that really got this going, even though I am with Ten now. I got a phone call out of the blue from some suit at Nine, and I went down and met Kerry Packer. He had plans for the coverage with a lounge room with an open fire, and so we all ended up sitting around in these chairs for a fireside chat – which worked well given it was the dead of winter and the middle of the night for most places in Australia. It's a wonder he didn't want us to smoke a pipe or something too.

My task was, and remains, simple. My job is not to say that the red car passed the green car, or the blue car passed the white car. You can see that. My job is to try and explain *why* and *how* it happened. The other part of the job is to be able to furnish some extra information that no-one else knows, which might be information about a driver – like some habit or superstition he has – or a peculiarity of a track – like the sheets of rain across the top of Bathurst – or about the car – for example, that the driver is now trying to extend the life of the tyres rather than going for all out speed, which will cost him time if he has to make a pit stop to change tyres. Hopefully people can say more often than not, 'I didn't know that.' If they do, I've done my job.

It is also not my job to sit on the fence: I say it as I see it. Like Bathurst in 2016: for me Jamie Whincup just went for an open door. I would have done that every day of the week. Scott McLaughlin left the door open, Whincup's going down there. Might have gone in a tad quick, might have slid a little bit more than what he would have liked to. Did go into the side of McLaughlin, but that's human error; that's called a mistake. Does he hold back and say I'd better not go for that gap just in case my car slides a little bit more than I anticipate? No way, you go in for it. Formula One's heading a bit in this direction now. Everyone's too shit scared to do anything for fear of a penalty. It's all just ring-up-your-mother stuff. Just get on and do it.

I think you have to ask what sort of motor racing do you want. I know what I want: racers, not people tippy-toeing around a track frightened to have a go.

The sanitising of the sport gives me the shits almost as much as the politics. To some degree, the politics is inevitable. Apart from the paddock being made up of incredibly competitive people, there is so much money involved that there will always be people playing games. There was, and still is, and always will be, a them and an us. When I was racing it was probably a little bit more nationalistic; the French against the English, for example.

Technically now the cars are a lot more sophisticated. Electronics is probably the biggest single difference. They've still got wishbones; they've still got discs; they've still got brake pedals. Some things do change: you brake with your left foot instead of your right foot, and you change gears with the things behind the steering wheel. Some things don't: you've still got to take a 250 kilometres per hour corner at 250 kilometres per hour. If you take it at 251 you're off into the boonies, and if you take it at 249 you lose time to your rivals.

I think there is no doubt the modern Formula One car is easier to drive. But I'll never find out, because I'll never fit in one. Everyone tells me that they're a lot easier to drive; in fact, they're too easy. They get around faster; the times prove that. Take Monza which hasn't changed much since my time: they are qualifying around 15 per cent faster than I was, and the race takes 10 minutes less over the same distance. A modern Formula One car has turned bigger circuits into what must feel like Monaco, because everything's coming up that much more quickly.

Even though the cars are that much faster, and they do it all on skinny little rubber too, they're infinitely safer. There's no doubt in my mind that if Fernando Alonso was in an aluminium monocoque car – as we were – at Albert Park, Melbourne at the beginning of 2016 he wouldn't be with us now. The car would be a crumpled up piece of tissue paper; instead he was shaken a bit and able to climb out of it. The carbon-fibre cars are just amazing. In some cases now it is just whether the body and brain can cope with some of the g-loads in a crash.

People were getting killed when I raced. Eight drivers I raced with or against lost their lives in a Formula One car. That's my mate Brian McGuire, Tom Pryce, Mark Donohue, Ronnie Peterson, Patrick Depailler, Gilles Villeneuve, Elio De Angelis and Ayrton Senna. And my era was safer than the one before, when drivers died virtually every year and often more than one a year. Now, we've only had one death since Senna back in 1994.

But I don't ever sit back and think it would be nicer to race now, or it would have been better in the 1960s. I had my day in the sun and I really enjoyed it. I wouldn't change it for anything. I'll always remember Stirling Moss coming up to me once and saying, 'Oh you blokes are getting paid so much money now,' blah, blah, blah. I thought, 'Jesus, don't ever let me turn into one of those.' I love Stirling, don't get me wrong, and me and Amanda, my second wife, get on really well with both him and Susie, but it made me think I never wanted to become one of those people who lamented what they had or didn't have.

And it balances out. If money is what counts, we were pretty much earning the equivalent of the guys today when you take everything into account. Formula One, for me, was never about the money. Overall my career may have been about money – whose isn't – but not Formula One.

When I was there I was going to make as much as possible, but money was not the motivation. Sure I would have jumped ship in 1981 if Frank Williams hadn't agreed to what I wanted, but I wasn't going to the back of the field to earn more money. Renault was up for it, and they had a good car. I always wanted a good and competitive car, and then I wanted as much money as I could get.

Let's keep things in perspective. I loved Frank, and I think he thought I was OK. But if I had killed myself in race three of the championship, Frank would have been looking for a driver for round 4. That's it. That's mercenary. That's the business. They call it a sport, but it's a bloody business. I always used to justify my stance because I thought Frank, like anyone else in pit lane, would be hunting for a new driver before they even thought of calling Bev.

Bev and Christian were my responsibility and I wanted to make sure they were protected as much as possible. At Kyalami there's a really quick right-hander coming onto the straight where Tom Pryce got killed. My left-hand rear wheel came off there once and I spun down the straight ending up almost where Frank was behind the pit wall. After I climbed out of the car I went up to him and said, 'That's why I want my money on time. If I'd just been killed then, would you have paid Beverley?' I added, 'Frank, no more, no less, just what I'm owed and on time.'

I had a good wage in my later years of Formula One and I had some fabulous endorsements. 'Akai's okay, OK!' I never understood, but as the cheques arrived it made enough sense. I was a member of the Marlboro World Championship team and that was a good earn too. And you never had to pay for much either; tennis racquets, watches, anything like that.

In some ways I wasn't ready for the money that came. George Robinson from Vegantune told me to get myself set up. 'Get a solicitor, get a company all organised because if you go as well as I think you're going to go, the money will come in very quick and you've got to be ready for it.' I thought, yeah OK whatever, but he was right. I did get myself set up. I had a company that I drove for and that company had a bank account in Switzerland. The money used to be sent there and then went from there to another bank, and eventually got lost in the valleys of Switzerland. It was money earned overseas, so I wasn't subject to tax when I came back to Australia. Life was pretty good.

But people started taking advantage of me. Like Dad, I liked to help people. It started with Bob Jane and that T-Mart, when I naively thought we were doing each other a favour. He was giving me a T-Mart and I was giving him publicity.

Of course to some people that's not enough. They've got to screw you, that's just their nature. I found plenty of people who would do that and I never really watched my back as much as I should have. Never got advice when I could have. Very impetuous, went into things probably a little too quickly. All the worst traits you can have in a businessman – I had them.

If I died tomorrow without a penny to my name – and that won't happen – I would not be the first ex-driver to go that way. James Hunt died broke, for instance. He probably got scammed by some of the same people as me. Then somebody they scammed using your name comes knocking . . .

Limited edition cars and boats, watches, jewellery and so on. I had a marine business called AJM, Alan Jones Marine, and we used to make boats called Fast Lane 40. For that they gave me a 40-foot boat, which was pretty slick. But I didn't make anywhere near as much out of it as the others did.

Another guy talked me into going into a business called Alan Jones Pit Stop, in competition with Bob Jane T-Mart. They bought a big ocean-going boat they called 'AJ' and kept in Sydney. When I went down to Sydney I had somewhere to stay and it was used to entertain . . . a completely unnecessary asset though. People like that were getting a lot of benefits out of the association, and using me.

After I came back home in 1982 I had car dealerships. I had a Porsche and Alfa dealership as well, one of only two Honda ones in Australia that had power products, bikes, and cars. When I had the opportunity to go back to Formula One, I got a childhood mate of mine to come in and run it. I gave him a percentage of the business too, and the opportunity to work his way up to 49 per cent. All he had to do was keep his horns in and keep it flowing. This Honda dealership in particular was going to grow, even if Porsche and Alfa might have struggled.

Then as soon as I went overseas he went berserk and ended up getting himself a race car. He bought a Ferrari and said he got it cheap and he'd be able to sell it for a profit, when in actual fact it was for him to prance around the Gold Coast in. Then I got a phone call from a guy who I had befriended at Borg Warner Finance, who financed all our stock. He called up one day and started with, 'I don't want to worry you, but . . .' The last thing I wanted to do was worry. When I did that deal I didn't want to be worried about business while I was over there racing in Formula One.

To cut a long story short, he told me that the bloke was actually selling the cars and not paying the finance out. The bloke also had a friend who came into the premises, put his own stock on the floor then they'd sell it and split the profit, completely bypassing me. All of that stuff was going on and I had no idea until I got that phone call. I came back and sold the businesses, which were now pretty much broke. My mate simply did the wrong thing by me. I gave him the best opportunity in the world but he got greedy.

I had people to give me advice, managers and the like to guide me through a whole bunch of things. Managers like Harry M Miller and James Erskine, who never really produced much but were happy to put their hands out when I brought something to the table.

I probably needed a bit more from Beverley, like I get from Amanda now. We had a very nice house with the tennis court and all the gear, and she always had a brand new car and she never worked. Our relationship in the end was only tolerable, and despite what she said in divorce court she didn't play that much of a role in me getting to where I got. It would have been good if I could have bounced things off her. It's good these days – Amanda pulls me into gear. She does my books and she is very successful in her own right working with IT in aged care and health, which I think is the big difference.

Around the end of 1984 I knew a deal with Beatrice Haas was around the corner. I wasn't getting much from Harry M Miller, so I went to him to cancel our deal. He wanted 20 grand to let me walk away, which I paid. Then later on I did the deal to go back into Formula One.

I still get approaches today for various things, and I am a lot less tolerant and open these days. But if someone walked in and I thought he was a nice guy and he had a good concept, I could possibly be conned again. At least I've got Amanda to shut me down.

Some people think they can get something for nothing out of me, that by offering me a good time I'll endorse their products. Australian businesses can really be so naive. I'm not interested in going to another function – you'll need to pay. And then they go on about plane flights and hotels and the like – seriously, they're the last things I want. I'd much rather stay home with my family.

One thing I did enjoy post-racing was my time on the board of the Australian Grand Prix after it moved to Melbourne. Ron Walker was the chairman and asked me to join because they wanted an ex-driver that could give them some information on what the drivers and teams want and need. There were some great people on the board: Dean Wills, who headed up Coca-Cola Amatil, James Strong who was then with Qantas and Brocky was there too.

That was a good time for me. I wasn't doing the TV at that stage because when it moved to Ten they didn't want any of the Nine people involved. Then Ten asked me to fill in for one telecast, when Craig Baird was unavailable. We did that out of Melbourne one night and it quickly turned into a regular job that is still going today.

I've worked there with both Greg Rust and Mattie White – both great blokes to work with and both very professional. With *RPM* I get to do some stuff with Mark Larkham, and he is very passionate about it all. You get in the car from the airport with him to go to the studio and by the time you get there he's on about 100 decibels because he revs himself up – he's self-revving. He studies, he draws, he gets totally into it. He'll spend the whole weekend doing diagrams. Technically he's very switched on, and he puts a lot of time and effort into staying on top of it all.

I love cars for the look and the way they drive and that's about it. If you took the body off and started going through the chassis, I couldn't care less. He'll come and explain how the twin turbo Merc works . . . He is genuinely passionate about motor sport and where he'd like to see it going – and anything else you'd like to talk about. He's a good bloke, I really like him.

Mark wanted to do Formula One, and today he lends a helping hand to anyone who he thinks has talent trying to get there. I've put money into drivers before, but I never had the time or the aptitude to mentor people like him. And we need that: we are not going to get our next Formula One driver from driving Supercars.

Barry Sheene

Barry was right up there with James in living life to the fullest. He is so much fun to be around. In many ways, it was no surprise they used to hang around with each other while Barry was still living in England, they were two peas in a pod.

He was an unbelievable character, no airs and graces about him at all, which was a bit like James too. He couldn't care how he dressed; if he was in jeans and a T-shirt he was happy. Barry was a mad smoker. He used to buy these cigarettes that were filtered because they were stronger than the unfiltered ones, and then he'd bite the filter off and smoke it. He had had a hole drilled into his helmet so he could keep smoking for longer until the race started.

I knew him when I lived in England and he used to come around to my house and ask me questions about Australia. What's it like here, what's it like there, what's it like in November, and just all these little bits and pieces. Even then he was sizing up Australia, maybe he knew with all his injuries a warmer climate was going to be better as he got older.

I bought a helicopter thanks to Barry. I was at Brands Hatch testing the Williams, and he flew up in his chopper. Knowing Barry as I do now, there was obviously a good commission in there for him, and he went into sales mode. We had a 45-minute or so break in testing, I jumped in the helicopter and he took me over the hills to one of the paddocks in Kent and then he let me fly it up and down in a straight line.

'I can get you one of these cheap, AJ.' I enjoyed helicopters more than planes, so I bought one. I got an Enstrom 280C Shark, which had a turbo-charged piston engine in it and I bought it off Barry's mates, who would insure it over the water. I thought it was going to be a great way to get around. Not so sure it was in hindsight, but I did enjoy it.

When he moved out here he moved to the Gold Coast and we had a great time together. He'd fly back with me on a Monday morning after we'd done something with Channel Nine or after a touring car race when he was commentating. We'd hop in a taxi and out would come the bloody fags and the butt was bitten off and it was lit up. I'd say, 'Barry, you can't do it, mate.' 'It's all right, it's all right,' was what he would say.

Sure enough, the taxi driver would turn around, 'Excuse me, sir, you can't smoke in here.' 'Yeah, what's up? Haven't I got windows down?' Oh, then of course the arguments would happen, that and the smell of things was enough for me and I ended getting my own taxi.

In keeping with his lifestyle, he ended up marrying a Penthouse pet, Stephanie. He would proudly overshare his exploits the morning after. 'Thanks, Baz, thanks for sharing that with me.'

Women loved him, he could walk up and be cheeky and they'd pinch his cheeks and say you're a cheeky boy. Whereas, if I did it I'd get a slap over the face. He just had this way of coming across as a cheeky little boy. He got away with murder.

22

A1 Grand Prix

THE A1 SERIES was a great idea, and to this day I think it could have been hugely successful if the right people had been running the show. I lent my name and was a part of the Australian entry, which is an interesting story in itself.

The cars were all built by Lola with Zytek engines, and our car was going to be maintained by Allan Docking Racing, which was essentially an Australian motor racing operation in the UK. The races were in the European off-season, it was to run all around the world, and the teams would represent nations, and the driver had to be from that nation, making it a sort of World Cup of Motorsport. It was an interesting concept and it took a little while to get going – about 18 months – but I was very interested.

I was in England when I first heard about it and it was supposedly owned by Sheikh Maktoum out of Dubai, so I decided to call into Dubai on the way home, ostensibly to look at the new circuit they had just built, but also to track down Sheikh Maktoum and have a chat with him. He was pretty full-on, he wanted a fee of something like $10 million for a three-year franchise and then he wanted control of everything . . . including where you put your advertising. I looked at the numbers and I thought there's no way I'm getting involved.

I got back to Australia and I got a phone call to say that a consortium of Australian business people had got together and organised A1 Team Australia and they wanted me to run it and have a little partnership in it. I thought this sounded like a load of bullshit, because if there was a consortium of Australian people that were going to do that, I think I would have heard something. Anyway I thought don't look a gift horse in the mouth and I agreed to do it. Like everyone else, I assumed at that stage that Sheikh Maktoum was the head guy.

The first race was at Brands Hatch in September 2005 and they spent a million bucks on hospitality at the Pangaea Club, complete with a new bridge to get across the track. I soon realised the Sheikh didn't have as much to do with it as I thought. He sold out his interest after one year of racing.

We had a guy called Adam Gotch looking after the engineering side of the operation; he runs a Formula Four team now in the national series. I used to call him Anal Adam because he was really well focused on the small things. He ran a good team, while I concentrated on the drivers and promotions.

Off the track a guy called Tony Teixeira, a South African diamond entrepreneur, was getting more involved. He used to run a lot of security for the mines and both he and the Sheikh were pumping money into this thing. I thought at the very early stages that it wasn't going to be sustainable, even a Rockefeller couldn't pour that sort of money in week in and week out, but it seemed Teixeira could. For a while.

Most of the nation's franchises were not bought as was originally planned and Teixeira and his mob were underwriting it all. They got Jan Lammers to look after Holland, Niki Lauda had Austria, Emerson Fittipaldi had Brazil and I had Australia. All these teams were being funded by A1 themselves. I'm not sure how many of the others were in the same boat.

Sheikh Maktoum had these dreams of taking on and beating Formula One, but that was never going to happen and they should have just focused on making the series as good as possible and the rest would have sorted itself out. Problem was, the sheikh wanted revenge on Bernie Ecclestone, who had awarded the first Gulf region grand prix to Bahrain, not Dubai. The sheikh sold Teixeira on the dream of being bigger than Formula One – they proceeded to sink a rumoured £100 million into it just in the first year.

But if he was told once he was told a hundred times, forget Formula One. They've got 50 years of equity, you've got 50 minutes. You're not going to be anywhere near Formula One. With that we went around the world racing A1 cars and it was a great concept. The average lay person could understand it; nation against nation. I used to call it the Admiral's Cup on asphalt.

After four years it was going well, but it wasn't giving a return on the substantial investment.

Then they started making some silly decisions. In the fourth season, 2008-09, they switched to a chassis built and designed by Rory Byrne at Ferrari and put a 4.5-litre Ferrari/Maserati engine in it. It was completely unnecessary and a great waste of money. The previous car and engine combination was really good, and they are still used in a series in Italy.

Ferrari used to send engineers and mechanics to every single race to monitor the engines. If you looked like you were having a problem with the engine they would tell you to change the engine, and that cost an unbelievable amount of money. On top of that Baz had these three or four birds running around the place looking at cars and photographing them every half an hour making sure that all the sponsorship was in the right place.

These were the same people who gave us grief after Peter Brock and Steve Irwin – the Crocodile Hunter – were killed in accidents in Australia. These were two iconic figures in Australian culture and we decided to honour them on our car. They came up and told me we couldn't do it. We had an argument about who they were and what they meant to Australia, but they didn't care. We ran it anyway.

If I wanted to find a new sponsor for the car I had to go through them and they wouldn't give you any information to use in the sales process. No Australian company was going to fork over 500 grand or a million bucks not knowing all the information, just because I asked them. That side of it was a disaster.

I never ceased to be amazed at the amount of people that wanted to stick their noses into the team, some of whom wanted to take control and all they did was take us backwards. Not the least of which was Alan Evans, who was with NRMA, and he said his business expertise was going to transform what we were doing, when all he really wanted to do was wear a set of gold headphones and look important. He was in cahoots with Rod Paech, who was some sort of consultant promoting the Eastern Creek race. But that wasn't enough for him, and like all consultants he knew everything, so he wanted to have an involvement in the team as well.

After a while, Graham Walpole was employed in England to oversee all the A1-owned teams, which included us. He in turn suggested a gentleman by the name of Daniel Zammit to come in and look after the Australian team. Daniel wanted to build a workshop in Parramatta Road with glass walls so people could see the car being prepared. He had no idea that after every race the cars went back to a central workshop near Silverstone, where they were all maintained.

Then there was this South African, Roy Peater, who they forced on our team because A1 borrowed some money off his brother in Perth to make sure the Eastern Creek race was run. Roy was living in Sydney and in he came like he owned the team, conducting interviews and questioning everything we were doing. It didn't take long before we had a major blowout. I told him to fuck off and get out. I couldn't stand him.

Just as it was getting traction, the South Africans stopped paying some of their bills. Then they were having trouble airfreighting the cars around because they couldn't or wouldn't pay the bills. I'd organised a race here in Australia where the IndyCars used to race and Emerson organised a race in Brazil. Had they been able to make those two first races they could have continued for the year, but the bloke that owned the transport business wouldn't release their cars and that was it.

Losing the Gold Coast race two weeks before it was due to run was a major embarrassment for me, but thank god the majority of people realised that it wasn't me at fault.

So that died a graceful death, when it could have been powering on. A1 was a great concept ruined by people who just didn't know enough about motor racing.

As a team we didn't get the results we wanted, but I got to run a lot of young guys in the cars. We started out with Will Power and he nearly won the first race, but he already had a deal to do Champ Car and he moved on to do that and eventually won that championship. We then ran my son Christian, followed by Will Davison, Marcus Marshall and Ryan Briscoe all in the first year. In the next three seasons we also added Karl Reindler, Ian Dyk and John Martin to the racing squad, while Daniel Ricciardo tested for us.

We tested Daniel at Silverstone and I was really impressed. He'd never been to Silverstone, he'd never driven the car and he was super quick. I wanted to sign him up but Helmet Marco had him tied up and wouldn't release him.

At one stage I was accused of giving too many people drives. There was no continuity in that sense, but for me it was a great way of looking at some young talent – and look at where most of those drivers are now. I'm proud of that.

I copped a bit for running Christian too, but he had won the Asian Formula Three championship and that meant he was a worthy choice. We had some heated father-son discussions at the time. I still believe he is a really good driver, but I don't think he was dedicated enough at the time. I said to him, 'Christian, you have to try twice as hard as anybody else because 99.9 per cent of the people are going to say you're here because of who you are and not what you are.'

He could have won the Porsche Carrera Cup two years in a

row too – he was leading the series when the car let him down. Porsche thought enough of him to fly him over to Stuttgart for the end-of-season dinner as a 'we're sorry' type thing for the car letting him down.

I was comfortable putting him in the car, just as I was the others.

What I really hoped was that we could show Australian companies what we could do if people got behind us, but it was a catch-22, because we needed them to come on board to show what we could do. Even in a one-make series, money buys speed.

If you head to Europe, which is where you need to be if you want to reach the top, and in my eyes everything else in motorsport is a lesser option and a cop-out, you'll see a lot of Brazilian kids with Brazilian companies sponsoring them. There's still people out there who remember that Yellow Pages helped Mark Webber. What the companies don't realise is that if they sponsor a young bloke, the benefits go on for years. Australian companies just don't have the foresight of those in other countries. They didn't when I started and they still don't.

That's why I make no apologies for how I went about my career. I have never paid for a drive in my life, I have earned money from pretty much everything I have raced, even it was just £2000 a season in the early days.

I may have had to sell my soul at times, but it was mine to sell and ultimately I built a great life out of it. Hopefully some of what I have given back to the sport will help other young Australians live their dream too.

Daniel Ricciardo

I really hope Daniel wins the World Championship one day; I really don't want to be Australia's last World Champion. I think he can do it too, he is a great driver. He is also so marketable, but what I like is that he seems to be the man that we see. He has a personality and he is not a wanker like some of the others.

Daniel's family's got a bit of money – they're not filthy rich, but they are not living by the seat of their pants either. His dad Joe's got a Ferrari, and he's got a couple of other good cars. He's a worker from an Italian family with good ethics. They've raised Daniel to be polite and happy and it shows.

I really wanted Daniel for the A1 team but I couldn't get him because of contracts, and he has got a lot better since then. He's just a really good kid – and very competitive. For all that smiling he is really what they used to call Glenn Seton: 'a smiling assassin'.

He grows horns when he races. He is there to win, and he's been able to do it without giving up his personality. As for drinking champagne on the podium out of a race boot – I can't think of anything worse, but he does it and now he owns it. The beauty for him is that he is loved all over the world because he is bloody fast and likeable. He's bankable.

Mark Webber

I have a lot of time for Mark Webber. He is very restrained and guarded, but he is typical of the modern Formula One driver, he'll roll out the lines you want to hear easily. He's a very proud Australian too and he has been a very good diplomat and promoter of the sport in Australia. If you think about it though, he's done nothing controversial. Boring.

He didn't win the World Championship, but he won nine grands prix. He should be proud of his achievements; it's hard enough to get to Formula One and even harder for an Aussie. On one hand, we're geographically disadvantaged. On the other hand, we're geographically advantaged, because we're far away from a lot of the shit that goes on in Europe and America. But you can't exactly zip over to Monza to walk the paddock.

I've tried to get Australian companies to understand what they can get out of backing someone like Mark, or Daniel now, but they just won't understand. There is not a lot of corporate vision in this country.

Eventually Mark made it there with not much support and he almost won the World Championship. He did end up with the World Endurance Championship and I think he is now running Porsche's racing programs, which tells you something about his intelligence and knowledge of the sport.

23

Racing Philosophy

WHEN YOU GO motor racing, you're there to win. Which means you must think you can win. There is no point getting out of bed in the morning and going to the track if you think otherwise.

If you don't think you are the best, or as good as the best, there is no point pursuing the career of a racing car driver. There is no point if you don't think, given equal equipment, that you can beat the others. You must go to the circuit with that philosophy. Except if you are getting fifty thousand in a brown paper bag and you are just going for that. That is still a win, just a different sort of win.

My philosophy was always to dot the I's and cross the T's at the beginning of each season. I was chasing the best equipment I could get. I was making sure all the insurance and other protection I needed were in place. I needed to know before I went onto the track that Beverley, and later Christian, would be okay no matter what happened to me.

Then get on with it.

You knew that you would have two or three good frights a year. I liked to get mine over and done with early. Just go out and go hard. It's as simple as that. When I sat my bum in the car I always gave ten-tenths, except for that one time I drove it off the track at Portugal. I'll give 110 per cent if I know the team is giving 100 per cent. If they are not, the tendency is not to drive your heart out. It was a psychological thing for me: I always needed to know it was as important to them to win as it was to me.

If the team was with me, I was going to be a very hard man to pass; anyone who wanted my spot was going to have to work hard for it. If anyone was in front of me, the slightest opening was seen as a gap. I would push people, let them know I was there . . . hello, here I am in this mirror, and now I am in this one.

It doesn't mean you are a pain in the arse just for the sake of being a pain in the arse. If you are being lapped, don't do anything silly or unexpected, and let the other driver through as easily as you can. You move out of the way, just as you do when you've done your qualifying lap and others are still going for it. For those guys that were unaware or just too ignorant to get out of your way . . . they were complete wankers. They were always given a bit of a talking-to afterwards, especially given some of them would be the same ones who'd whinge when it happened to them.

I always knew who was in front of me and knew what liberties I could take with each them. Like, with Gilles Villeneuve, you had to take into account that it was Villeneuve and that you had to be well and truly past him before you did anything. He'd hit you before he'd blink his eyes. There were others that if you stuck your nose in they would move over.

In terms of where you raced, you tried not to have favourite tracks and least favourites, because that would just be asking for trouble. It's hard though: I liked Silverstone and the Österreichring before they were altered; big, fast, sweeping curves that were a challenge to the driver and required balls. I tried like hell not to think about how much I disliked Monaco because I wanted to go well there too. It was all in the head.

Regardless, I used to just treat them as they came. I didn't get excited about a circuit I liked or flat about a track I didn't. Like or dislike, it was a venue where I had to race. I always used to say, 'The circuits I like the best are the ones closest to a hotel and an airport.'

Above all else, I was a driver. I didn't break down my driving style and analyse my speed in corners, check my pulse and then see if my cheeks had colour. Frank Williams used to say the only training I ever did was by lifting my arm at the local pub. In reality I did more than that, but relaxation to me was important for my mental state on a race weekend.

Today I would have hated debriefs . . . hours of looking at computer screens and talking about why I did what I did there because the data said my left eye twitched on my first qualifying run and it was the right eye on the next run. Once I'd raced, I just wanted to get out of the track as quickly as I could. I would debrief with Patrick Head, tell him everything I could remember and then let him do what he did best. Frank was always a bit of a character. He'd sit there with his clipboard and at the appropriate time he would say, 'Driver comfort?' That was Frank's input. I always used to say, 'Yeah, good! No dramas.' One day I said, 'No, I think the steering wheel's off-centre a bit.' He looked satisfied – he had something to write down.

One of the guys at the factory said I was hard on the gearbox, but I had very few mechanical failures that were my fault. I had very few non-finishes due to riding the car too hard. And I probably saved a few engines by having a very good feel for vibration and noise. I couldn't say what it was or why it came about or what to do about it, but I could come in and say, 'This has got a vibration.' And it did.

Touring cars were slightly different in terms of tolerance, but again I didn't break many because I was ham-fisted or changing gears too hard. One of my philosophies is that when you hop in a car, you drive 100 per cent (unless you are so far in front you don't need to). You change gears as quickly as you can, you brake as late as you can and you jump over curbs if you can. If they haven't built a car to take that, well tough.

Today I feel a little sorry for the drivers. The cars are so good there is little room for a driver to have the same impact we did. Our braking distances were longer, so there was more room to get on the brakes later. Today, there's no such thing as 'out-braking'. The cars are so similar, and the performance of the brakes is so good, you just put yourself in a position where you spoil a bloke. If that means running into a corner side by side, he'll have to relent. In the old days you would go desperately late and hope it was going to slow enough. Which is what we saw Senna do so brilliantly at Donington in that wet race, his car control that day – and most days – was just phenomenal.

It was like the day at Hockenheim 1981 when I out-braked

Alain Prost at Sachs Curve and slipped between him and René Arnoux. That was a big opportunistic move. I knew Prost was cautious and we caught his teammate at just the right spot, and wham. There I was. It looks spectacular on the TV, and it felt great in the car. That was the sort of feeling I went racing for.

I'm not saying the drivers aren't important today, but I think in terms of pure race craft we had more of an impact. But no matter what happens with rules and cars, the cream always still rises to the top, and that is what tells you the driver still has real value.

I used to go back to the hotel every night and think about how I could improve my lap. I used to think, 'Maybe in turn 4 I could try this,' but that was about the extent of it. It was just a corner that had to be taken and you took it. If you could work at a better, slightly quicker way, then you do that. You may even do it by paying attention to others, but I was a race driver more than a thinker.

Today I enjoy my role as a race steward when I get to it. I think it is important to have ex-drivers in the decision-making process, and we have such amazing technology at hand. We have three or four big screens. We have the ability to replay an incident from many angles, we can call up their radio and listen to what they had to say. We can access their telemetry, so we know everything they know in the pits. We can see if they lifted under yellows or not, which is important.

It is also important that more than one person is involved in the process. Charlie Whiting is the Formula One racing director, and he sits in race control, where he might spot something and then refer it to us. We might already be on it though, and we'll make a decision on whether it was stupidity or bad luck or intentional. If it is stupidity, we determine what penalty we'll give him, based on what the manual tells us we can do. There's a bloody book for everything these days. Sometimes we do it afterwards and talk to the drivers, which gets in the way of me leaving the track quickly. I do it for the honour of doing it – they meet our expenses, but that is it.

For me though, it keeps me involved and I love that. I love car racing, and I love that I can still be involved now that I am in my 70s.

24

Family

THINGS GET COMPLEX in this chapter, but one thing that is clear is that I love my family, all of it. Even the ones I was never really a father too, and yes, I have regrets there but I can't change the past.

Nothing I do is uncomplicated and obviously I get myself into these binds. The broader family has few kids from many different ways and directions. None of it, except Christian, was planned. I spoke earlier about the early days with Beverley, so I don't plan to do that here. Suffice to say my divorce from her in 1997 was more about financial pain than anything else, we had grown to a point where that was the best thing for the both of us.

When I first got to London it was so different to Australia, it was alive and so free and open. All the stories you hear about the place in the late 1960s, they're all true. And for a confident young lad from Australia this was like a lolly shop. And maybe I took after the old man more than I realised; when it came to the desires of the flesh I was like him. I'm not now of course, but when I was younger I was a bit weak in that department.

Carnaby Street was in full swing and Earl's Court was a lot of fun with all the Aussies. I was 19 and had a big share apartment with a bunch of other Aussies and there were parties on virtually all the time. We had various people coming and going at all times of the day and night. There was always something happening.

Kay was one of the girls who came around, a 'counties girl' who used to find her way to our place when she was in London. You've got to remember it was a very different time back then. We had some fun together and that led to the bedroom, but it was never very serious. After a while she hooked up in a more permanent way with one of the blokes sharing the apartment, Joe. She ended up staying with him in the apartment for a few weeks. One day there was a knock on my bedroom door and the two of them were standing there.

'We want to have a talk with you. Kay's pregnant, and you're the father.' I was already packing for my trip back to Australia and they were happy together, so that was it really. I don't think they were after anything from me and I think they were happy with my approach.

They were together for a very long time and even moved to Joe's native Tasmania. Emma was born and eventually they had two other daughters too. I think Emma had some sort of inkling that she wasn't Joe's daughter, but you'd have to ask her that. Her sisters are both natural blondes and she has jet black hair. It was when Joe and Kay split up that Kay and Emma had a bit of a talk one night around a fireplace and over a couple of glasses of red. I think that's when it came out about me being her dad.

The first meeting with Emma was pretty emotional. She came up to Symmons Plains when I was there one weekend, and she turned up with her dog in the back of the station wagon. We all got together and went back to the hotel that I was staying at and had a big dinner and that was it.

She was in her 20s at that stage. Now 20-20 hindsight is a wonderful thing to have, but what has happened has happened and I cannot change that. Of course I would have liked to have been there, but from Emma's point of view, she had a father and she was happily living with her family in Tasmania. It wasn't for me to knock on the door and upset that.

I think between Joe, Kay and me we had an unspoken thing that they were going to bring her up and I would stay out of it until such time as they chose to tell her or she found out. I'm not a doorknocker and I respected that until it all came to its natural conclusion.

Emma and I talk nowadays, but I do wish I'd been there for the growing up. To watch her grow into the woman she has become. But as they say, such is life. She has two daughters now, so I have two grandchildren and that is special too.

Christian was next, the only one who was planned. We'd tried for quite a while to have children. Bev and I spoke about it for a while and we decided to adopt. It is one of the best things we ever did. One of the best things *I* ever did.

Christian was born and given immediately to Beverley. He was born on 27 September 1978. I was driving car number 27 and I was at the end of what was my best season to date. I left England for the Canadian and United States grands prix without any children and came home to a baby.

I couldn't love Christian any more or any less, and as far as I'm concerned, Christian's my son, end of story. I love him dearly. I hope that I've been able to give him all the things he wanted in life – except a Formula One drive. I had a fair crack at helping him out with that, but in his eyes I just didn't do enough there. In my defence, I don't think he pulled his weight fully in that arrangement.

He won the Asian Formula Three Championship. He came third and fourth in the Porsche Carrera Cup Asia when, and I know this sounds like a typical father talking, he failed to win both of them through no fault of his own.

Christian's got a lot of ability and could be out there racing competitively today if he put his mind to it. But that is up to him.

It is funny, we look very similar and people often say he's a 'chip off the old block, it must be in the genes'. Particularly when he won the Asia Formula Three Championship but no, to his credit it was simply because of his ability. I think he was more inclined to go motor racing because he was my son than if he was a butcher's son. I think you're influenced by your surroundings and he shows that talent behind a wheel doesn't need to be inherited.

Camilla is my next child and I suppose she helped me with my divorce from Beverley, whom I was still with when I met Robyn, her mother, through a mutual friend. Well, one thing led to another and we ended up in some sort of relationship, some people might call it an affair. I don't think Bev was overly impressed with the situation when she found out; if only I was an Arab and was allowed more than one wife. Bev didn't see it that way.

So Camilla was the result of that union, and she's a lovely girl, very bright and very pretty. She's currently working for lawyers in Canberra.

I don't see her as much as I'd like. There have been several occasions where she's been in Brisbane and I've had to go overseas. I'm sure a lot of the time she thinks I'm avoiding her, which I'm not. I do love Camilla, she's my daughter and I wish I could spend more time with her.

So from that part of my life, the only regret I have is not being able to spend enough time with either Emma or Camilla. Today, I have a young family with twins that are still children – although they probably don't see it that way – and that takes my time. Distance is also a major factor; I've got Christian and the twins up here with me on the Gold Coast, but Emma is in Tasmania and Camilla is in Canberra for the time being.

That brings me to Amanda, who I met a few months after I had separated from Beverley. Maybe 20 years ago, one of Amanda's best friends was going out with a guy I know up here on the Gold Coast. I was out on the Broadwater on my boat and Bob – the boyfriend – was on his boat. We used to hook our boats up and tie a rope onto the bow, let it run the whole length of the boat in the current down to the back of the boat, and then the kids that were with us would jump off and follow the current, then grab the rope and come back on the stern. Along with those kids was me too.

Amanda came over on a jet ski to see how her daughter Amber was getting on and I thought, 'Oh that's not a bad sort.' I did a bit of work there, but she didn't want a bar of me. Initially, I think she only saw the bad side of me the first couple of times, the jungle juice. Eventually I wore her down and we went out to lunch and from that point on we've never really been apart.

This was me in salesman mode, I had to sell myself. I wore a shirt and tie to lunch in Surfers Paradise – that was working hard I can tell you now. People must have been laughing at me. But I was putting on Mr Nice Guy. It has worked out really well, Amanda is my best friend and I can't imagine not being with her. It helps that she is successful in her own right. She is very bright and good at what she does.

Amanda had Amber and she was living with us when Amanda and I moved in together. Amber now lives up in the north of Queensland working as a teacher, but I think we thought that was it for us in terms of kids. The twins were not planned, in fact we thought we weren't going to have kids together. I'd known Amanda for about four years when we were away for the Goodwood Festival of Speed and then went for a holiday in Spain. One day after we returned home, she asked, 'Do you want the good news or the bad news?' and then she told me she was pregnant with twins. I'm not sure which part of it she felt was the bad news.

As it turns out one was conceived at Goodwood and the other in Spain. Jack is the mellow one, so I'm sure he was England and Zara is feisty, so she's got to be Spain. I prefer to think of it that way than to picture Zara as a feisty little me, and Jack as an Amanda.

I was already into my 50s when they were born, and now that I'm 70 they keep me both young and old. It's given me a second lease of life. It's good, I like it, I love it.

Amanda is a really great mother, and I'm not just saying this to earn brownie points. But she is a great mum and as a result they are growing up as great kids. Well I am old and I know it, so parenthood today is no challenge for me, I just hand them over to Amanda when I need to.

We all sort of fit in pretty well. Diane, that's Amanda's mum, lives up here and she's terrific. She'll come round and look after them or stay with them if we're both away, given we both travel for work and often can't change our travel dates. Diane has been an absolute godsend.

From the outside it all seems very complex, but for me it works. I can't say it works or has worked for each of the kids, but I can't change that. All I can do is look to the future and what can happen from there.

They're all happy, healthy, good looking and great people. All is good. We've never all got together but I'd dearly love for that to happen. Who knows? There's always next Christmas.

25

AJ Today

WHEN I DID my first book back in 1981, I said, 'So far, I have expressed my life in my racing, and who I am will not come out until I've finished.'

So who am I? We all know about my racing, I was a Formula One World Champion, and while millions have had that dream, only 33 have pulled it off. I was the 18th to do so – the second Australian, and hopefully not the last.

But I am more than that. I have been both a good and an equally poor father, and I have been the same as a husband. I love my family, all of them.

Above all else though, aside from a few times of stress, I have always been able to sleep at night without fear or shame. I try to be a good person, I act with honour and I am honest, which is why I fire up if someone questions that.

Deep down though I am just a bloke who is as happy sitting in the corner at the bowls club having a beer with himself, as I am walking the paddock and talking car racing with people, or even attending the odd function in a dinner suit. Just the odd one, mind you.

I am 70 now and trying to slow down. The twins – Zara and Jack – are in their last years of school, but I would imagine education is not nearly done for them, so there is no freedom on the near horizon.

I have a few things I am working on in addition to the TV, which I really do enjoy. I am an ambassador for a few different products – Lexus cars, Ageless supplements – and I enjoy all of those in my own little way.

I am not the sort of person that could just stop and do nothing. I found that out on the tractor all those years ago – not that cutting hay is exactly doing nothing. I'm actually getting very close to perfecting drinking; I've been putting a lot of work into that and I'm nearly there.

I was grifting and grafting in the 1970s to make enough money to live and to invest in my career. With Brian I was buying and destroying racing cars and working on a dream. When I needed help from people, they weren't there then. When I was successful and didn't need it, they were everywhere.

I don't know if it is any easier or harder today than when I was young. One thing I know is that there is no use sitting in a pub somewhere drinking another pint and lamenting what might have been.

Winning my World Championship was a ten-year exercise; I was not an overnight success. I was great with the mind games,

I was able to read people and know exactly what to say. I didn't write things down, and while my memory has never been that great for many things, it worked really well when I needed to remember the weakness of a competitor, or the trick I used to get through that bloody right-hander at Zandvoort.

My life has been an amazing journey with few regrets. I said earlier in the book, I wasn't going to make the same mistakes as my father. I was not going to leave this earth without having given my all to get to the top.

As it turns out, I did get to the top. Hopefully this story will help inspire a young driver to make sure I am not Australia's last world champion – but that is out of my hands.

Afterword – Andrew Clarke

Alan Jones means more to Australian motorsport than he ever cares to admit. Or perhaps even understands.

He brought Formula One to our TV screens in the late 1970s and ultimately a Formula One grand prix to our shores in the mid-1980s, which remains to this day. As a young motorsport fan who liked Formula One more than touring cars, this was truly significant to me. The people I had read about were now on the TV screen in Australia. And like many of us down here, when our TV screens burst into life at some ungodly hour in the middle of winter to the sounds of Murray Walker and James Hunt, we were doing it to watch AJ win grands prix and then the World Drivers' Championship in 1980.

What Alan did, without realising it, was to change the motorsport landscape here in Australia. If he hadn't been successful enough to inspire the Nine Network to come on board, we wouldn't have our Formula One grand prix.

It was 40 years ago that he joined Williams, and within three years the combination of him, Patrick Head and Frank Williams had built a dynasty. AJ's brilliance as a driver was as much the catalyst as the technical genius and financial wizardry of the other pair.

And have no doubts, he was a bloody good driver. The best of his day. His mind was strong and he had a great ability to weaken the spirit of his rivals off the track, before beating them on the track. He was at his brutal best when he had to fight. He could overtake and because he had sublime car control he was a gun in the wet. I've always admired racing car drivers, not mathematicians, behind the wheel, or politicians away from the track.

If he hadn't walked away at the end of 1981, who knows what the record books would have reflected. He would certainly have more wins and more titles beside his name, but we'll never know how many.

My first contact with AJ was when he returned to Australia after his Formula One career was done. He started racing for Tony Longhurst's Benson & Hedges Racing team and he was hard to connect with. He was distant but palatable, he wasn't friendly or warm like Glenn Seton, but he also was not gruff like Allan Moffat – he was somewhere in between. Today I know a different AJ. He is no different to most of us in that he carries his memories within his heart.

The seeds for this book were born out of a chance conversation with my old mate Mark Larkham at the end of 2015. He said AJ was ready to tell his story, but he wanted it done right. So AJ and I started to talk.

We spoke to Alison Urquhart at Penguin Random House, with whom I had worked before. She jumped at the concept and gave it life, embracing the worldwide concept as much as the Australian. And then she brought her team on board and today you hold the results in your hands, and both AJ and I are indebted to them for the work they have done for us.

There were many websites used for fact-checking, and the people over time who have studiously kept these records are to be thanked, particularly formula2.net, oldracingcars.com, primotipo.com, racing-reference.info, f3history.co.uk, autosport.com, grandprix.com, touringcarracing.net and conrod.com.au.

Thanks to Keith Sutton (sutton-images.com), my first port of call for any international motorsport images, John Crawford, Mike Dixon and Peter Kostas and the rest of the crew who run the Lexus drive days.

As ever, my personal inspiration comes from the racers I have loved watching. Drivers like Ronnie Peterson, Ayrton Senna and now Daniel Ricciardo, and down here in Australia, Allan Moffat, Dick Johnson and Marcos Ambrose. And of course AJ, who belongs in both groups.

I have been honoured to work with Alan on this book and I hope you gain some insight. Success doesn't happen by chance, it's one per cent inspiration and 99 per cent perspiration, as they say. In the sporting parlance, it means there is no use having talent if you don't have the determination to do the hard work. AJ did that hard work.

Thanks to my two great kids, Byron and Gabi, who understand when I am tired and have lost track of time and forget to get them out of bed because I'm deep into the story. To my father who helped foster my love of motorsport and gave me the courage to follow my own dreams. As with AJ and his family, it is my family that gives meaning to my life.

Andrew Clarke, 2017

ABOUT THE AUTHOR

Andrew Clarke is a writer and journalist and lives in Melbourne. This is his 19th book.

Index

Citibank 144
competitiveness 7, 16, 122, 174, 230, 239
Concorde 305
Concorde Agreement 245
Constructors' Championship 179, 215
Cooper Climax 12, 21–2, 33
Cooper Mini 850 12
corporal punishment 6–7
corruption 42
Costanzo, Alfie 237
crashes 95, 158–63
    throttle stuck open 161–2
Crawford, Jim 59
Crichton, Neville 291, 323
Crichton-Stuart, Charlie 124–5, 129, 130–1, 138, 184, 202, 229, 231, 292
Cullen, Warren 259, 290
Custom Made 58

Daly, Derek 140
DART (Dobbie Automobile Racing Team) 45, 51
Davison, Will 361
De Angelis, Elio 222, 347
death of car drivers 42, 101, 112, 134, 213, 267, 273, 284, 347–8
Dennis, Ron 286
Depailler, Patrick 41, 66, 168, 169–70, 171, 182, 205, 213–14, 347
Dick Johnson Racing 339
Dijon 1977 107
Dobbie, Denys 45, 51–2
Donington 171, 262
    crash 1980 160–1

Donohue, Mark 66, 74, 107, 347
Dormobiles 31–2
drugs 28
Dumfries, Johnny 130, 131
Dutch Grand Prix 90, 133
    1973 42
    1975 72
    1976 90
    1977 112
    1979 177–8
    1980 162, 216–18, 219
    1981 257
Dyk, Ian 361

Earl's Court 31–2, 52, 152, 372
    Ford Thunderbird crash 163
Eastern Creek
    1994 329
    Triple Challenge 1995 330
Eastlake, Darrell 328, 335, 344
Easton Neston 62
Ecclestone, Bernie 38, 71, 134, 200, 208, 210, 296–7, 298, 307–8, 342–3, 358
Eckersley, Wayne 184, 236, 269
Elgh, Eje 314
Embassy Hill 66, 71, 75
England
    1966 26–9, 371
    1968 30–3, 37
Ensign 41–2
Erskine, James 351
Ertl, Harald 89
Evans, Alan 359

Falcons 326